Multicultural Celebrations

MULTICULTURAL CELEBRATIONS

Today's Rules of Etiquette for Life's Special Occasions

NORINE DRESSER

THREE RIVERS PRESS

NEW YORK

Published by Three Rivers Press, a division of Crown Publishers, Inc., 201 East 50th Street, New York, New York 10022. Member of the Crown Publishing Group.

Random House, Inc. New York, Toronto, London, Sydney, Auckland
www.randomhouse.com

THREE RIVERS PRESS is a registered trademark of Random House, Inc.

Printed in the United States of America

Design by Mspace

Library of Congress Cataloging-in-Publication Data
Dresser, Norine.
    Multicultural celebrations : today's rules of etiquette for life's special occasions / Norine Dresser. — 1st ed.
        p.   cm.
    Includes index.
    1. Etiquette—United States.   2. Manners and customs.
3. Pluralism (Social sciences)—United States.   I. Title.
BJ1854.D74   1999
395.2—dc21   98-29809
                                                                      CIP

ISBN 0-609-80259-3

10 9 8 7 6 5 4 3 2 1
FIRST EDITION

To those whose celebrations we have shared—
drawing us close together.

CONTENTS

Acknowledgments xiii

How to Use This Book xvi

Introduction 1

1 Expecting 9

TRADITIONAL RITUALS AND BELIEFS 10
Hawaiian 10
Indian (Brahman) 10
Korean 12
Mexican 13
Native American 13
Thai 14

DISCOVERING THE SEX OF THE CHILD 14
Anglo-American 14
Latina/Caribbean 15

EMERGING TRADITIONS 15
In Honor of Pregnant Women 15

2 Giving Birth 19

TRADITIONAL RITUALS AND BELIEFS 20
Cambodian 20

Egyptian (Coptic) 25
Ethiopian 25
Hawaiian 26
Hmong 28
Indian (Brahman) 30
Japanese (Buddhist) 31
Jewish 32
Korean 36
Lao 37
Mexican 38
Native American 38
Samoan 40
Thai 41
Tibetan 42
Vietnamese 43

NAMING CEREMONIES **44**
Chinese 45
Indian (Brahman) 46
Jewish 47
Native American 49
Nigerian 50
Protestant Christenings 52
Roman Catholic Christenings 53

DETERMINING THE BABY'S FUTURE **55**
Armenian 55
Korean 56
Vietnamese 57

BIRTHDAY ANNIVERSARIES **57**
Japanese 57
Korean 59

EMERGING TRADITIONS   **60**
Alcoholics Anonymous   60

3 Coming of Age   63

TRADITIONAL RITUALS AND BELIEFS   **64**
African-American   64
Indian (Brahman)   66
Japanese   66
Jewish   67
Latina   70
Native American   73
Roman Catholic   79
Thai   81

EMERGING TRADITIONS   **83**
New Age Queens of Fertility   83
Latina *Cincuentañera*   85
Croning   87

4 Marrying   91

TRADITIONAL RITUALS AND BELIEFS   **92**
Afghani   92
African-American   98
Amish   101
Anglo-American   103
Armenian   104
Cajun   106
Cambodian   108
Chinese   110
Egyptian (Coptic)   111
Ethiopian   113

Filipino   114
Greek Orthodox   115
Hawaiian   116
Hmong   117
Indian   120
Iranian   122
Italian   124
Japanese (Buddhist)   126
Jewish   127
Korean   131
Lao   133
Mexican (Roman Catholic)   136
Nigerian (Ibo)   137
Samoan   138
Thai   139
Tibetan   141
Vietnamese   143

EMERGING TRADITIONS   **145**
Las Vegas Weddings   145
Same Sex Weddings   147
Vampire Weddings   150
Later-in-Life Weddings   153
Divorce Party   154
Divorce Cleansing Ceremony   156

5 Healing   159

TRADITIONAL RITUALS AND BELIEFS   **161**
Hmong   161
Jewish (Sephardic)   162
Lao   165
Native American   166
Thai   169

PILGRIMAGES **170**
El Santuario de Chimayó 170
Saint Anne de Beaupré 173
Tomb of El Niño Fidencio 175
Tomb of Rabbi Menachem Mendel Schneerson 176
Labyrinths 179

EMERGING TRADITIONS **181**
Caribbean/Latino Santería or Orisha Worship 181
Teddy Bear Medicine 182
Vibrational Healing 184
End-of-Therapy Rituals 188
The Goddess of Hysterectomy 189

6 Dying 193

TRADITIONAL RITUALS AND BELIEFS **196**
African-American New Orleans or Jazz Funeral 196
Amish 197
Armenian 198
Buddhist 199
Cambodian 200
Chinese (Buddhist) 201
Egyptian (Coptic) 203
Ethiopian 204
Hawaiian 205
Hmong 206
Indian (Brahman) 209
Japanese (Buddhist) 210
Jewish 212
Korean 215
Lao 217
Mexican 218
Muslim 220

Native American   221
Rom (Gypsy)   225
Samoan   228
Thai   229
Tibetan   231

EMERGING TRADITIONS   **232**
Lapel Ribbons   232
The AIDS Memorial Quilt and NAMES Project   232
Project Blue Light   235
Children's Bell Tower   235
Surfer Service   236
Memorial Walls   238
Sidewalk Shrines   239
Gang Members' Funerals   242
Hospice Ritual   243
Missoula Demonstration Project   246
Do-It-Yourself Home Funerals   248
Write-On Caskets   249
High Tech   250
Cyberspace   250
Outer Space Funerals   251

Looking for More Information?   **253**
Print   253
World Wide Web   263
Organizations   264
Videotapes   266
Other Sources   266

Index   **267**

Acknowledgments

My favorite part of writing is the research. Hunting for data at the computer or digging through volumes at the library is captivating. However, what exhilarates me most is that candid moment when a human being opens up. The names that follow are those of people I spoke with who energized me by providing information, sharing customs, or leading me to other informants. You spurred me on to completion of this project. Thank you for your generous contributions.

Victor Agbo; Chris Aihara, Director of Community Programs, Japanese American Cultural Community Center; Kristine Alvarez; Barry J. Ancelet, Ph.D.; Ruth E. Andersen, Ph.D.; Lynn Ballin; Robin Baltic; Armine Berberian; Réjean Bernier, Lay Pastoral Worker, Shrine of Saint Anne de Beaupré; Vivian and Joe Besbeck; Ramaa Bharadvaj; Bruce T. Bliatout, Ph.D.; Nancy Blumstein, M.D.; Rebecca Blustein; Rabbi Daniel Bouskila, Sephardic Temple Tifereth Israel; Ann Bradley; Dwan Bridges, Ph.D.; Mogus and Dereju Brook; Vanessa Brown; Heather Bryan; Norma E. Cantú, Ph.D.; Sra. Berta Castillo de Torres; Suellen Cheng, Chinese Historical Society of Southern California; Soo-Young Chin, Ph.D.; Tenzing Chonden, Friends of Tibet; Diane Cohen; Carolyn Cole, Project Director, Shades of L.A.; Jeanne Córdova; Star Coulbrooke; Rabbi Boruch Schlomo Cunin, West Coast Director of Chabad Lubavitch; Mrs. Dawa; Luisa Del Giudice, Ph.D.; Ann Del Signore; Kieran Devane; James R. Dow, Ph.D.; Sue Duncan; Yossi Edelstein, M.D.;

Robin Evanchuk, Ph.D.; Claire Farrer, Ph.D.; Joseph F. Fennelly, M.D.; Heng Foong, Project Director, Pacific Island Asian Language Services; Million Gebreyesus; Clarice Gillis; Jane Goldberg, Ph.D.; Officer Ken Greenleaf; Del Howison; Kimberly Hughes; Jean Tokuda Irwin; Athina Kenekeo; Anne Marie Khalsa, M.D.; Margaret Kim; Sojin Kim, Ph.D.; Julie Kirkpatrick; Rev. Masao Kodani, Senshin Buddhist Temple; Provost Donald B. Kraybill, Ph.D., Messiah College; Im Jung Kwuon; Cecilia Ledezma; Isaac J. Levy, Ph.D.; Rebecca Amato Levy; Pat Luce, Director, Samoan Affairs Central Region; Ellen Mark, Levy Sephardic Library; Riem Men, Southeast Asian Health Project; Doug Metz, Mortuary Science, Cerritos Community College; Teferi Michael; Ann Milton; Father Al Montalto, St. Bartholomew's Episcopal Church; Chanida Mumanachit, Tourism Authority of Thailand; Blair Murphy, Empyre Films; John B. Niazi; Clarice W. Nuhi; Jon Olson, Ph.D.; Natalie Olson; Tracie Owens; Jane Ka'ala Pang, Hawaiian Civic Club; Florence Pou, Samoan Community Center; Harihar Rao, the Music Circle; Meg Reed, Preternatural Productions; Sister Jean Roche, Chaplain, St. Peter's Hospice; Arpi Sarafian, Ph.D.; Jeannie Shade, R.N.; Nancy K. Shimamoto, Hispanic & Asian Marketing Communication Research, Inc.; Sherry Skramstad; Connie Spittler; Father Tom Stehle; Theresa Sterling; Sharon Suh, Ph.D.; Hany Takla, President, St. Shenouda the Archimandrite Coptic Society; Frances Tally, Ph.D., UCLA Archive of Popular Belief and Superstition; Judith Terzi; Waraporn Tiaprasith; Barre Toelken, Ph.D.; Chue Vang; Vlad; Bibian Vosgien; Eleanor Wachs, Ph.D.; Mary G. Wentz; Anne G. Wilcoxen, Ph.D., Director, Center for Cultural Fluency, Mount St. Mary's College; Patchara and Vibul Wonprasat, Thai Community Arts and Cultural Center; Mai Xiong; Jack Yaffe; Dean Eri Yasuhara, Ph.D., California State University, Los Angeles; Gerald D. Yoshitomi, Executive Director, Japanese

Cultural & Community Center; Jeanne Youngson, Ph.D.; Arina Zahid; Fahimeh Zand.

Additionally, I salute my research assistants for their enthusiastic work: Zachary Berk, Jim Gillette, Juan Hernandez, Leila Sharafi. And hats off to the nameless, always gracious reference-desk staff at the Glendale and Pasadena Public Libraries, who attentively answered my countless phone queries.

My appreciation goes to Rabbi Stephen Stern of the Arden Heights Boulevard Jewish Center and Congregation Etz Chaim on Staten Island for judiciously examining Jewish entries.

I wish to acknowledge dear friends, my cabal—a staunch circle of consultants unconditionally checking copy, submitting suggestions, pondering ideas, or finding facts: Virginia Crane, Marilyn Elkins, Kay Enell, Montserrat Fontes, Janice Garey, Michael Owen Jones, Morrie Polan, Julie Benton Siegel, Rachel Spector, Jan Steward, Lucia Van Ruiten, Dolores Wong, and Fay Zachary.

My New York team was invaluable, as well—agent-consigliere Sheree Bykofsky and editor PJ Dempsey, an astute ally who enlivened me with daily doses of E-mail humor.

To this thank-you list, I add my family, who gave me comfort and terrific leads: Mark, Andrea, Amy, my children; Carol, my favorite daughter-in-law; plus Mickey, the best of brothers; and Mom, proud of me, no matter what. Of course, the biggest booster in the writing of this book and everything I do is that sweetheart of a husband, Harold.

I offer all of you my love and gratitude.

How to Use This Book

In my earlier book about cross-cultural differences in customs (*Multicultural Manners* [Wiley, 1996]), I offered guidelines for successful interactions when people from different backgrounds came together—at work, at school, and in social settings. I gave advice about proper forms of greetings and appropriate choices of colors, numbers, and gestures to help readers avoid inadvertent offenses.

Multicultural Celebrations takes the reader to the next level of intimacy. Now you're invited to a Cambodian wedding. What do you bring? What do you wear? You want to go but don't want to insult anyone, nor do you want to just sit there observing without understanding. *Multicultural Celebrations* offers signposts to guide you through your multicultural adventures. View it as a practical adviser for culturally unfamiliar situations.

Multicultural Celebrations is reader friendly. The entries are designed as a quick study, offering a thumb-through look at ceremonies, complete with details never before collected in one book. Chapters are arranged according to the way we encounter the life cycle: pregnancy, birth, coming of age, marriage, healing, and death. Traditional rituals and beliefs appear at the beginning of each chapter in alphabetical order by named ethnic or religious group. Emerging traditions are found toward the end of the chapter. In time, these newer ceremonies may become established American traditions, as some people would argue is the case for the taking-a-cake ritual of Alcoholics Anonymous.

Multicultural Celebrations tells what to expect when you are invited to attend a ceremony and what is expected of you. It suggests what kinds of gifts to bring, how to dress, what to say, and what kinds of behavior to avoid; whenever possible, I make recommendations for such actions following the celebration descriptions.

Note that in some instructions I have indicated taboo colors or numbers. No mention of taboos means none apply. Additionally, in describing the various ethnic celebrations, I have incorporated numerous non-English words. These are transliterations which, by their nature, lead to spelling variations. Many of these words are transliterated phonetically, but where needed, I have inserted a pronunciation guide in brackets.

"Expecting" features ceremonies and beliefs surrounding pregnancy, such as the Indian bangle-bracelet party and the Korean conception dream.

"Giving Birth" documents naming ceremonies, parties to determine the baby's future, and birthday anniversaries. It supplies samples of birth rituals—the Navajo first-laugh party and Samoan *alaalafaga*.

"Coming of Age" delineates events marking the change of status from child to adult, such as the Apache mountain-spirit dance, Jewish bar mitzvah, and Roman Catholic confirmation. The "Emerging Traditions" section contains queens of fertility paying tribute to the onset of puberty. Croning and other ceremonies now applaud old age, a formerly dreaded stage of life.

"Marrying" characterizes the medley of practices celebrating unions. Customs range from African and Anglo-American jumping the broom to Cajun shivarees to the Italian *la busta*. Emerging traditions encompass Las Vegas, same-sex, and vampire-theme weddings. You will also discover later-in-life remarriage and divorce rituals.

"Healing" describes the milestones of the dramatic change a human makes in moving from sickness to health. Pilgrimages and ancient rituals are included as well as the emerging ceremonies of teddy bear medicine, vibrational healing, and the goddess of hysterectomy.

"Dying" details the most strictly followed ceremonies. This chapter notes variations in honoring the deceased and comforting the mourners, including Amish, Buddhist, Mexican Día de los Muertos, Rom (Gypsy), and Lakota reburial rites. "Emerging Traditions" contains the AIDS Memorial Quilt and NAMES Project, the sidewalk shrine to Diana, Princess of Wales, do-it-yourself and outer-space funerals.

"Looking for More Information?" presents categories of research sources: print, World Wide Web, organizations, and videotapes. This is in addition to the large number of informants whom I have already cited in my acknowledgments.

What if the description of a celebration practiced by your group is different from how you observe it? Unless customs are dictated by holy scripture, which rarely occurs, variety is the rule, even within the same culture. People can't refrain from putting their individual stamp on a tradition. This paradox of being similar and unique is what makes human nature fascinating.

If you are invited to a ritual that is not included in this book and have questions about how to behave, don't hesitate to ask an insider. She will appreciate your interest. However, avoid yes/no questions. Ask open-ended ones such as "What do you recommend that I wear?" "What would be considered an appropriate gift?" "What is the most respectful way to greet the celebrants?" Be sure to ask what colors, numbers, or behavior should be avoided. At the event, be observant and follow cues, but above all, enjoy the adventure of participating in another culture's celebration.

Multicultural Celebrations

INTRODUCTION

"And many more"

The tag line "And many more," from the song "Happy Birthday" and its accompanying rites, embodies the essence of milestone celebrations. Humans feel joy when gathering around a glowing candlelit cake, waiting expectantly to see if a celebrant will blow out the candles in one breath, cheering when he or she is successful, groaning if not. "And many more" signifies our desire for honorees to live additional years and for us to share that pleasure with them.

Social scientists use the term *rites of passage* to distinguish the major stepping-stones in an individual's life. We begin with birth, move to coming of age, then marriage, and finally death. While these changes represent the major markers, in between are graduation, moving into one's first home, retirement, divorce, remarriage. The celebrations, customs, ceremonies, and rituals that accompany these life-cycle changes are the focus of this book.

1

HOW DO WE BENEFIT FROM LIFE-CYCLE CELEBRATIONS?

While many of us don't think of these life-cycle transitions as precarious, we find ourselves thrown off-balance because they upset the status quo. For example, consider how unsettling it is to have a new child enter the family, in spite of the anticipated happiness. It requires financial, spatial, physical, and emotional alterations. Most rites of passage entail these adjustments. Consequently, at these important times, family and friends observe appropriate customs to help people cope with the changes. While variations exist, certain ritual elements remain constant: gifts, lights, flowers, music, special words, clothing, and food.

Although skeptics might dismiss life-cycle celebrations as frivolous occasions, they have important functions. They allow for "conspicuous consumption," a term anthropologists and folklorists use to label the material aspects of the celebrations, which commonly are displays of the hosts' extravagance. Through these activities, wealth circulates within the community. Honorees receive useful goods; shopkeepers profit; community employment increases to accommodate the needs of the event.

Beyond material considerations, celebrations give us a break from our workaday routines. They force us to take time out from the mundane to savor precious moments. Some encourage fantasy and playfulness; some evoke powerful emotions causing goose bumps, tears, laughter, and awe. Celebrations surrounding life-cycle transitions, in particular, cause us to take inventory of who is still among us, who is no longer here. They make us stop and reflect on where we are in life. Perhaps that is what makes tears spring to our eyes at these events—the awareness of our own journey, its beginning and its approaching end.

These celebrations give us something to look forward to; they buoy us and can even lengthen our lives. Witness the ninety-fifth birthday celebration of Harry Asimow. After being incarcerated in a Russian prison for inciting revolutionary activities while serving in the czar's army, he was released and fled to the United States, where he became a union organizer in the sheet-metal industry. Following retirement, he took adult education classes and began writing poetry and essays. Later, he helped found the first senior centers in Southern California and in his eighties became actively involved in the Israel Levin Senior Center in Venice, California.

Each year, Harry's devoted family prepared a large birthday party for him at this Venice center, where he always gave a speech. However, by the time he reached his ninety-fifth birthday, Harry was quite frail. Still he insisted that he attend the party and read a speech containing an important message: he was leaving money for five more birthday parties to be celebrated in his honor, whether he was here or not.

For this special occasion, 150 friends, relatives, and center members attended. Part of the time, Harry rested backstage on a cot using the oxygen that his family had provided. After lunch, Harry mustered all his strength, gave his speech, received accolades, sat down at the table, folded his hands, and died. While many of those who attended believed that the angel of death had waited until after Harry's speech, others might say that Harry's anticipation of the celebration and the honor he was to receive from family and friends sustained his life. Harry's story is not unique.

We need symbolic action to draw us together and keep us going. That's what celebrations do. They make us feel that we belong. This feeling comes through the creation of *communitas*—a feeling of oneness. When friends and family come together to sing "Happy Birthday," to toast the bride and groom, or to bid final farewell to a loved one, they demonstrate that happiness and grief can be shared. These symbolic moments are communal hugs.

NEED ALL LIFE-CYCLE CELEBRATIONS BE TRADITIONAL?

Close-knit societies or ones governed by strict religious institutions do not welcome deviation from standard ceremonies. On the other hand, in a diverse United States, where individuals may be unaffiliated with institutionalized religion, or where institutions are free to innovate, humans express *communitas* by creating new rituals to fit new circumstances beyond the walls of churches and temples.

In Oklahoma City after the April 19, 1995, explosion at the Alfred P. Murrah Building where 168 lives were lost and over 500 injured, grieving families and the public expressed sorrow and offered solace by transforming the chain-link fence surrounding the rubble into a makeshift memorial wall; they attached cards, messages, poems, photos, American flags, flowers, and teddy bears. The expression of grief was spontaneous. No one needed instructions. Some inner need drove people to this act, which brought comfort to those who participated and a lump in the throats of those who observed.

On June 2, 1997, 774 days after the bombing, when a jury found Timothy McVeigh guilty of the crime, people again took ritual action. Dozens of survivors and relatives surrounded a slippery elm located across from the bomb site. This tree had become the "survivor tree"; even though the concussion of the blast had blown off its limbs and leaves, the tree still lived. On the day of the verdict, human survivors surrounded it, then took plastic bottles of water to pour over its roots. Using water to represent their tears, mourners poured only as much as seemed fitting to their stage of grief. Symbolically, the survivors shed their sorrow and emphasized life by nurturing the tree with water.

In less somber situations, people may take a standard celebration and use it as a model to create a new one. For example, Prof. Norma E. Cantú of Texas A&M International University in Laredo, Texas, adapted the *quinceañera,* the traditional celebration for fifteen-year-old Latinas, to celebrate her fiftieth birthday. She called it a *cincuentañera.* Others take classic ceremonies and customize them to fit their interests; some wedding couples have created vampire-themed nuptials to express their love of the Gothic. Some people may find this shocking; others may see nothing wrong with a bride dressed in black or the presence of a flower ghoul in the wedding party.

Through croning ceremonies, women's groups have created new rituals to pay tribute to older women and their wisdom. Some of these ceremonies have roots in Native American traditions; others are based in pre-Christian rites; still more have combined elements from the two sources. Purists may shudder at this mix-and-match attitude, but it is an ancient practice to borrow customs that please us.

In aboriginal times, when different tribes shared water from the same river, they had the opportunity to learn about other styles of body decoration, food preparation, or storytelling, and they embraced what suited them. Today the media have replaced the shared river, and we witness how others celebrate. From these myriad customs and beliefs, we adopt and adapt what attracts us.

At Cypress Hills Cemetery in Queens, New York, a Puerto Rican mother borrows a Jewish mourning custom by leaving small rocks on the gravestone of her eight-year-old. Instead of leaving sticky rice, soy chicken, or other traditional Chinese-food graveside offerings, a Chinese mourner leaves White Castle miniature hamburgers.

Many people today are familiar with the chair dance, where, as a celebratory act, men hoist the bride and groom, seated on chairs, into the air and carry them above the guests' heads. This is an Orthodox Jewish wedding custom that has spread to other forms of Jewish weddings and Armenian weddings, as well. Additionally, the custom has been adopted for bar and bas mitzvah celebrations, where hardy guests lift the seated celebrants overhead to demonstrate their newly elevated status.

As some rituals fade, such as the *prekante*, which combats the evil eye, others emerge, for example, the *santiguo,* a procedure that ameliorates women's gynecological problems. These examples show that as much as we like to think of traditions as Perma-Prest activities, they are not. They continually metamorphose to accommodate changing conditions and innovation.

How Is Multicultural Celebrations Useful?

Multicultural Celebrations details life-cycle rituals of all kinds, religious and secular, from the staid to the seemingly bizarre, the traditional to the innovative. *Multicultural Celebrations* presents a vantage point for observation and satisfies a curiosity about the behavior of those different from ourselves. It furnishes a peek at some unusual events that many of us will never be privy to observe. It may be that we have not yet had the opportunity to be placed on appropriate guest lists for these occasions, or outsiders are not allowed in.

Multicultural Celebrations documents and illuminates a wide spectrum of ritual behavior. It is a commentary on and exaltation of our heterogeneous society, honoring American culture for nurturing variety. The book reveals the vigor of new traditions being born, old ones being adapted, and some even being cast aside when they conflict with American laws. For example, in 1996, when Iraqi immigrant parents in Nebraska observed their Old World custom of arranging marriages of underage daughters to men ten years their senior, the grooms were sentenced to four to six years in prison. In the United States, Iraqis no longer practice this custom.

The more familiar rituals, such as graduations, retirements, and traditional church weddings, are not included in this book. If we have not attended, we have at least seen such events on television and in movies. At a wedding, for example, no matter the religious denomination, we know more or less what to expect when we get there. Therefore, we are not shocked when, in the middle of the reception, the bride lifts up the long skirt of her formal white gown to expose her thigh and blue garter. We know why unwed women surround the bride and push and shove to catch the bouquet she tosses in the air. Without instructions, we understand that we must throw the rice at the newlyweds.

The ubiquity of such events and space limitations have dictated what I include in this book. I have focused upon uniqueness, on eye-catching differences, on the unexpected qualities that make events memorable. I did not envision this volume as an encyclopedia, but rather as an entertaining look at the variety of ways in which we celebrate our humanness.

Not surprisingly, the longer immigrant groups have been in this country, the more Americanized they have become. Consequently, there are fewer distinctions in their rites of passage, and obviously, I have included less about them in this book.

In the pages that follow, the emphasis is on the newest arrivals because they are in a transitional stage and still maintain their homeland's ways. Nonetheless, some groups have been here for hundreds of years, such as the Amish, who have deliberately preserved their seventeenth-century traditions with minimal changes. I have included some of their rituals because of their uniqueness. But be aware: not all Amish observe customs in exactly the same way. Variations exist because of separate locations and branches of the religion.

Different countries of origin cause distinctions as well. For example, U.S. Muslim customs vary because Muslims may be from Iran or Afghanistan, and each country has added its own flavor. Further, not everyone within a Native American tribe celebrates its rituals in exactly the same way. Most tribes have different branches, each with its own specialization. Other group variations occur because of economics and social status. Individuals, too, add their personal touch to tradition.

I have written this book from a folklorist's perspective because folklorists often examine rites of passage, customs, beliefs, and ceremonies in order to understand human behavior and culture. This research has been my occupation and preoccupation for over twenty-five years, lecturing at California State University, Los Angeles, delivering papers at academic folklore meetings, publishing books and articles and a newspaper column about ceremonies and traditions.

I have been attracted to this study because life-cycle celebrations provide comfort by giving people something to do during unsettling times—"Don't just stand there. Do something." These celebrations bind us to our communities; they furnish creative outlets for the human spirit. They allow us to nonverbally express our emotions. Life-cycle celebrations, whether they elicit laughter or tears, confirm spirituality and authenticate life.

1 EXPECTING

"She's got one in the oven."

"Don't drink from that cracked cup or your child will have a harelip." "Don't reach up high or the cord will strangle the baby." Well-meaning family and friends bombard the pregnant woman with advice. Most of it centers on desires for a healthy child and an uncomplicated delivery; don't make a bonnet for the baby before it is born. People shield the woman from unpleasantness and may prohibit her from attending funerals. Both sadness and fright might "mark" the unborn child, causing deformity, a birthmark, or abnormal behavior.

Many believe in special dietary rules and that the pregnant woman's food cravings should be indulged. Other beliefs dictate how to ensure pregnancy: eating many eggs brings about conception, as does rubbing one's stomach against the stomach of a pregnant woman. Some customs predict the sex of the child and relate its temperament to the

9

mother's behavior; if she reads scholarly books, her child will be clever.

TRADITIONAL RITUALS AND BELIEFS

HAWAIIAN

During pregnancy, the woman wears an open-ended lei rather than one in a complete circle. Hawaiians believe that the circle must be severed or else the baby might choke. Especially on the islands, pregnant women are protected from extremes in nature such as fires and major storms because Hawaiians are in tune with land and nature. They interpret violent changes in the weather as a negative communication from the gods.

INDIAN (BRAHMAN)

Valaikappu [vell-lay-kap-pú] (Bangle Bracelet Ceremony)

When the woman is in her seventh month, women gather to decorate her with many glass bangle bracelets, sometimes as many as twenty-five to thirty on each wrist. This celebration acknowledges the positive influence of sound on the fetus. The clinking of the bangles against each other is believed to aid the mental health of the baby and to protect it from evil influences. The sounds of the women's laughter on this jolly occasion advantageously affect the baby, as well. In India, the presence of a priest and the vibrations of his chanted mantras enhance the well-being of the unborn child.

❂ *Gifts:* Only bangles.

FOLK WISDOM

If you swallow a watermelon seed, you'll have a baby.

If you want to get pregnant, have another mother lay her baby on your bed.

At a bridal shower, if the bride-to-be breaks the ribbon, she will have a baby in the first year.

To tell the proposed name of a baby before it is born is bad luck.

If a pregnant woman picks up a dropped handkerchief by the corner, the child will be a boy.

If a pregnant woman craves strawberry ice cream, she will have a redheaded girl.

If a pregnant woman cans fruit, it will spoil.

If a pregnant woman ties knots during her pregnancy, she will have a difficult birth.

Paint fumes and strenuous horseback riding will produce an abortion.

To ensure the birth of a boy, forcefully wish for a girl.

If a pregnant woman looks at a dead body, her baby might die.

✪ *Words:* "Congratulations" and other felicitations.

✪ *Clothing:* Remove shoes and socks before entering the home. Avoid black.

KOREAN

Tae Mong [téh mong]

Many Korean Americans retain their Old World tradition regarding a woman's conception dream, called *tae mong,* which they believe precedes conception. These dreams depict fruits, chestnuts, and red peppers, which the mother either plants, picks from trees, or receives as gifts. They believe that fruits, flowers, and small objects represent girls, while animals symbolize boys. To dream of a pig is a good omen; the child will become wealthy and have good fortune.

The pregnancy dream need not be the dream of the future mother herself but may be that of a close relative or friend. One woman's friend dreamed about a tiger, and even before the male child was born, his parents thought of him as a powerful man with the potential of becoming president of the United States. A friend of another woman who desired to become pregnant dreamed of a beautiful pearl, which was interpreted to mean that her friend's future child would be a beautiful girl. Sometimes Korean parents plan their child's name according to the dream.

Tae Kyo [téh gyo]

Tae kyo are pregnancy taboos that some women observe for protection of themselves and the fetus. For example, a woman may not look at a house on fire; she must avoid killing any living creature; she should avoid eating twenty different taboo foods including rabbit, associated with harelip; duck, an omen of fused extremities; eggs, a sign that the fetus might not have a backbone; and chicken, which forebodes a sharply pointed mouth or goose bumps on the newborn.

MEXICAN

Some women believe they should prevent their babies from becoming too large and will keep working and moving about during the pregnancy to keep the baby small. Taboos exist against reaching high with the arms, crossing the legs, and sitting near cool breezes, even near evaporative coolers. Other dangers include moonlight, night air, and a lunar eclipse, all of which might endanger the fetus. For protection during an eclipse, pregnant women wear a piece of steel or attach a safety pin to their underclothing to prevent their child from being born with a cleft chin. Some also believe that if the pregnant woman looks at the moon, her baby will have a mole *(lunar* [loo-nár]*)*.

NATIVE AMERICAN

MIWOK AND MAIDU

Blessing the Baby Cradle

Prior to the baby's birth, the grandmother, mother, or aunt makes a basket cradle. The woman decorating it uses whatever materials she chooses including bone, feathers, and porcupine needles. When the cradle is ready, she brings it to a spiritual leader to be blessed so that the baby will be protected.

NAVAJO TABOOS

Husbands of pregnant women may believe the following: if you try to count stars, you'll have too many children; if you kill birds, the baby will look like a bird; if you kill any animal, the baby will not be normal. If you wear two hats, you'll have twins. If you hit a sheep's legs, the baby will be crippled.

The pregnant women themselves may observe prohibitions: If you look at any wild animals, the baby will look wild. If you eat a lot of sweets, the baby will be weak. If you look at a dead person or dead animals, the baby will not be strong.

THAI

Thais believe that if the woman drinks a large amount of coconut juice throughout the pregnancy, it will cleanse the baby, so that upon delivery the baby will not be coated with a cheesy substance called the vernix caseosa. They also avoid hot chilies, believing that they cause the baby to have dark and bumpy skin.

DISCOVERING THE SEX OF THE CHILD

ANGLO-AMERICAN

People from a wide variety of ethnic groups believe that by attaching a sewing needle or the mother's wedding ring to a string and suspending it above the pregnant woman's abdomen, they can learn the sex of the child. If the needle moves in a circle, the baby is a boy; if the needle moves in an oval, the baby is a girl. Others say that if the object moves clockwise, it is a boy; counterclockwise, it is a girl.

An alternative method is to examine the shape of the pregnant woman. If her stomach is pointed or all out in front, it will be a boy; if rounded or the woman has gained weight all over, the baby will be a girl. If the woman carries high, she will have a boy; if she carries low, she will have a girl.

LATINA/CARIBBEAN

At baby showers, Latinas and Caribbean women often play this game: The pregnant woman must choose to sit in one of two cushioned chairs. If she picks the chair that has a knife hidden under the cushion, she will have a boy. If she chooses the one hiding a scissors, she will have a girl. Variations may be a fork for a boy and a spoon for a girl.

EMERGING TRADITIONS

IN HONOR OF PREGNANT WOMEN

Belly Masks

Since 1986, Francine Krause of Guerneville, California, has been making belly masks of pregnant women. A belly mask is a mold made of a pregnant woman's belly that, when dry, may be decorated, then hung on the wall as an object of beauty and a memento of this transitory stage in life. An artist and maskmaker, Krause created the first one for herself during her own pregnancy. Thrilled with how it made her feel and how it affected her relationship with her son, she now helps other women experience the same joyful bonding with their unborn children.

Krause wants people to relate to pregnancy in a more positive way, to celebrate it through personal imagery, to show reverence for the beginning of human life. She believes that a pregnant-belly cast empowers women by honoring the female process. The benefits extend beyond the expectant mom. Ordinarily, fathers feel cut out of pregnancy, but those who witness the belly mask making or participate in it have a bonding experience with their partners and with the baby. It is a sensual, nurturing, fun experience. For one father, making the belly mask was one of the highlights of his wife's pregnancy.

For the baby, Krause is confident that anything that can be done to help moms bond with their babies prenatally is helpful, especially in our culture with so much disconnection between mothers and children. When the youngsters grow up, they are proud to have the belly masks, to show that they were inside. It makes clear that their moms were proud to be carrying them, that they were immortalized as sculptors within the body.

Here's how the process works. Before an expectant mom arrives at Krause's studio, she brushes the room with smoke from burning sage to clear it and make it joyful. Then she burns some light-scented incense, lights a white candle, and plays soft music in the background.

Before the mother-to-be arrives, Krause cuts eight-inch-wide plaster gauze strips from a fifteen-foot-long roll. She dips the strips into warm water and places them in layers on the woman's naked body, covering the entire torso, molding and smoothing the gauze until she creates a precise replica of the body, including nipples and belly button. As the plaster form dries, it swaddles the woman's torso like a chrysalis. The process takes about an hour, during which time Krause and her client talk about birth, pregnancy, and relationships. When finished, the woman steps out of the cast, amazed at the results. Since most pregnant women feel clumsy with their enlarged bellies, hips, and breasts, objectifying their shapes lets them witness, then endorse, the beauty of their own bodies.

Afterward, Krause applies several coats of gesso to the mask, which prepares it for embellishment. She encourages the women to paint and decorate the masks, but often they are reluctant, fearing that artistically they cannot do them justice. Some choose to leave them unadorned; others decorate them with paint or found objects, including fabric, fiber, shells, feathers, and crystals. Sometimes friends or family members help in the decorating. Whether the result is primitive or sophisticated, the final product and symbology come from the woman's heart.

Mask decorations feature Native American or East Indian themes, colorful geometric designs, a child's face in the center of a giant sunflower, motifs of dolphins, hearts, the lotus, moons, and stars. One woman equated her painting with a meditation where she felt the sacred connection of all mothers throughout time. Another said that what she painted was not related to her but to her unborn child, that one day he would be able to decipher the meaning of the symbols she felt compelled to paint.

Krause has had four gallery showings of belly masks in Northern California, which evoked powerful responses. The exhibits consisted of embellished belly masks of thirty different women hung next to their statements in poetry or prose about their pregnancy, birth, and early parenting, along with a photo of them and their babies. Visitors to the exhibit invariably cried when they read the statements by these mothers who so loved their children.

For women who cannot travel to Northern California, Krause has created a Women's Do-It-Yourself Pregnant Bellymask Kit. (See "Looking for More Information?"/World Wide Web, p. 263; "Other Sources," p. 266.) It contains the materials and instructions for making your own belly mask.

2   Giving Birth

"Have a cigar."

To ensure that the fragile new life survives without harm, families observe various customs and employ protective devices: Middle Easterners pin blue beads to children's clothing; Eastern Europeans affix red ribbons to the crib or baby carriage; Puerto Ricans tie a black and red charm on a baby's bracelet; Mexicans hang a "deer's eye" from a red string around the baby's neck; Orthodox Jews place a talisman near their baby's bed to keep away the preying Lilith. These practices thrive throughout the United States.

The newborn child represents unlimited potential. At the same time, fears for its future abound. Consequently, the family anxiously looks for omens, good and bad. For example, some believe that a baby born with a caul (membrane) over its face foretells of second sight, that the child is destined to become a healer.

Which day of the week the baby arrives has meaning,

too, inspiring the well-known nursery rhyme "Monday's Child . . ." (see p. 22). The significance of the birth date accounts for the popularity of horoscopes, a feature found in magazines and daily newspapers, often with a special insert: "If your child is born on this day . . ." The day and time can be so wrought with meaning that expectant mothers may consult with astrologers before selecting a date for a C-section, as sometimes happens in the Chinese immigrant community.

TRADITIONAL RITUALS AND BELIEFS

CAMBODIAN

Seven days after its birth, the family has a party at home to bless the baby. Sometimes the grandparents sprinkle water on the baby.

❂ *Gifts:* Baby clothes or money in an envelope of any color.

❂ *Words:* Any sentiment offering the mother and the father long life and happiness for the new child. While in Cambodia, they observed a taboo against complimenting the baby. Although that custom is fading, use discretion when complimenting the baby in front of an older person.

❂ *Clothing:* Cambodians remove their shoes inside their homes. Guests should do the same. Non-Cambodians who respect their no-shoes tradition are appreciated.

❂ *Body Language:* Use the *wai* [why] form of greeting. With hands pressed together in a prayerlike gesture, bring them up to just below the chin and nod slightly. Avoid male/female body contact.

FOLK WISDOM

Put a sharp knife under the pillow of a woman in labor to cut the pain.

To help a teething baby, rub its gums with a gold wedding ring.

If you cut a child's hair before its first birthday, it will never walk.

When a baby begins to walk, mark a straight line in front of him to help him follow a straight path.

A child born on its father's birthday will be lucky.

Don't keep a cat in the house with a newborn or it will suck the baby's breath and kill it.

When seeing a newborn baby, touch it, so it won't get the evil eye.

Never allow a newborn to look at itself in a mirror or it will become sick.

Like father, like son.

If you kiss a baby, you bring it good luck.

If you burn or throw the afterbirth in water, the mother will not recover.

Monday's child is fair of face,
Tuesday's child is full of grace,
Wednesday's child is full of woe,
Thursday's child has far to go,
Friday's child is loving and giving,
Saturday's child has to work for its living,
But a child that's born on the Sabbath day
Is fair and wise and good always.
—"MONDAY'S CHILD IS FAIR OF FACE"

BIRTHSTONES

January	Garnet	Constancy
February	Amethyst	Sincerity
March	Aquamarine or bloodstone	Truth
April	Diamond	Innocence
May	Emerald	Happiness
June	Pearl or moonstone	Health
July	Ruby or carnelian	Love
August	Peridot or sardonyx	Felicity
September	Sapphire	Wisdom
October	Opal or tourmaline	Hope
November	Topaz	Fidelity
December	Turquoise or zircon	Success

Astrological Signs

Aries: March 21–April 19

The Ram. Enthusiastic and forceful, they never admit defeat. They have great willpower and confidence in themselves.

Taurus: April 20–May 20

The Bull. Passionately loyal to friends, they are also extremely jealous. They are stubborn and execute their own ideas with skill.

Gemini: May 21–June 21

The Twins. With curiosity and quick minds, they often lack self-discipline. They are the salesmen and communicators of the zodiac.

Cancer: June 22–July 22

The Crab. Moody at times, they are also shy. Establishing and protecting domestic security is their greatest goal.

Leo: July 23–August 22

The Lion. Charismatic and organized in leadership, they tend to be bossy. They are the entertainers of the zodiac.

Virgo: August 23–September 22

The Maiden. Creative yet modest, they tend to be highly critical of others. They are attracted to the medical profession.

Libra: September 23–October 23

The Scales. Hard workers, they demand the same of their partners. They have a strong sense of justice and are romantic, as well.

Scorpio: October 24–November 21

The Scorpion. Known as the sex symbol and detective of the zodiac, they can also be vindictive, sarcastic as well as heroic.

Sagittarius: November 22–December 21

The Archer. Idealistically and spiritually drawn, they can easily become fanatics. They are sometimes accused of being tactless.

Capricorn: December 22–January 19

The Goat. With their need to be in charge, others may accuse them of being slave drivers. They are practical, worriers, and cautious.

Aquarius: January 20–February 18

The Water Bearer. True in friendships, innovative at work, they are also stubborn and argumentative. They are drawn to politics.

Pisces: February 19–March 20

The Fish. Gentle and supportive, they are blind to the faults of those they love. They are compassionate and have an interest in serving others.

EGYPTIAN (COPTIC)

On the seventh day, the priest anoints the baby with water, and the family holds a party. The priest pours water into a basin, adds a small amount of salt and oil, and lights seven candles. After saying a prayer of thanksgiving, he offers incense. Later, when a girl is eighty days old and a boy is forty days old, the infants are eligible for baptism, and by this time the mother is strong enough to attend a church service held on a Sunday before the regular service. Baptism, communion, and confirmation transpire on the same day.

⚙ *Gifts:* Money or standard baby gifts.

⚙ *Words:* Some older and more traditional people prefer that the baby not be complimented. Younger or more educated Egyptian Copts tend not to practice this taboo associated with the evil eye. Observe others and use discretion.

⚙ *Clothing:* Women avoid wearing pants in church. No required ties and jackets for men, although older men generally wear them.

⚙ *Body Language:* In church, men and women sit separately.

ETHIOPIAN

After the baby arrives, guests bring the new parents congratulatory cards and flowers, especially red roses. To make the new mother strong, the family feeds her *genfo* [gun-foe], a mushy, oatmeal-like grain that is easy to digest. When people come to greet the new child, the family feeds them *genfo* as well, to welcome them to the new family situation.

In Ethiopia, the new mother stays in bed at least one month, and her mother, aunts, and sisters take care of her. In this country, Ethiopians have dropped this custom.

✪ *Gifts:* Baby gifts rather than money, which people give only when in large amounts.

✪ *Words:* Baby compliments are appreciated.

✪ *Body Language:* Ethiopians show babies great affection. Frequently they kiss the hand of the newborn or touch the baby's cheek or forehead with their fingers, then bring the fingers to their own lips in a kiss.

Baptism

This is not a naming ceremony. Boys are baptized at forty days and girls at eighty days. The babies are completely immersed. If the child is a boy, the godfather brings the baby to the priest, who, when finished with the immersing, blessing, and anointing of the child, hands the baby to the mother. The same procedure takes place with a baby girl except that the godmother brings her to the priest.

Adults may be in national dress. After the baptism, while still in church, everyone partakes of unleavened bread *(injera* [een-jay-rah]*),* tea or coffee, or soft drinks. Later they adjourn to a big luncheon at the home of the newborn's parents. A priest or one of the elders says a prayer over the unleavened bread. Then they feast and party. No formal gift-giving takes place at this time.

HAWAIIAN

The birth of a child is significant because it means the continuation of the culture. In the old days, if the firstborn was a girl, the maternal grandparents would *hanai* (adopt) the child—the child lived with the grandparents, who assumed the responsibility of teaching the Hawaiian culture and genealogy to the girl. If the firstborn was a boy, the paternal grandparents adopted the child, *punahele* (favorite child), and teaching Hawaiian culture and genealogy to the boy was their responsibility. In the old days, when Hawaiian culture was strictly an oral tradition, ensuring the transmission of the lore to the next generation was vital to the survival of the people. This is the motivation for such adoptions.

Nowadays, the structure and pressures of modern living have made adoptions less feasible. Add to this the common separation of families with some on the mainland and others in the islands. As a result, the tradition has been modified by having the firstborn spend vacations and as much spare time as possible with the appropriate grandparents. If no grandparents are available, an elder aunt or uncle takes over.

When the baby is born and at the first birthday, the family has a luau, which must have the basic traditional foods of the gods: roast pig prepared in an underground oven, fish, banana, sweet potato, taro, coconut, *kinolau* [key-no-lau] (spirit forms of the gods). Hawaiians eat these foods not only for nourishment but for spirituality. As they ingest the foods, they become godlike and strengthen their mana, insight, and wisdom.

The luau is a gathering of friends and family, a joyous event with singing, dancing, and food. Customarily, each person brings a dish, and all lend a helping hand. Each person has individual responsibilities: set up tables and chairs; decorate; prepare *emu* (roast pig); serve the food; clean up; play music; bring ukuleles, guitars; dance the hula as a gift for the honored child.

✪ *Gifts:* Close family and friends contribute to a potluck meal. Standard baby gifts or money from others. Certain family members prepare traditional handcrafted gifts. In the past, when a woman was pregnant, a quilt design for the new baby would appear in the mother's or grandmother's dream. She made the quilt during the pregnancy and presented it upon the baby's birth. Quilts are treasured heirlooms for the child as are other labor-intensive gifts such as a *lei hulu* (feather lei) or a pandanus-leaf fan or *lauhala* (pandanus) basket.

✪ *Words:* Avoid complimenting the baby, or the gods might take it away. To protect the child, admirers pick out an unfavorable physical characteristic to comment upon. "Oh, what a flat nose spread out all over its face." "Oh, what big ears," meaning just the opposite. Sometimes Hawaiians use uncomplimentary words as terms of endearment. *Pupuka* [poo-pookah] means what an ugly child, but when spoken in a loving manner has the opposite meaning.

✪ *Clothing:* Sandals without socks, aloha attire (floral clothing, muumuus for women, tropical-print aloha shirts for men), shorts for outdoor luaus, slacks for indoor luaus. Clothes should be comfortable because participants may be sitting on the ground or floor while eating.

HMONG [MONG]

During labor, Hmong women prefer not to cry and reveal their pain. Moments after birth, the baby receives a silver necklace to warn the spirits that the child belongs to the family and is not a slave. In some Hmong communities, the women sew caps covered with flower designs *(paj ntaub* [pah-dow]*)* to fool the evil spirits into thinking the baby is a flower.

If doctors are willing to give them the placenta, the Hmong bury it in the backyard, an adaptation of the home-country custom of burying it beneath the central pole of their homes. If the firstborn is a male, they dry the umbilical cord and use it for medicine made by boiling it with a piece of oak. They feed it to a seriously ill person.

For one month following childbirth, three times a day

the new mothers eat only boiled chicken and broth and rice. They may add special homegrown herbs. The chickens must be freshly killed each day to meet the mother's nutritional needs. Store-bought chickens are unacceptable.

Three days after birth, the Hmong have a ceremony where they announce the baby's name and call back the baby's soul, which might have been frightened away during birth. If the family is Catholic, they may delay the ceremony until one month. For the baby's protection, they tie white strings around its wrists, which remain until they fall off or disintegrate on their own. These strings install the protective spirits within the body and prevent the soul from being abducted. (See "Giving Birth"/Lao, p. 37; "Giving Birth"/Thai, p. 41; "Healing"/Lao, p. 165; "Marrying"/Lao, p. 133; "Marrying"/Thai, p. 139.)

✪ *Gifts:* Baby clothes and toys.

✪ *Words:* Most of the older generation believe that if they compliment the baby, evil spirits will take it away. While the younger generation claims not to believe in this, refrain from commenting positively about the child. The Hmong themselves make comments such as "The baby smells of poo-poo." By acknowledging the child, they are revealing their admiration, but by saying something uncomplimentary, they are protecting the baby, too. For some of the older Hmong, the prohibition against compliments extends to grown children.

✪ *Body Language:* Older Hmong avoid body contact with members of the same and opposite sex. A married woman disrespects her husband by smiling at or shaking hands with a man. In contrast, the younger generation is beginning to adopt the hugging traditions of their American schoolmates. To be prudent, avoid all body contact.

INDIAN (BRAHMAN)

Baby's First Birthday

Most prefer to go to India for this ceremony, where they offer a temple the baby's hair, which is later used for wigs. Girls' heads are completely shaved, and boys' heads are shaved except for a small tuft at the back of the head. In the United States, they do it symbolically by snipping a piece of hair and saving it in a plastic bag for their next journey to a temple in India.

During the ceremony, they build a fire in a two-foot-by-two-foot brick square. Several priests pray for the well-being of the child and pour ghee (clarified butter) to make the flames flare higher, for the fire is considered the witness that will carry the prayers for the child to heaven. If, according to the astrologers, the child is in danger because of harmful positioning of the planets on its birth date, the priests request that the gods be gentle and not harm the child too much.

✪ *Gifts:* Baby clothes and other typical baby gifts.

✪ *Words:* Although it is permissible to compliment the child, it is better not to say too much. To counteract the evil eye, after someone compliments the baby, a family member rubs her palm over the baby's forehead, then cracks her knuckles, one at a time. The sound of each cracked knuckle forces away the evil eye.

✪ *Clothing:* Elegant dresses, silks only for Indian women. Avoid black. Remove shoes and socks.

✪ *Body Language:* Use the *namaste* [nah-mah-stay] for greetings. With hands pressed together in a prayerlike position, bring them up to just below the chin and nod slightly.

JAPANESE (BUDDHIST)

First Haircut

Many Japanese do not cut their baby's hair until their first birthday. In Japan they use the hair to make a *sumi* [sue-me] brush (used for calligraphy). Some Japanese Americans still observe this tradition by sending the baby's hair to Japan to be made into a brush.

Hatsu Mairi [hot-sue mah-ee-ree] (First Temple Presentation)

Once a year, parents present new babies to the temple. They are given *juzu*, a string of beads, white or crystal for girls and red for boys. The babies wear kimonos. In the past, they were wrapped in adult kimonos and dressed in red. (See "Giving Birth"/Japanese, *Kanreki*, p. 58.)

⊙ *Gifts:* After the child is born, grandparents present grandsons with a *kabuto* (warrior's helmet) and a warrior doll, which are never used for play. Families display them on Boys' Day, May 5. After World War II, during the American occupation of Japan, the United States banned Boys' Day because of the militaristic emphasis symbolized by the warrior objects. They changed the name to Children's Day. In the United States, they still call it Boys' Day.

Similarly, grandparents present new granddaughters with a set of dolls representing the emperor and empress and their royal court dressed in traditional royal garb and exhibited on five tiers. Since only the wealthy can afford such expensive dolls, paper replicas may be substituted. These dolls are shown only on Girls' Day, March 3. If they remain on display on any other day, many believe that the newborn girl will never marry.

Nongrandparents give any kind of gift, including money. If possible, place the cash in special envelopes decorated with baby motifs, which may be purchased in Japanese shops. (See "Marrying"/Japanese, p. 125.) If these envelopes are unavailable, use any kind. In all circumstances, bills should be clean, preferably new, and wrapped in white paper placed inside the envelope, never directly placed inside.

✪ *Words:* Compliments are acceptable.

JEWISH

Brit Milah [breet mee-láh] (Circumcision)

Brit Milah means "covenant," commonly called either a *brit* or a *bris*. It refers to an agreement made between God and Abraham (Genesis 17:2) wherein God promises to bless Abraham and allow him to prosper in exchange for his loyalty. This covenant was symbolized by circumcision—where the foreskin of the penis is removed. Ever since then, Jewish families enter the covenant when the son of every Jewish mother is circumcised on his eighth day.

A ritual specialist called a *mohel* [móy-ell] performs the ceremony. The godmother brings the child into the room, and the godfather holds him during the prayers. The child is then handed over to the one who has the most honored role, the *sandek* (godfather, in Greek), who is often a good friend or a grandparent. He holds the infant on his lap during the procedure, which is brief, generally taking less than ten minutes.

Jews believe that the prophet Elijah is present at each Jewish child's circumcision. To represent his presence they set aside a special chair, known as the chair of Elijah. Just prior to placing the baby in the *sandek*'s lap, the godfather momentarily sets him on the chair as a symbol of Elijah's blessing.

During the operation, they ease the baby's pain by giving it a pacifier to suck on or a small sponge filled with sugar water. Often the *mohel* takes a wine-dipped cloth and places it in the infant's mouth, which not only acts as an anesthetic but becomes the first partaking in the blessing of wine. After the procedure, the *mohel* bandages the baby and hands it back to the father. Sometimes, the father buries the removed foreskin.

In the past, the ceremony was frequently celebrated in the synagogue; nowadays, it is more commonly held at home. They bless the wine (kiddush) and give the baby his Hebrew name. The family then serves a celebration meal.

Spirits are high at this event, which is generally attended by the immediate family and close friends. Because of the delicate nature of the procedure, much joking takes place, for everyone is acutely aware of the need for precision. While on the surface, jokes on this occasion might be considered in bad taste, they serve to relieve the tension felt by both the men and women.

One new mother described the tension in the room when the Hasidic *mohel* arrived. A hush fell as non-Jewish and Jewish guests tensed. The rabbi broke the silence: "Okay, who's first?"

What did the father of the newborn say to the *mohel*? "You can keep the tip."

✪ *Gifts:* Typical baby gifts or money. If money, use units of 18, the numerical value of the two letters that make up the word *chai* (life) (yod = 10, chet = 8).

✪ *Words:* "Mazel tov." "Congratulations."

Because the former USSR prohibited Jews from being circumcised, many adult Russian males elect to have this procedure when they come to the United States. It takes place in a hospital, where rabbis are present to give blessings and bestow Hebrew names. Families partake of food and wine before leaving the hospital.

SEPHARDIC [SAY-FÁR-DICK] VARIATIONS

Since Sephardim [say-far-déem] (descendants of Spanish, Portuguese, and Middle Eastern Jews) name their children for living relatives (see "Giving Birth"/Jewish, Giving Hebrew name, p. 33), it is likely that at least one of the newborn's relatives will bear the same name and be present at the circumcision ceremony. Consequently, when a child of Judeo-Spanish ancestry is given his name at this event, everyone else attending the ritual slaps those who bear the same name. This reminds them that the qualities they developed as a result of their name and their soul will now be shared by the new member of the Jewish community.

Pidyon Haben [pid-yon hah-bén] (Redemption of the Firstborn Son)

If the firstborn child is a male, this ceremony occurs on his thirty-first day. It is a reenactment of a biblical tradition that the firstborn must be consecrated to the lifelong service of the Lord. However, in biblical times a father could redeem his son through the proferring of redemption money. So, too, fathers today redeem their sons from priestly service through payment of a ransom.

Generally, the mother enters the room carrying the infant on a pillow and hands him to the father, who places the child and the pillow on a table. The rabbi asks the father if he wishes to surrender his son for priestly service or ransom him for five pieces of silver.

After the father announces his intention to keep his son, he makes a blessing and gives the rabbi five silver dollars. The rabbi accepts the money, announces that the child is redeemed, and blesses the child, the bread, and the wine. The rabbi often donates the money to charity. Family members may say a few words. Sometimes the parents make speeches about aspirations for their son.

Exemptions to this ceremony occur if the child is born by C-section, if the mother's first pregnancy ended in a miscarriage, or if the child is the firstborn male child of a Kohen (priest) or of a Levite. If the thirty-first day falls on the Sabbath or a Jewish holy day, the ceremony is postponed one day.

✪ *Gifts:* Traditional baby gifts, clothes, money—especially in units of 18. (See "Giving Birth"/Jewish, *Brit Milah,* p. 32.)

✪ *Words:* "Mazel tov." "Congratulations."

✪ *Clothing:* Not too casual.

Upsherin (shearing) (Baby Boy's First Haircut)

Orthodox Jews in Israel annually observe this event thirty-three days after Passover, known as Lag b'Omer. Thousands bring their three-year-old sons to Meron for a haircutting ceremony. Meron is the site of the tomb of the famed Rabbi Shimon Bar Yochai, author of the *Zohar,* a cabalistic work. The rabbi died on this date and in his will declared that there should be a party on his day of death.

In the United States, Orthodox and some secular Jews observe the first-haircut ceremony when a male child is three years old. The child becomes analogous to a tree that is prohibited from being cut until it is three years old. Until that time no one takes its fruit because it is underdeveloped, but if left untouched for three years, the fruit becomes sweet. Humans, too, should not be touched for the first three years. After that, they are ready to move on to the next stage of life. Fittingly, at three years of age, a haircutting ceremony marks the beginning of the boy's next stage—his acceptance of responsibility to begin studying the Torah.

Observances vary. Among the Orthodox, the child may be brought in to meet his rebbe (teacher), who blesses him and places tzitzit [tsi-tsiss, rhymes with *kisses*] (a short-fringed jacketlike garment worn under the coat or vest) on him. The rebbe goes through the *aleph-bet* (Hebrew alphabet) to introduce him to the learning of the Torah, then he cuts off a few locks of hair. Afterward, the child may be taken to a barber or the barber may be present and finish the job. A party with lots of food follows, and the parents feed the child honey for a sweet life. They also distribute small packages of candy to all children who may be present.

At other celebrations, all present participate in cutting off the hair, which by the time a child is three may be so long as to reach the waist. While non-Orthodox Jews provide a standard haircut, Orthodox Jews cut all but the *peot* [pay-oat] (side locks). Each person who cuts a curl places some money in a charity box to be distributed to Jewish charities.

This event stresses the importance of charity and the responsibility of learning. After the haircut, eating and general frivolity take place.

✪ *Gifts:* Children's gifts of any kind, especially books.

✪ *Words:* "Mazel tov." "Congratulations."

✪ *Clothing:* The event is informal, but if held at the home of Orthodox Jews, women have modest necklines, arms covered, and midcalf hemlines.

KOREAN

One Hundredth Day Party

Whether Christian or Buddhist, Koreans have a celebration of life when the baby reaches its one hundredth day. They have an abundance of food, but the hallmark of this event is the presentation of a one-layered, un-iced, round, white cake made of rice flour. It is always present at this event and has no candles.

✪ *Gifts:* Gold for girls or boys: rings, necklaces, bracelets. If unaffordable, any other baby gift.

⚙ *Words:* Compliments are acceptable.

⚙ *Clothing:* To the hosts, what guests wear is unimportant.

LAO

Sou-Khouanh [sue-kwanh]

Sometime between the first and second months after birth, the Lao have a party. The highlight of the event is a well-wishing ceremony called *baci* [bai-see] or *sou-khoanh*. (See "Giving Birth"/Hmong, p. 28; "Giving Birth"/Thai, p. 41; "Healing"/Lao, p. 165; "Marrying"/Lao, p. 133; "Marrying"/Thai, p. 139.) The ceremony welcomes the mother and the baby home from the hospital. Because of the violent nature of childbirth, the Lao believe that the souls of the mother and the baby may have been frightened away. Their straying souls are brought back by wrapping white strings around the wrists of the baby and the mother. The strings remain in place for three days, after which they are removed.

Everyone who attends participates in tying on the strings. Monks are not required. A grandmother or grandfather may officiate. A feast follows.

⚙ *Gifts:* Any baby gift. Money in a white envelope. Hand it to the mother or father.

⚙ *Words:* When tying on the strings, wish the mother and the baby good health and happiness. When the Lao were still living in Asia, they avoided complimenting the baby lest the evil spirits come and take it away. Since most Lao have now been in the United States since the 1980s, that belief is fading, especially among the younger people. If you decide to compliment the baby, use discretion if older people can hear you.

⚙ *Clothing:* Remove shoes inside homes.

MEXICAN

Recent Mexican immigrants often have a strong belief in the power of the evil eye, which may harm the baby. This may occur when a stranger compliments the child, as a Spanish-speaking American couple discovered while riding a crowded bus near the Texas/Mexican border.

Noticing a young Latino couple holding an adorable baby, the American woman smiled at the parents and said, "*Qué chula.*" (How darling.) Troubled by the comment, the young parents left their seats, pushed through the crowd, and handed the baby to the American woman, requesting that she touch him. By so doing, the American would no longer be a stranger and the child would not be vulnerable to an attack by the evil eye, which might bring about illness or worse.

NATIVE AMERICAN

CHEROKEE

At four days, the mother brings the baby to a priest, who takes the child in his arms and walks to a river. Facing the rising sun, he places himself at the water's edge and leans toward the water seven times as if to plummet the child into the river. However, he keeps the baby safe, never allowing it to touch the water.

While performing this act, the priest says a prayer to himself asking for a long and prosperous life for the child. When finished, he passes the baby to the mother, who gently rubs water onto the baby's face and chest.

If for some reason the ceremony cannot take place on the child's fourth day, it may be postponed to the seventh. Both four and seven are sacred numbers to the Cherokees.

NAVAJO

First-Laugh Feast

Navajos adore new babies. Family and friends lovingly welcome the child, play with it, watch over it, especially encouraging the baby's first laugh, which always comes as a surprise, generally anywhere from three to eight months. This joyful sound is cause for celebration.

Whoever makes the baby laugh for the first time must prepare the first-laugh feast, which consists of corn in mush form, on the cob, or canned, mutton or beef stew, vegetables, fried bread, and berries for a sweet life. The berries can be wild, canned, or served in a pie.

To make the baby laugh first is a great honor. It is also a lot of work. The person who inspires the first laugh must prepare food for the twelve to fifty guests who participate in this significant meal. Guests include immediate and extended family, friends, and visitors. They welcome non-Navajo, too.

The guests line up with their food-filled plates to greet the baby, who sits on the lap of the person who made it laugh. The child holds rock salt tightly in one hand. In its other hand, the baby sometimes grasps a miniature Navajo wedding basket. As each guest steps up to the baby, the person holding it helps the baby release some of the salt from its fist onto the guest's plate. By so doing, the baby learns to be a giving person. Through this act, Navajo families instill the importance of generosity.

After the guests receive the salt, they shake the baby's hand, hug it, or give it a kiss. It is an uplifting occasion, and guests receive blessings by receiving the salt. The rock salt represents tears, the result of either laughing or crying, and although they might seem like opposite emotions, to the Navajo they are the same. The Navajo treasure both. The first-laugh feast signals what lies ahead for the child.

✪ *Gifts:* Small gifts for the child. Additionally, the host family may give small gifts to the guests, such as earrings or trinkets.

✪ *Words:* After guests receive salt from the baby, they may say "Thank you," for reminding them of their own first happiness.

✪ *Clothing:* Informal but modest.

Ear Piercing

At approximately two weeks, mothers pierce the ears of their newborn sons and daughters. They do this so that their children will heed their mothers' words throughout their lives. Although the earrings are usually of silver and turquoise, the piercing matters more than the material placed into the earlobes in teaching the child to obey. Nonetheless, the Navajo consider silver and turquoise the earth's treasures and call turquoise the umbilical cord attached to Mother Earth.

SAMOAN

Alaalafaga [ala-ala-fanga]

When the mother and child arrive home from the hospital, the family has a formal thanksgiving for their healthy return. Extended family, a minister, *matais* [mah-ties] (chiefs), from both sides of the family attend, and the families exchange fine mats to celebrate the occasion. If the birth of the child has been difficult, family members may invite any medical personnel believed to have aided in the successful delivery.

Depicted as a kind of potluck party on the mainland, on the islands it is more like a baby shower. Because they have adopted the baby shower tradition stateside, fewer baby gifts are given at the *alaalafaga*. They sing, read from the Bible, and say prayers for the child, mother, and family.

After the prayers, the chief thanks the minister and they eat. Since eating heartily is an important Samoan tradition, in addition to the eating at the party, food is sent home with each guest. Close friends and family members bring money and food to contribute to the feast.

Alaalafaga always takes place at night after sundown in Samoa. Stateside, they have it at 7 P.M. or 8 P.M. They also observe this ceremony when a patient returns home from the hospital or when someone new comes to visit.

✪ *Gifts:* Baby gifts. Do not bring liquor, considered offensive among traditional Samoans.

✪ *Words:* They welcome compliments.

✪ *Clothing:* Avoid shorts or cutoffs.

THAI

Well-wishers tie white strings around the wrists of the mother and the child upon their return from the hospital. (See "Giving Birth"/Hmong, p. 28; "Giving Birth"/Lao, p. 37; "Healing"/Lao, p. 165; "Marrying"/Lao, p. 133; "Marrying"/Thai, p. 139.) The mother wears the strings for two to three days. The baby wears them longer. The white strings must not be cut off, but can be removed by pulling them apart or untying them.

When the baby is seven days old or one month old, parents bring the baby to the Thai Buddhist temple to be blessed by a monk. There is no special party, but friends and family may give gifts. In Thailand, they do not celebrate birthdays, but when Thai children attend school in the United States, they request parties just like their classmates. Parents usually acquiesce.

✪ *Gifts:* Regardless of its sex, after the baby is blessed, friends and families give the baby gold: chains, necklaces, and bracelets. They also give money in envelopes. In the past, the envelopes were generally white. Nowadays, some people put money in pink envelopes for girls and blue envelopes for boys.

❂ *Words:* In Thailand, people do not compliment the baby for the first three months. If they were to say that the baby was pretty, the bad spirits might want it. To discourage compliments, they used to put a black smudge on the baby's face. Most Thai living in the United States do not follow this custom. Nonetheless, to avoid upsetting the older generation, use discretion when commenting on the child's appearance or demeanor.

❂ *Clothing:* Remove shoes when entering a temple. Step over the threshold, not on it, an inauspicious act.

❂ *Body Language:* People greet one another with the *wai* [why]. This is the most respectful form of greeting. With hands pressed together in a prayerlike position, bring them up to just below the chin and nod slightly. However, Thai customs in the United States are relaxing a bit. Some Thai may use the handshake when greeting non-Asians. Watch cues and follow suit.

TIBETAN

Bhansel [bahn-sell] (Cleansing Ceremony)

This is the baby's first official bath, which takes place at home two days after the birth of a girl and three days after the birth of a boy. Friends and family gather, and after they wash the baby, they sprinkle it with holy water. Guests offer a white, filmy scarf to the baby, wrapping it around the infant while blessing the baby and wishing that it serve its parents well and have a long life and good health. As guests each place a scarf around the mother's neck, they slip her an envelope made of homemade Tibetan paper containing money.

Note: In Tibet on auspicious occasions, flowers for offerings are not available because of the harsh weather. Instead, they use white, rectangular rayon or silk scarves for offerings and prayers, a tradition maintained in the United States. (See "Marrying"/Tibetan, p. 141; "Dying"/Tibetan, p. 231.)

✪ *Gifts:* Non-Tibetans bring baby clothes, blankets, and other useful items.

✪ *Words: "Tashi delek"* (May all auspicious signs come to this environment). In the United States, it is permissible to compliment the baby.

✪ *Clothing:* Dress up for this important occasion. Women should wear jewelry. Depending on the family, note whether or not they remove their shoes inside their homes and follow suit.

✪ *Body Language:* After saying *"Tashi delek,"* Tibetans may briefly stick out their tongues to one another, indicating respect and affirmation. They use the *namaste* for greetings (see "Giving Birth"/Indian, p. 30), but the younger generation may also shake hands with non-Tibetan guests.

VIETNAMESE

They believe that during birth the mother loses body heat, which must be restored. After delivery, they keep the mother warm by piling on blankets and hot-water bottles or electric blankets. Other postpartum practices include avoidance of cold drafts, cold drinks, bathing, and shampoos.

When the baby is one month old, they have a big party, especially if the child is male. They light incense on their home altars, thank the gods for the new baby, and pray for blessings on the child. Although some Vietnamese have parties for newborn girls, the celebrations are not as large as those for boys, and some families opt not to have a party for girls. Whether the babies are boys or girls, families send gifts of boiled pork and red- or pink-dyed eggs to their neighbors.

❂ *Gifts:* Gold jewelry for the baby girl or boy shows the highest respect and reflects on the donor's class and generosity. If unaffordable, baby clothes.

❂ *Words:* Avoid complimenting the baby.

❂ *Clothing:* No restrictions.

❂ *Body Language:* The older generation avoids male/female contact. The most prudent acknowledgment is a slight nod. However, younger people may shake hands or even give hugs.

NAMING CEREMONIES

A person's name is her most valued possession, which must be protected. One may have power over others simply by knowing their names. The Rumpelstiltskin fairy tale demonstrates this when the queen, to avoid giving her firstborn child to the strange little man, destroys him by merely uttering his name, "Rumpelstiltskin." In real life, some Native American tribes never reveal to outsiders the true name of a child. Others believe that revealing the baby's proposed name before it is born brings bad luck.

Selecting the right name for the child is one of the most complex decisions facing new parents. To continue the link of generations and cement family ties, parents may name the child after another family member, living or dead. They may consult with books and elders about this important act. The ceremonial bestowal of names is charged with implications for the child's future.

CHINESE

Red Egg and Ginger Party

In China, they called it the completion-of-one-month party, a time to introduce the baby to the family and give the child its name. Held thirty days following the birth of a child, this celebration dates back to the Zhou dynasty in the first millennium. However, in those times, due to high mortality rates, it was more frequently celebrated when the child was three months old.

Chinese Americans more commonly call the festivities red egg and ginger parties, which take place anytime after the baby's first month. They write the invitations on red paper, and at the parties, families distribute red-dyed hard-boiled eggs. The eggs symbolize fertility and wholeness; the red represents good fortune. The eggs are eaten with thinly sliced, sweet pickled ginger, believed helpful in restoring the new mother's energy. Sometimes the eggs are piled high into a basket for guests to help themselves. In more formal situations, hosts place one red egg with ginger at each table setting.

Today, as in ancient times, the celebration introduces the baby to friends and family. Since most American children are named within the first few days of life, at this party they announce the child's Chinese name. Parents dress the baby in its best clothing, and guests compliment the baby's appearance and alertness.

Many Americanized Chinese families place announcements of the event on the society pages of Chinese-American newspapers, and the party often takes place in a

Chinese restaurant. More traditional families do not announce the event in the paper and more frequently have parties at home.

✪ *Gifts:* Typical baby gifts. Chinese guests frequently give money in small red envelopes available for purchase in Chinese gift shops.

✪ *Words:* Compliments are acceptable.

✪ *Clothing:* Whatever is appropriate for the setting, restaurant or home, but not too casual.

INDIAN (BRAHMAN)

Namakarma [nah-mah-car-mah]

On the baby's eleventh day, the priest comes to the home to bless the baby, who is dressed in ordinary clothes and lying in a cradle. In fear of the evil eye, parents place a black dot on its face, often on the chin, to detract from the child's appearance. This also deters people from complimenting the child. If someone inadvertently compliments the baby, the power of the evil eye can be removed by one parent placing salt in each hand, waving it over the baby's whole body, then dissolving the salt in tap water and letting it run down the drain. After the child reaches the age of one, fear of the evil eye lessens.

After the baby's birth, parents consult with an astrologer about the baby's planetary influences. The astrologer suggests an appropriate ritualistic name, which the priest announces along with a calling or modern name. Often the ritualistic name is that of one of the gods or goddesses, so that in everyday life if there is no time to pray, just by calling the name of the child the parents are also mentioning the name of the gods.

The priest blesses the child and so do the guests.

✪ *Gifts:* Typical baby gifts.

✪ *Words:* Avoid compliments. One should not look at the baby too much or too long.

✪ *Clothing:* Indian guests wear silks. Non-Indian guests wear good clothing as they might for a church christening. Avoid wearing black. Remove shoes and socks when entering the home and/or temple.

✪ *Body Language:* Indians greet each other and out-siders with the *namaste* [nah-mah-stay]. With hands pressed together in a prayerlike position, bring them up to just below the chin and nod slightly.

JEWISH

Generally, parents select an important family member to name their child after. They may choose the same Hebrew name and/or the initial letter to use for the secular name. While Ashkenazic [osh-key-náh-zick] Jews generally name their babies after a deceased relative, Sephardic [say-fár-dick] Jews name them after someone who is alive. In the lat-ter tradition, the first son is named after the father's father, the first daughter after the father's mother, the second son after the mother's father, the second daughter after the mother's mother. (See "Giving Birth"/Sephardic Variations, p. 48.)

Hebrew names are used on religious documents and during rites of passage. Boys receive their names at a *brit*. (See "Giving Birth"/Jewish, *Brit Milah*, p. 32.) However, if they are circumcised at the hospital as part of a surgical procedure immediately after birth, a special ceremony may be held in the synagogue or at home. Today, girls are be-ginning to receive their Hebrew names in *brit bat* cere-monies, which can be held in a temple or at home (see below). After a baby girl is named in temple, Sephardic Jews distribute bags of nuts and candy. They call this ritual *sha sha*.

BRIT BAT [BREET-BAHT] (ALSO KNOWN AS SIMCHAT BAT [SIM-KHA-BAHT])

American parents have become innovative in developing welcoming ceremonies for their newborn daughters. Past emphasis on paying ritual attention to boys and not to girls has been the motivation for these celebrations, especially in a society that struggles to promote equal rights for females.

These events can take place at eight, fourteen, or thirty days after birth, on the first day of the new moon, or on the Sabbath. When held at home, the new parents generally officiate; when held in the synagogue, the rabbi conducts the ceremony. Because this ceremony is evolving, it stimulates innovation and manipulation of traditional symbols of readings, prayers, poetry, blessings, including the presence of Elijah's chair to petition angelic protection. Often there is a formal greeting, reading of prayers, followed by the blessing of the wine, sometimes with a drop given to the baby. In a parallel act to circumcision, whoever presides may wash the baby's feet or hands, representing the child's entrance into the covenant.

This occasion usually provides the opportunity to bestow names upon daughters. A celebratory meal follows.

✪ *Gifts:* Baby gifts of any kind; monetary gifts, particularly in denominations of 18. (See "Giving Birth"/Jewish, *Brit Milah*, p. 32.)

✪ *Words:* "Mazel tov." "Congratulations."

✪ *Clothing:* Not too casual. This is the equivalent of a church christening.

SEPHARDIC VARIATIONS

Among those of Judeo-Spanish ancestry the baby girl is brought into the room on a pillow carried by a young relative dressed as a bride. They call this ceremony *las fadas,* during which they seek the blessings of good spirits. Each guest blesses the baby, including the rabbi. Afterward, they sing songs and enjoy a bountiful meal.

NATIVE AMERICAN

(See "Coming of Age"/Native American, Lakota, p. 77.)

CHEROKEE

When the baby is seven days old, they take it to the river they call Long Man, where the medicine person prays for the new child while holding it over the water. The medicine person offers the baby to the water seven times. The mother dips her fingers in the river, then brings the water to the baby by softly touching her fingers on the child.

HOPI

Twenty days after birth, the paternal grandmother arranges the naming ceremony. This is the first time the father sees his new child. At sunrise, the mother and father's mother present the baby to the sun and repeat the new name.

MIWOK/MAIDU

The child receives its Indian name after its personality evolves. One child was named Sharp Eyes because at an early age he could see his grandmother coming down the road. Another was named Owl because when learning to speak, he kept asking, "Who?"

NAVAJO

In a private ceremony at birth, babies receive a Christian name and a traditional name, which may be bestowed by a relative or medicine man. Later, when children enter puberty, marked by a boy's voice change and the first menses for girls, they receive adult names given to them by a different person. This symbolizes that they have already walked the way of a child and are closing the book on childhood and must now look toward the future. This, too, is a private ceremony, where they are taught to protect their spirit names lest people use those names to harm them. Their name carries them through their whole life.

PUEBLO

The mother chooses a relative or friend to bring the newborn outside and present it to the sun. At this time, they give the baby a name. However, if the name brings bad luck or makes the child fretful, they change the name.

NIGERIAN

IBO [ÉE-BOW]

The name is so important that, if a child is wrongly named, it may become sick and die. Sometimes, parents go to a traditional healer, who after consulting with the spirits advises what name to choose.

Generally, the baby is given its traditional name four months to one year after birth. The first son is usually named after his paternal grandfather and the first daughter after her paternal grandmother. When making these decisions, the Ibo consult with the paternal grandparents.

Sometimes the grandparents may travel from Nigeria to perform the ceremony, officiated by the eldest male on the paternal side. The Ibo place the child on the floor, and in addition to bestowing a name, they give the child a pen, signifying their hopes for the child's education. This is one of the most prized desires for newborns, both male and female. The Ibo also put the child in touch with its roots. If the baby came from a family of farmers, parents will let it touch something related, such as a hoe. If from a weaving family, the child will be handed a weaving stick to touch. If the family have been peanut traders, they will place a peanut in the baby's hand. Baby girls participate in the same ritual.

⚙ *Gifts:* Baby clothing and money. Place the bills directly in the baby's hands. If guests give money to the parents instead, the parents show it to the baby.

⚙ *Words:* Advise babies that when they grow up, they should take good care of their parents.

⚙ *Clothing:* Dressy.

YORUBA [YÓUR-OO-BAH]

The following description applies to those Yoruba who are not Orisha [oh-rée-sha] followers. Seven to nine days after birth, they name the baby. Otherwise, traditional Yorubas believe it will not outlive its parent of the same sex. The ceremony takes place at home beginning in the afternoon when guests arrive with gifts. Later, all gather around a table bearing ritual food and objects. After singing an opening hymn, the pastor allows the baby to taste or touch each of the foods and objects on the table. He describes the symbolism of each article, expresses prayers for the child's well-being and good character, then circulates the items for all to taste or touch. Afterward, the minister announces the baby's first and second names.

Next, while singing and bearing candles, the minister leads the parents, family, and baby into the baby's room to bless it and the baby's bed with prayers and hymns. Some may recite poetry created for the occasion. Afterward, everyone returns to the living room to enjoy traditional foods such as fried plantain, goat stew with *fufu* (a glutenous substance made of boiled and pounded cassava), boiled yams, and fowl. Later more guests arrive for music and dance, which may last all night.

Frequently the parents and the baby wear new African

clothing. If the grandmothers are still in Nigeria, they send their choice of names for the baby. When the baby visits Nigeria for the first time, grandmothers will call the baby by the names they have chosen. In Nigeria, this ceremony takes place outdoors, where they touch the baby's bare foot to the ground, signifying that its first steps will lead it in the right direction.

○ *Gifts:* Money, layette sets, clothing, blankets.

○ *Words:* Congratulate the parents.

○ *Clothing:* Dressy.

PROTESTANT CHRISTENINGS

These are generally held during the Sunday service after the sermon. The child's godparents and parents stand at the font, and one of the godmothers holds the baby, dressed in a white cap and christening gown. The godmother stands on the minister's left, and after the start of the ceremony, she places the child in his left arm. The minister asks the godparents to speak on behalf of the child and make promises to God and renounce the devil. The godparents announce the child's name and the minister says, "I baptize you in the name of the Father and of the Son, and of the Holy Spirit." He then sprinkles or pours blessed water on the child's head. In some churches, baptism may be by immersion. The minister repeats the child's names and makes a cross on the baby's brow and hands it back to the godmother.

On some occasions the godfather holds a lit candle and the minister says, "I give you this sign to show that you have passed from shadow into light." He makes a final blessing and reminds the parents and godparents of their commitment to God and the baby. Afterward, the family or fellowship may serve cake and coffee or perhaps a light lunch.

✪ *Gifts:* Typical baby gifts.

✪ *Words:* "Congratulations."

✪ *Clothing:* Guests should dress up for this occasion. Modest clothing. Avoid shorts and beachwear.

ROMAN CATHOLIC CHRISTENINGS

Since Sunday-morning Mass is the busiest time, they frequently hold these twenty- to thirty-minute ceremonies separately in the afternoon in the middle of a Mass between the reading of Scripture and the priest's sermon. The Eucharist follows. Big parishes often have groups of twenty to thirty at a time.

Sometimes this ceremony is called baptism. In past times, christening took place soon after a child's birth. Urgency stemmed from the fear that an unbaptized child might die and be unqualified for salvation. However, nowadays, the more common belief is that the mercy of God will take care of the child, and parents may wait months, even years.

The mother dresses the baby in a white cap and long gown, symbol of the wedding garment; some baby boys may wear a white shirt, vest, and short pants. Others have hand-me-down dresses that have gone through many generations that sometimes become yellow. Most commonly, the priest or deacon pours water on the baby's forehead, but some churches have a baptismal font containing heated water so that the baby may be immersed.

After welcoming the child, the priest asks what name will be given, and one of the godparents replies with the selected name and adds one of a saint. Commonly, they bestow a saint's name to give the child a model of good behavior. Godparents are generally relatives and are frequently asked to take a preparation class to learn their duties. In general, their role is to be attentive to the child's religious upbringing in the event that something happens to the parents. They serve as mentors and models and remind the child that he or she is baptized in the faith.

Standing in front of the font, the mother or godmother holds the baby. The priest or deacon asks the following questions of the parents and godparents: "Do you believe in the tenets of the faith?" "Do you resist evil?" "Do you wish _____ (name of child) to be baptized in the faith?" After receiving positive answers to these questions, the priest asks the godmother to hold the baby over the basin. He takes a cup of holy water, sometimes from a seashell container, and says, "I baptize you in the name of the Father, Son, and the Holy Spirit." He anoints the child on the breast with holy oil and hands the parents and god-parents a lighted candle, symbol of the light of faith. Then he speaks a prayer for all of them.

The priest places a white veil or cloth over the child's head for a moment and says a final prayer over the baby's ears and mouth so that the child will receive the word of the Lord and proclaim his or her faith. The priest concludes by blessing the parents. He reminds them of their religious duties and to thank God for this child's life.

✪ *Gifts:* Traditional baby gifts and money. Sometimes godparents give the child a little prayer book and rosary.

✪ *Words:* Simple words of congratulations.

✪ *Clothing:* In church, respectful attire.

✪ *Body Language:* Kneeling is not required of non-Catholics or Catholics who have physical limitations.

✪ *Communion:* If the ceremony takes place during Mass, non-Catholic guests need not feel uncomfortable. Remain in place while others pass in front of you to proceed to the front of the church to accept the host and wine.

DETERMINING THE BABY'S FUTURE

All parents have high hopes for their offspring, and this type of celebration expresses ambitious desires for them. To foretell the baby's future, families from a variety of ethnicities have parties where they utilize commonplace objects to divine what lies ahead for the child.

ARMENIAN

Although the Armenians are a disparate people, no matter where they live, Turkey, Lebanon, the former USSR, the United States, they participate in this event. The party occurs when the baby's first tooth appears. Thus it is called *agra* (tooth) *hadig* [ha-deeg] (wheat), a traditional food served at this event.

The mother props up the infant on a table or on the floor and places up to five objects in front of the child. Whichever object the child selects first reveals the baby's future occupation. If the child picks a book or a bible, it means the child will be a scholar, teacher, or clergy person. If the baby chooses money, the child will become a banker, a financier, or very rich. If it selects a hammer, the child will enter the building trades. A knife symbolizes a doctor or surgeon; a scissors foretells a life as a seamstress or tailor; a comb means a barber or hairdresser.

Hosts boil whole wheat and add sugar and spices, covering the mixture with pistachios, cloves, and cinnamon. When the baby is about to make its selection of objects, the mother throws some of this mixture on the baby's head, which has been covered by a towel.

Sometimes only females attend and only sweet foods are served. Among other families, they invite all family members and serve a lunch with many sweets. This is a gleeful event with clapping and singing to the baby and holding of the baby to make it dance. Although merriment prevails, underlying the gaiety lies a genuine concern for the future well-being of the child, its social status and economic survival.

While Armenian-American celebrations generally do not include negative portents, in other parts of the world, if a child picks up a scissors, they believe the child will become a murderer; dirt can signify an early grave; a glass can foretell the life of a drunkard; and if the child chooses a deck of cards, its life as a gambler is assured.

✪ *Gifts:* The first person to discover the tooth brings the baby an undershirt. Others bring small gifts.

✪ *Words:* Praise the baby, wishing it to grow up to be gentle, kind, the pride and joy of the family.

While the first tooth sets the timing for this divinatory event among Armenians, among other cultures it frequently occurs when the child is one year of age. Americans of Irish, English, Russian-Jewish, Polish, Greek, and German descent in the South, Midwest, Pennsylvania, Wisconsin, Nebraska, Colorado, and Utah have similar parties. Outside American borders, the custom has been recorded in Germany, China, and Czechoslovakia.

KOREAN

They call the celebration *tol* [tuhl], held when the baby is one year old, when it is considered fully human. The baby wears a colorful traditional costume, and among its choices are noodles or a piece of string for longevity, a pen or pencil for becoming a writer, a book for wisdom or knowledge, and money for wealth.

VIETNAMESE

A ruler predicts life as a teacher; a mirror symbolizes a beautician; sticky rice in brilliant colors of orange, green, and purple means the baby will eat a lot; a pen represents a writer; a book indicates a scholar; a toy car signifies a mechanic; a scissors means a dressmaker.

BIRTHDAY ANNIVERSARIES

Like first-year celebrations, certain other birthdays have special meanings: sweet sixteen; decade markers, especially the "big five-oh." Among the Vietnamese, forty, fifty, sixty, and seventy are special. Yet among certain cultures, particular birthday numbers are taboo and thus go uncelebrated. For example, Chinese immigrants may ignore the fortieth and forty-first birthdays because of the death connotations connected to the sound of four. Chinese men celebrate the twenty-first, thirty-first, fifty-first, sixty-first, seventy-first, and eighty-first birthdays, while traditional Chinese women celebrate their twentieth, thirtieth, fiftieth, sixtieth, seventieth, and eightieth birthdays. The differences between the men and women are tied to yin and yang principles. Yang, for males, stresses the odd numbers, while yin, the female principle, emphasizes even numbers.

JAPANESE

Yakudoshi [yah-coo-doe-shee]

Yakudoshi celebrates a man's forty-second birthday but is often observed on his forty-first birthday because traditionally Japanese are one year old at birth. The ritual prepares the celebrant to be on guard and protected through difficult years ahead, to help him avoid a midlife crisis. *Yakudoshi* represents the calamitous years. In Japan, friends and family present him with one thousand origami [oh-ree-gah-mee] (folded paper) cranes as a symbol of protection. In the United States, they more frequently use a thousand cranes for felicitations at weddings and birthdays rather than as omens for protection.

Kanreki [kahn-ray-key] (Return to Origins)—Age Sixty

Originally for men only, women are now celebrating it as well. The Buddhist calendar contains twelve zodiac signs and five branches. One completes the cycle at age sixty and is considered reborn and entering a second childhood. A party, hosted by the celebrant's children, often takes place at a restaurant, and the celebrant wears either a red jacket, vest, or sweater, and a red hat *(chan chan ko)* like a baseball cap. Red is a distinctive feature of the event, tied to the old Japanese tradition of dressing newborns in red caps and vests, a custom rarely followed today in the United States (See "Giving Birth"/Japanese, *Hatsu Mairi*, p. 31.)

This party is lighthearted, like a roast. Family and friends give gifts. The family may display a thousand red origami cranes made by all the children and grandchildren. These serve as symbols of longevity and good fortune. The party may be repeated at age eighty-eight and called *beiju* [bay-ee-ju].

✪ *Gifts:* Money or typical gift items, especially red ones.

✪ *Words:* "*Omedeto*" [oh-meh-det-oh] (congratulations or good luck), a felicitation used at weddings and New Year's, as well.

KOREAN

Hwan'Gap [hwon-gop]

In the United States, the children and wife give this party for the sixty-year-old man. Sixty signifies five times around the lunar calendar and the return to one's birth year. Rather than being a birthday party, it is more a rite of passage into old age.

If the celebrant's parents are still alive, he wears brightly colored clothing. If they are not, he dresses in all-white, traditional Korean drawstring pants, loose shirt, and vest. Wearing white signifies that he need not work anymore, that others have to serve him. One at a time, and starting with the eldest male, each of his children and their spouses followed by the rest of the kin approach the celebrant and his spouse. In turn, they bow, pour a cup of rice wine, circle the cup in front of the celebrant, then offer it to him. Men bow twice; women bow four times.

Other fixtures of the ritual include a table that looks like an ancestor worship table (see "Dying"/Korean, p. 215) filled with foods presented in a formalized order going from sweet to sour, in order of auspiciousness: piled-up plates of dried fruits, fresh fruits, cookies, rice cakes, pancakes, dried meats, pan-fried foods, and salads.

The heart of the ritual occurs when an emcee recounts the life history of the celebrant, and family members and others add their testimonials. Drinking and dancing follow.

The elaborateness of the celebration depends on the economic and social class of the involved families. Some children may not give their parents a big party but instead send them on a cruise or on a trip to Korea.

✪ *Gifts:* Koreans put cash inside a double envelope and give it to a family representative, who tallies amounts so that reciprocity may be maintained for future gift-giving. Non-Koreans often give personal gifts believing it to be a birthday party rather than a rite of passage into old age. Avoid giving knives.

✪ *Words:* "Happy birthday" is acceptable even though it is not strictly a birthday party.

✪ *Clothing:* Dressy clothing with suits and ties for men. Older Koreans may wear traditional clothing. Remove shoes if the celebration takes place at home.

✪ *Body Language:* Among the older generation, bowing is the official form of greeting. Avoid body contact unless initiated by others.

EMERGING TRADITIONS

ALCOHOLICS ANONYMOUS

Taking a Cake

Alcoholics Anonymous meetings take place mornings, afternoons, and evenings, seven days a week throughout and outside the United States. One of the highlights is the ceremony called taking a cake, which celebrates a member's sobriety.

Generally, meetings last from one to one and a half hours, depending on the time of day. Often a topic is suggested by the lead speaker, who for five to ten minutes explains that he qualifies as an alcoholic and has the right to lead a meeting. If the meeting is large, members step up to the podium to share their feelings and experiences. At smaller gatherings, members may sit at tables. Afterward, the secretary asks a series of questions:

"Does anyone want to take a welcome chip?" This is a

way of asking if any persons are first-time attendees. The person might answer, "Yes, I'm here for the first time. I live in Tulsa, Oklahoma," or he might say, "Yes, I have two days of sobriety and I'm hoping for more," which brings applause from the other members. AA members believe that newcomers are the most important persons at meetings. Consequently, they are very welcoming.

The secretary continues the questioning: "Does anyone have thirty days of continuous sobriety?" A person with thirty days will raise his hand and everyone will applaud. That person goes up to the secretary and receives a hug and a chip with "30 Days" on it. The person may say, "My name is John and I have been trying for a year to get thirty days together. I'm very grateful." Members applaud and John sits down. The same procedure occurs for sixty days, ninety days, and six months of sobriety.

Then the secretary asks the key question: "Is anyone celebrating a birthday?"

The presenter, who may be a sponsor or a friend of the celebrant, lights the cake in the kitchen and brings it out all lit up and holds it in front of the birthday honoree. Those in attendance sing "Happy Birthday," but instead of singing the tag line "And many more," they substitute, "Keep coming back," which means that the celebrant should keep returning for more meetings and stay sober. Then the celebrant blows out the candles. Note that there is never an extra candle for good luck on the cake because this would contradict the AA philosophy of "one day at a time."

After the celebrant extinguishes the candles, members applaud and the presenter hugs the person and puts the cake on a table to be cut and served. Then the honoree steps up to the podium and receives a chip in the form of a key chain or metal token designating the number of years of sobriety. The secretary then hugs the celebrant.

This process is repeated until all persons celebrating their birthdays have taken their cakes. At some meetings, as many as ten cakes may be presented. They generally honor the youngest birthday first. At times, the person being honored only receives a cupcake or doughnut. Since the celebrant generally observes the cake ritual for a whole week at different meeting places, bringing a cake to each gathering would be too costly. "Taking a cake" in a variety of locations boosts the morale of the celebrant as well as others struggling to overcome their alcoholism.

✪ *Gifts:* Congratulations cards. While gifts are not required, drug and alcohol rehabilitation centers have shops that sell appropriate items: T-shirts, coins, and coffee mugs with the number of years on them, key chains and bumper stickers with AA, NA (Narcotics Anonymous), CA (Cocaine Anonymous), and MA (Marijuana Anonymous) mottos on them; e.g., "Clean and Serene," "Fearless," "One Day at a Time," "Keep It Simple."

✪ *Words:* "Congratulations" and other words of encouragement.

3   COMING OF AGE

"Today I am a man."

When does a boy become a man? When does a girl reach womanhood? The ages marking the crossover from childhood into adulthood vary, depending on cultural background. Some celebrations occur in the secular world: a debutante ball at eighteen, a party at sweet sixteen; others occur in religious settings: a bar mitzvah at thirteen; a *quinceañera* at fifteen. We expend time and money on these occasions that announce to the world that our children have become adults and that we parents have achieved enough status to afford extravagant observances.

Ironically, the dominant event marking entry into U.S. adulthood is one devoid of ritual fanfare—obtaining a full-fledged driver's license. Across ethnic and gender borders, this act awards physical freedom to children, granting them the same mobility as their parents. While ceremonial expenses may be nil, the immediate costs of music, food, garb, and guests are replaced by long-range financial burdens.

TRADITIONAL RITUALS AND BELIEFS

AFRICAN-AMERICAN

SECULAR

A variety of organizations across the country have developed rites-of-passage programs, aimed at boosting self-esteem, for girls and boys to help them cope with the challenges of contemporary life. (See "Looking for More Information?"/Organizations, p. 264.) The programs declare ideals, set forth tasks that must be accomplished, and ceremonially reward achievements. All emphasize African traditions.

Organizations may work with children as a means of building self-confidence before they enter their turbulent teens, or they may target those already at risk. African American Women on Tour offers five conferences a year around the country with three-day workshops. "Joining the Circle of Women," for girls twelve to eighteen, deals with family life, goal setting, teen sexuality, African cultural heritage, and holistic empowerment practices. A program administrator describes the results of these workshops: "When the girls come to registration, they generally have a hands-on-hips attitude, but in only three days they are transformed into receptive, responsible, responsive, affection-giving and -accepting women."

African American Women on Tour have another program called "Under the Village Tree," for girls nineteen to twenty-five. Here they emphasize that women don't need men to be complete, that what they must do is polish and appreciate the prize within themselves. They explore their spirituality as well as deal with educational goals, personal fitness, sexuality, and childbearing.

The West Dallas Community Center Rites of Passage Project helps children break negative habits, working with fifty African-American adolescents between the ages of nine and twelve for five years. They focus on overcoming substance abuse, school failure, teenage pregnancy, and runaway behavior. They provide youngsters with the opportunity to move to a higher level of human, social, and educational development. In doing so, the youngsters must complete certain requirements, eventually earning the community's respect.

Each organization has its own ceremony of achievement. At the West Dallas Center, they base it on African rituals. Participants, including parents and mentors from the community, dress in traditional African garments. The initiates perform African dances and songs, and the honored youth deliver speeches on their accomplishments and the knowledge they have attained. Based upon their profession of knowledge, the community welcomes the adolescents.

At the African American Women on Tour ceremony, the girls exchange affirmations with their elders in call-and-response style: "I will honor and respect the wisdom of my parents. I will appreciate the efforts and prayers of my ancestors and make them proud of me. I will appreciate my African-American heritage."

✪ *Gifts:* Check with organization sponsors about requirements.

✪ *Words:* "Congratulations." Affirmations of all kinds.

✪ *Clothing:* Check with the organization's sponsors about requirements. Some may request African-styled clothing.

INDIAN (BRAHMAN)

Upanayanam [oopah-náyah-nam] (Sacred Thread Ceremony)

This major ceremony heralds a boy's initiation into learning; he is now ready to study the Vedas [vay-duhs] (ancient Sanskrit scriptures). The event occurs on one of the boy's odd-numbered birthdays, generally the seventh, ninth, or eleventh, but sometimes as early as the fifth year. To symbolize his change of status, he wears white threads that go over the left shoulder, fall onto the chest, then loop under the right arm. Once initiates put on the white threads, they must wear them at all times and recite certain mantras twice a day.

- ✪ *Gifts:* Clothing, books, items related to learning.
- ✪ *Words:* "Congratulations."
- ✪ *Clothing:* Best clothing. Avoid black. Men need not wear jackets or a tie, but wear a good shirt. Remove shoes and socks when entering the temple.
- ✪ *Body Language:* Use the *namaste* [nah-mah-stay] for greetings. (See "Giving Birth"/Indian, p. 30.)

JAPANESE

First Menses

To honor the occasion of their daughters' first menses, mothers prepare a special dish, *osekihan* [oh-sek-ee-hawn] (red rice). *Osekihan* consists of sticky rice cooked with red beans that stain the rice red. By serving this dish, the mother announces to other family members that the daughter has officially crossed the line from childhood to womanhood.

In Japan, they serve the red rice in recognition that the

daughter is now a full-fledged woman who can marry and have children. *Osekihan* is served on other celebratory occasions, as well.

JEWISH

Bar Mitzvah

At the age of thirteen years and one day, a Jewish male becomes a "son of the Commandment," allowing him to become fully incorporated into Jewish life. This entitles him to participate in a minyan [mín-yon] (a prayer quorum) in the synagogue; he can be called to testify in a Jewish court of law; and in ancient times he could enter into various legal contracts, including marriage. Theoretically, from now on he assumes responsibilities for his own actions.

Preparation includes years of a Hebrew-school education where he learns Jewish history and traditions. He learns to chant blessings over the Torah [tow-rah], recite the haftorah portion (selection from the Prophets), and sometimes to chant from the Torah portion itself.

The ceremony takes place wherever the Torah is being read, but most commonly occurs in the synagogue during Sabbath services. The young man receives the honor of being called up to the pulpit to read a portion of the Torah and sometimes from the haftorah. Following the reading, he usually makes a speech about his relationship to Judaism and his ideals and goals. He then thanks his parents and teachers for guiding him to this moment of achievement.

After the ceremony, the parents provide wine, bread, and sweets for the entire congregation. Often they have a luncheon or an evening party for relatives and friends. New traditions may be initiated.

In 1965, to honor the Los Angeles bar mitzvah of Mark Dresser, Jan Steward, family friend and artist, created twelve individual cloth banners, depicting the twelve tribes of Israel. In stitchery and appliqué on contrasting fabrics, these colorful, three-by-four-foot standards bore bold tribal symbols such as a lion, tents, a serpent, and a sailing vessel. They added a striking historical link between contemporary and ancient traditions. Charmed by their symbolism and beauty, friends borrowed them to display at their sons' bar mitzvah celebrations. Thirty-one years later, the still-vibrant banners began hanging again at ceremonies for offspring of the original bar mitzvah boys.

Nowadays, to avoid the conspicuous consumption aspects of the festivities, some rabbis encourage parents to put the mitzvah (good deed) back into the celebration. As a result, celebrants visit the sick or keep mitzvah journals showing how they fulfill the commandments, such as helping to build a community playground or helping to restore a synagogue. Akin to this, families may give 3 percent of the costs of the celebration to an organization called Mazon [mah-zóne] (hunger): A Jewish Response to Hunger. Mazon is a contemporary interpretation of an ancient tradition when no meal at a joyous occasion *(simcha)* could commence until poor people joined the table. Instead of inviting the poor to share the meal, today's families may donate money for hunger prevention and relief. (See "Looking for More Information?"/Organizations, p. 264.)

✪ *Gifts:* Items emphasizing learning, such as books, or items related to the individual boy's interests. Money gifts in units of 18. (See "Giving Birth"/Jewish, *Brit Milah*, p. 32.) In the 1940s a popular bar mitzvah joke punch line was "Today I am a fountain pen," erringly announced by the bar mitzvah in his speech referring to the abundance of gift pens received.

✪ *Words:* "Mazel tov." "Congratulations."

✪ *Clothing:* In Orthodox and Conservative temples, Jewish and non-Jewish men must wear yarmulkes [yáhr-mull-kes] (skullcaps). This may be an option in Reform synagogues. For those not owning their own, extras are usually placed at the sanctuary entrance. Orthodox and Conservative congregations require Jewish men to wear the tallit [tall-éet] (prayer shawl).

Married women attending Orthodox synagogues must cover their heads with hats or kerchiefs, wear long sleeves, and have modest necklines and midcalf hemlines. If there is an evening party, women wear dressy outfits and men wear suits and ties.

SEPHARDIC [SAY-FÁR-DICK] VARIATIONS

In spite of efforts by rabbis to discourage the practice lest an injury occur, after the reading of the haftorah portion of the ceremony, well-wishers throw candy-covered almonds and other sweets at the bar mitzvah. This practice has now spread beyond the Sephardim and occurs at other ceremonial occasions, as well.

Bas [bahs, sometimes baht] Mitzvah

An innovation in Jewish ritual life, this female equivalent of the bar mitzvah caused shock waves when for the very first time a woman—Judith Kaplan, daughter of Rabbi Mordecai M. Kaplan, in New York in 1922—stepped forward to read from the Torah. Since that time, especially in Reform and Reconstructionist congregations, girls have celebrated their coming of age like boys, but with one difference. Girls can achieve bas mitzvah at twelve years and one day, one year earlier than the boys, although many families observe it at thirteen years.

Like their male counterparts, girls prepare for several years by attending Hebrew school, where they learn to read Hebrew and receive a good education in Jewish history and tradition, learn to chant blessings over the Torah, to recite from the haftorah, when appropriate, and sometimes to chant from the Torah portion itself. During the bas mitzvah, held by Reform and some Conservative synagogues, everything is the same as it is for the bar mitzvah. However, since Orthodox and some Conservative Jews oppose having women called to the Torah, they do not have bas mitzvah ceremonies. On the other hand, some modern Orthodox Jews and Conservative Jews allow them, but instead of reading from the Torah, the young women make speeches about it.

The celebratory aspects of the event are identical to those of the bar mitzvah. Parents serve sweets, bread, and wine to the entire congregation. Later, a private party for friends and relatives takes place, generally away from the synagogue. Some of these events can be quite elaborate, but new ways to celebrate the event instead of by having expensive parties are being introduced as a way of returning to spirituality.

✪ *Gifts:* Same as bar mitzvah.

✪ *Words:* "Mazel tov." "Congratulations."

✪ *Clothing:* Same as bar mitzvah.

LATINA

Quinceañera [keen-say-ah-nyéra] (Fifteen Years Old)

(See "Coming of Age"/Latina *Cincuentañera*, p. 85.)

Observed in the United States for over one hundred years, this all-day cultural, social, and religious event marks fifteen-year-old Latinas entry into womanhood and the church. During this transition they move from being *niñas* [nee-nyas] (girls) to *señoritas* (young women). Through this ceremony, they enter into the Catholic community as young adults. The Mass of Thanksgiving for Life and the party held afterward are popular in Central America, Cuba, Puerto Rico, and wherever one finds Mexican populations on both sides of the Mexican-American border. In cities away from the border, the *quinceañera* has been altered, and families may celebrate it one year later and call it either a "sweet sixteen" or "presentation."

Regional or personal variations may occur, but in all instances, the *quinceañera* resembles a wedding with its formal clothing, printed invitations, and many-tiered cake. It is a costly ritual, but family friends, *madrinas* [mah-drée-nahs] and *padrinos* [pah-drée-nose] (godparents or sponsors), help finance the event. Often their names are printed on the invitation with their duties, which include supplying the cake, limo, flowers, favors, rental hall, and traditional gifts, such as the rosary and missal, and birthstone ring. The *madrina de muñeca* [moo-nyay-caw] is the sponsor who presents the young woman with her last doll. This last vestige of childhood concretizes the dramatic transition the *quinceañera* is about to make. The wearing of makeup, high heels, and jewelry, her own missal and rosary, mark her new status as an adult.

To attend the ceremony, commonly held at a Saturday Mass, the girl travels with her entourage from home to church in a limo. Frequently, she wears a long, white gown, but in some places the dress must be pink or another pastel shade. A headpiece ornaments her ornate hairdo. It may be a tiara with glass stones or made with silk flowers and ribbons.

The entourage includes the girl's parents, grandparents, godparents, and court of honor. The court consists of fourteen couples, one couple for each preceding year of the honoree's life. The girls, *damas,* have identical gowns of a specially selected color, and their male escorts, the *chambelans,* don tuxedos with bow ties and cummerbunds in colors often matching the girls' dresses. The honoree's mother wears a long, formal gown, her father a tuxedo.

They enter the church in the following order: the court; a flower girl and boy carrying baskets of flower petals or party favors. The flower girl may also carry an altar pillow on which the honoree will kneel. The parents may walk with the *quinceañera* or she may follow alone. She stands at the front of the altar alongside her godparents. Her parents and her court stand in the first section of pews.

During the middle of the Mass, the priest directs his words toward the *quinceañera* and reminds her how lucky she is to have her parents sacrifice to give her such a celebration. He proclaims that she is now a woman and delivers words to inspire her to further study and achievement. She receives a religious medal on a gold chain, often the Virgin of Guadalupe imprinted with her name and the date. The girl delivers a speech giving thanks to her parents, the guests, the Church. Sometimes she reads from the Bible. She and her court receive Communion, and as her last act, the *quinceañera* makes a flower offering to the Madonna and returns to the pews.

When the entourage leaves the church, the girl walks out accompanied by her male escort. Guests offer congratulations, and often the family distributes party favors. The limo then carries the family and attendants to a special location for a photo session, most popularly a park setting or outside a local landmark.

Later, the family sponsors a reception in a hall, restaurant, hotel, or at their home, festively decorated with flowers, balloons, and streamers. After abundant food and drink, guests dance to music provided by a deejay or a band. The girl and her father dance the first dance, which is a waltz. The next dance includes her court. Regional differences occur. Mariachi music is traditional, but other Latino dance rhythms are played as well: salsa, cumbias, boleros. Miami *quinceañeras* reflect their Cuban connection particularly in the dancing. They begin with the traditional nineteenth-century waltz, followed by a *danzón*, then move into the mambo and conga, sometimes finishing with Miami disco, Gloria Estefan, and hip-hop.

Regardless of geographical location, the girl cuts the cake, which is topped by a porcelain, crystal, or plastic replica of a fifteen-year-old girl. Guests bring gifts to the reception that she later opens at her home. The young woman receives objects representing her transition to adulthood: jewelry, religious medals, high heels, her own missal (religious guide) and rosary, rings, earrings, and bracelets.

To shift the focus away from the partying aspects to the more serious meaning of this event, priests now hold meetings with the *quinceañera,* her parents, and the court. The priest counsels about God, the Bible, and appropriate behavior. In addition, he reminds parents to be thankful for the fifteen years they have had with their daughter, emphasizing their responsibility in preparing her for womanhood.

Some Latino families may celebrate the event across the Mexican border so that grandparents and others left behind may participate in this significant life passage.

❂ *Gifts:* Money, clothing, jewelry, and personal items.

❂ *Words:* "Congratulations." *"Felicidades."*

❂ *Clothing:* Shirts, ties, and jackets for men. Respectful church attire for women.

NATIVE AMERICAN

Whereas girls may have one public ceremony, boys frequently repeat a vision quest ceremony over their lifetime as a way to renew their connection with their guardian spirits. Although traditions vary with the tribe, generally the boy prepares for his vision quest through a purifying ritual by bathing in a river or going to a sweat lodge. (See "Healing"/Native American, Sweat Lodge, p. 166.) After receiving instruction from a male elder or medicine man, the boy leaves his people behind and ventures to live alone in a simple shelter. He must fast for four or five days, and while in this altered state, a vision comes to him, often in animal form. Once he receives his vision, the young man returns to his people and seeks interpretation of it from an elder or a medicine man. If he receives no vision or cannot complete his fast, he must repeat the process the next year.

APACHE (MESCALERO)

Mountain Spirit Dance

This is only a small part of a girl's puberty ceremonial paying tribute to the achievement of womanhood, held after a girl's first menses. It sanctifies the role of woman. More than one girl may be feted, and variations exist at different Apache sites, for example, San Carlos, Cibique, and Mescalero.

The ceremony is a four-day/four-night coming-out party, and at Mescalero always includes the Fourth of July. Like puberty rites of other cultures, it is costly. Friends and family consume huge quantities of food over the four days, and the singers and dancers must be compensated. Although many Native American ceremonials are closed to outsiders, non–Native American guests are welcome at the Mescalero summer event. An outline of main features follows.

On the first day, tribal members construct a tepee of four main and eight subsidiary structure poles to house the young girls and their godmothers. Celebrants wear buckskin ceremonial garments painted yellow or bleached white, with beaded symbols. Yellow represents sacred pollen and God's generosity. Singers apply the pollen to the girls' bodies.

The Mescalero Apaches reenact the legendary journey of White Painted Woman, the mythological figure who brought this ritual to the Apaches. The Mescalero say they invented the ceremonial to honor and commemorate White Painted Woman. During the four days, physically and emotionally ailing tribe members approach the initiates, who are known to possess curative powers at this time in their life as the embodiment of White Painted Woman. The initiates treat them through touch and blessing and exchange pollen blessings. They must also behave according to strict rules. For example, they are not supposed to smile or laugh as this will cause premature wrinkling.

On each of the four nights, holy singers each sing at least sixty-four different songs and retell stories of their people. On each of the four nights, mountain spirit dancers bless the encampment and through their performance drive away evil spirits. Groups of four dancers impersonate the mountain spirits. Clowns and young boys dance with them. At the beginning of the ceremony, the dancers approach the central fire and the girls' ceremonial tepee four times.

The "owner" of a set of mountain god dancers sings and drums as the dancers perform. Additionally, initiates must participate in a minimum of two hours of strenuous dancing on each of the four nights. During the day, they run around a basket four times to symbolize the life cycle: infancy, childhood, adulthood, and old age. At the end of the fourth run, their uncles or brothers spill baskets of tobacco, candy, piñons, fruit, and money over them. This sets off giveaways by members of the girls' families. Folklorist Claire R. Farrer describes how relatives throw gifts of candy, oranges, apples, and cigarettes from the beds of pickup trucks. Others scramble to pick up these goodies because they consider the food and tobacco blessed.

When the fourth day has ended, and after the initiates have again done four ritual runs, the tribe dismantles the tepee and visitors leave. However, the family stays until the ninth day when they purify the girls in a yucca suds bath. In the old days, at this point girls were considered eligible for marriage; now they finish school before marrying.

Note the significance and appearance of the number 4 in this Apache ritual. The tepee has four primary wooden supports; the ritual lasts four days; there is a minimum of four dancers; they apply pollen to the girls in four places; the girls run around the basket four times; dancers approach the ceremonial tepee four times as a blessing. Emphasis on the number 4 as an omen of harmony and balance is common to many Native American tribes.

✪ *Gifts:* If you attend as a tourist and pay for entrance, no gifts are expected or necessary. If you are visiting a particular girl's family, substantial gifts of food are welcome because the family must feed everyone three meals a day for the four days. Choose four among the following choices: twenty-five pounds of flour, five pounds of lard, ten pounds of sugar, a sheet cake, fifty pounds of potatoes, four to six dozen eggs, watermelons, and cantaloupes.

If you are visiting the owner of a set of mountain god dancers, give him a Pendleton blanket (about $120) or Indian tobacco or cattail pollen or a good unset piece of turquoise or the largest-size Swiss army knife.

✪ *Words:* There is little opportunity to convey verbal felicitations. One's presence implies congratulations. Additionally, an announcer or family member may request that an observer participate in an Apache dance. This honors the family and is a nonverbal expression of "Hurrah!"

If you are a woman, and a family personally invites you to attend, demonstrate your happiness for them by saying, "I'm ready to cook." This means you are willing to help the family with food preparation or serving. Men say, "I can chop wood or carry water," to show, rather than speak, their praise.

✪ *Clothing:* For women, jeans, skirts, dresses, and slacks, but no shorts. Men cannot be shirtless. Avoid wearing sandals without socks because naked feet are displayed only to one's closest intimates.

✪ *Taboos:* They prohibit all recording devices: cameras, audiotape recorders, video cameras, notebooks, and sketch pads. If discovered, equipment will be confiscated and perhaps not returned. Credentialed journalists may be exempt from this rule, but only if they apply in advance for a camera permit to the Apache Tribe at P.O. Box 176, Mescalero, NM 88340. Permission is not always granted. Families who hire photographers to document their ceremonial may also be exempt, but only if they receive permission from tribal officials, who issue permits that must be hung from the cameras.

LAKOTA

First Menstrual Flow

The ceremony is announced a year in advance so that family members can begin gathering traditional foods and sew, bead, and quilt gifts as well as purchase blankets, towels, and dishes for the feast and giveaway. At the celebration, red paint is applied to the young woman's forehead and three marks to her chin to mark her entrance into womanhood. For the Lakota, red symbolizes dedication to truth as well as the Red Road. Menstrual blood signifies the woman's capacity to create. In addition to the red with its symbolism, the Lakota also include white, associated with virtue, represented by a white golden-eagle feather tied to the initiate's hair.

Seated in a chair of respect covered with a star quilt, one or more girls go through the outdoor ceremony. This can take place just before or right after the young woman's first menstrual flow. Initiates are reminded that they are Lakota and should live as good Lakota people. Ceremonial heads offer chokecherry juice and pemmican to the grandfathers, the elderly, and Mother Earth. At this time, the girls may be given new spirit names to supersede childhood names. The new ones will be used for all future ceremonies but will rarely be spoken.

In prereservation days, women isolated themselves for four days every month. That no longer occurs. However, not all young women participate in a public ceremony. Nonetheless, all girls upon becoming women receive advice from older women about how to behave when they have their menstrual flow. This includes taboos against sitting around, cleaning house, or sewing. They should not cook or chew their nails or step over any men's clothing lying on the floor. They must wash their clothes separately. Most importantly, elder women emphasize the ideals of having a good home, of being good mothers and wives.

⊙ *Gifts:* In tribute to each child being honored, the Lakota give gifts to visitors in something called a give-away. They distribute gifts according to protocol. Items include towels, blankets, cigarettes, or bolts of cloth. They also give away food left over from the feast, where they expect guests to stuff themselves, then take home the leftovers in special containers to share with friends and relatives.

NAVAJO

Kinaaldá (Making Her Cake)

Although most initiation rites are closed to outsiders, in 1995 some Navajo invited writer Susan Hazen-Hammond to witness a coming-of-age ceremony with the understanding that certain information not be documented, that it was to remain within the tribe. Dawn, the initiate, did not have the ceremony at her first menses, but waited until a school break. Those present included her parents, her sisters, a medicine woman, and other elder women.

In preparation for the cake-making ceremony, Dawn's father dug a fire pit for baking; the old women blessed the hogan by applying corn pollen to the walls in each of the four directions. They washed Dawn's skin and hair with yucca root and rubbed corn pollen on her; they combed her hair and chanted and touched corn pollen to her tongue and hairline. In addition, Dawn performed ritual runs to the east and back prior to making the cake and while it was cooking.

To make the cake, they mixed eighty pounds of cornmeal with ten pounds of wheat flour and a handful of ashes in plastic buckets of hot water. When it reached the necessary consistency, Dawn stirred the batter in a zinc tub with a bundle of greasewood sticks. After two hours of stirring, she sewed two corn husks together in the shape of a cross. When the fire pit coals were red-hot, the elder women pulled them out and lined the pit with aluminum foil. They placed the stitched-together corn husks on top and poured in the batter. Dawn sprinkled white cornmeal over the batter to bless the four directions; then family members added their blessings. Just prior to sunset, they covered the mixture with more corn husks and foil and topped it with earth and hot coals. The next morning, when the cake was removed from the oven, one of the elders cut out four pieces, one for each direction. Dawn presented these to the medicine woman. At this point they requested that Hazen-Hammond leave so that Dawn could spend the next four days at the hogan contemplating her life as a woman and a Navajo.

ROMAN CATHOLIC

First Holy Communion

This occasion marks the first time the young Christian is officially invited to approach the altar and participate fully in the Eucharistic celebration called the Mass, commemorating the Last Supper. Catholics understand Communion as receiving the body and blood of Christ, symbolized by the host (wafer or unleavened bread).

Generally, the first Communion takes place when children are seven or eight years of age and after approximately two years of Christian education or catechesis. The candidates participate together in this ritual on a special day on a weekend following Easter. The boys usually wear a white or dark suit, and girls wear white dresses and veils with white shoes.

First Holy Communion ceremonies occur once a year at a Mass, although a large parish may have several first Holy Communion Masses. The pastor officiates over numerous elements including an entrance song, penitential rite, readings from the New and Old Testament, singing of a responsorial psalm, and a proclamation of the Gospel followed by a homily and Communion. Commonly, family members bring up to the altar gifts of bread and wine.

Often a reception is held in the parish hall to celebrate the event with food, music, and dancing. Some families may elect to celebrate away from the church with family dinners or barbecues.

✪ *Gifts:* Catholic religious gift and book stores can be helpful in making suggestions. Guests may give a child's missal, rosaries, a daily prayer book, stories about saints, money.

✪ *Words:* Christians may say, "Congratulations. You will be able to receive Communion when you attend Mass." "Congratulations, God is within you." Others say, "Congratulations."

✪ *Clothing:* In church, respectful attire.

Confirmation

Confirmation is a sacrament of maturity and commitment. It grounds young Catholics' connection to the Church and generally occurs when participants are in high school, but may occur earlier depending on the local diocese. It is a onetime event where the Holy Spirit enters the person to root them more deeply into divine affiliation. Confirmation is an initiation into the parish community and calls forth a more mature commitment to being an adult. To qualify, candidates often participate in parish community-service projects. Confirmation preparation takes two years, with groups of candidates focused on study and prayer. Theirs is a journey toward a maturing faith within the faith community.

At the ceremony, the bishop comes to the parish community and anoints candidates and gives them a new name. This name, chosen by the candidate, is usually that of a saint who has special meaning to the initiate. The young persons wear their Sunday best, often adding a red stole or a red carnation to symbolize the fire of the Holy Spirit. During the ceremony, a sponsor accompanies each initiate as he or she approaches the bishop to receive the anointing of confirmation. The sponsor is a confirmed Catholic, one who walks the faith journey—supports, inspires, and challenges the one to be confirmed. As part of the ceremony they celebrate the Eucharist. (See the preceding entry.) Following the religious service, the parish community hosts a reception to welcome the new members of the community.

✪ *Gifts:* Books, a Bible, rosaries, tickets to a good movie or the theater, money.

✪ *Words:* "Congratulations. You have received the Holy Spirit. Now you may bear witness to the Christian faith in words accompanied by deeds." Non-Christians may just say, "Congratulations."

✪ *Clothing:* In the church, respectful attire.

THAI

As young as six and up to twenty-one years, boys may participate in a rite of passage that teaches them how to live as Buddhists. The boys, called novices, live and study with monks at the temple for as little as two weeks and for as long as a summer. This is a commonplace ceremonial event in Thailand and is beginning to be observed in the United States where Thai Buddhists have a large enough community to support a temple and monks.

The occasion begins with family members taking turns to cut locks of the boy's hair and placing them in a golden bowl. Afterward, a monk finishes the job by shaving the boy's head. The act demonstrates how vanity must now be set aside. After the shaving, the novices put on white robes and move to the front of the temple where they join a procession of musicians, dancers, friends, and family members. They walk around the temple three times to show their respect for Buddha and then kneel before the monks. The head monk explains the ten rules of Buddha's teaching and in ritualized question-and-answer form asks if the boys wish to proceed. After agreeing, the novices change from their white robes into saffron ones to begin their spiritual journey.

From then on, the boys steep themselves in the teachings of Buddha. They live and study at the temple, sleep on floor mats, give up play, music, laughter, and eat only two meals a day, the last one at noon.

✿ *Gifts:* No gifts.

✿ *Words:* "Congratulations" to the boys and their parents.

✿ *Clothing:* Respectful attire. When entering the temple, shoes must be left outside.

✿ *Body Language:* When entering the temple, avoid stepping on the threshold. Step over it. As an outsider, it is not necessary to prostrate oneself as believers do. To avoid feeling conspicuous, sit at the back of the room. Chairs are usually provided for visitors and the infirm. If no chairs are available, sit on the floor. As a sign of respect and greeting, they use the *wai* [why] sign. With hands pressed together in a prayerlike position, bring them up to just below the chin and nod slightly. When people greet you this way, you should return the gesture. If this makes you feel uncomfortable, just nod.

EMERGING TRADITIONS

MENARCHE

NEW AGE QUEENS OF FERTILITY

This retreat welcomes girls to their coming of age and was created by Tamara Slayton, founder of the Menstrual Health Foundation in Sebastopol, California (see "Looking for More Information?"/Organizations, p. 264). Slayton teaches girls to celebrate menarche (onset of menses) rather than face it with dread.

Slayton has been a part of the women's self-help health movement for over twenty years and has been conducting these female coming-of-age ceremonies for six years. At least a thousand girls have participated. She says, "The shaming of girls at adolescence is part of how our society puts girls in their place. The message is that something is wrong with them." Slayton is attempting to remedy the terrifying bleeding-without-dying syndrome and is a key figure in the emerging menstrual-awareness movement.

She holds "Camp Fertility" weekends where pubescent girls engage in a number of activities such as building a twenty-foot-long fertility sand goddess lying on her back, with large, full breasts and pregnant belly. The girls make a seashell necklace for her and decorate her head with tangled seaweed hair. Then they lie between her legs to receive her birth blessing and afterward place twenty-eight pieces of driftwood around her representing the days of the menstrual cycle.

The girls also use pastel crayons to draw rainbow wombs. At the same time, Slayton explains the woman's complex body system and encourages them to see their fertility cycle as feminine power. Afterward, the girls form a circle and in dance portray the cycle. They ascend toward ovulation and descend to menstruation, coming out to be with others, going in to be alone.

Initiates also work with heart imagery. They make drawings of the heart or create stuffed felt hearts to establish the connection between the womb and the heart. Slayton has the girls draw their wishes for the world: "I wish to create world peace." "I wish to end poverty."

Parents attend the closing celebration and bless the girls and place gold crowns on their daughters, crowns that the girls have made themselves and decorated with lace, ribbon, glitter, and feathers. Slayton asks the parents to repeat words taken from a quote by Ntozake Shange: "Remember, you are a river. Your banks are red honey where the moon wanders." Then Slayton says, "In beauty let it begin. In beauty, let it end. Blessings on your cycle. Let us eat cake." The new queens of fertility and their parents have a party with red cranberry juice and a cake covered with flowers.

✪ *Gifts:* Flowers, especially red roses. Any memento from the family lineage of women, such as jewelry, clothing, or any object handed down through time. Candles, journals, or jewelry made especially for the girl to honor this special event. Avoid something that insists she's a woman. She is not. She is just getting there. Fertility jokes and gags are offensive.

✪ *Words:* Avoid such sentiments as "You don't know what's going to happen to you." "Better look out for the real world." "Keep an eye on those boys."

✪ *Clothing:* The more color, the more flowers, the better. Festive clothing creates a positive image and warm memories.

ON BECOMING ELDERS

Attempting to counter "over the hill" attitudes, older women are developing new traditions to honor rather than disparage age. Newly created ceremonies, sometimes based on combined elements of traditional forms, pay tribute to wisdom and wrinkles.

LATINA CINCUENTAÑERA [SEEN-COO-ENTA-NYÉRAH] (CEREMONY HONORING FIFTY-YEAR-OLD MEXICAN WOMEN)

Norma E. Cantú, professor of English at Texas A&M International University, had a *cincuentañera* on January 4, 1997, at Laredo, Texas. As a model, she drew from memories of her own *quinceañera* (celebration for fifteen-year-old Mexican women), research on *quinceañeras* (see "Coming of Age"/Latina, *Quinceañera*, p. 70), and another *cincuentañera* given by a colleague in Corpus Christi.

Like Cantú's *quinceañera,* her *cincuentañera* included a Mass, but this time held the evening prior to the reception instead of on the same day. On both occasions, family and friends participated, this time two hundred. She wore a white, traditional, formal dress like the one for her *quinceañera,* but at this event it was a long one.

Cantú selected forty-nine family members and friends as *madrinas* [mah-drée-nas] (sponsors). She instructed them to wear anything they liked but to wear rebozos [ray-bów-sews] (traditional shawls) over their outfits. Cantú wore a red one over hers. During the ceremony she called up each *madrina* by name and title to make assigned formal presentations, e.g., *madrina de* AARP, who gave her an AARP membership. The *madrina de recuerdos y deseos* (sponsor of memories and desires) placed throwaway cameras at each table and brought a blank book where guests wrote their thoughts and memories of the honoree. The *madrina de flores* (sponsor of flowers) was unable to attend, so she sent money for the purchase of Cantú's favorite flowers, *nardos* (pungent spikenard flowers), which graced the main table. The forty-nine *madrinas* helped to defray the costs of soft drinks, music, Cantú's bouquet, earrings, corsage, champagne, decorations, and candles. After paying tribute to each *madrina*, the honoree presented each one with a tiny medal of the Virgin of Guadalupe.

For the reception, Cantú and her sisters decorated the Woodman of the World Hall with piñatas and *papel picado* (paper cut designs) of the Virgin of Guadalupe. Mariachi music, boleros, Tejano, and *conjunto* music, from a sound system and two different bands, entertained the crowd, sated with margaritas and traditional foods: tamales, rice, beans, chicken, beef, *champurrado* [chom-poor-ráh-doe] (a traditional Christmas drink), cookies, and celebration cake. The cake had three tiers, each one decorated with symbolic objects representing Cantú's life. The first tier held a baby carriage representing her birth. The second tier showed a *quinceañera* doll recalling her fifteen-year ceremony. The upper tier displayed a woman in a cap and gown, a replica of her book, *Canicula* [caw-née-cue-lah], with the number 50, marking her current status and scholarly accomplishments.

During the celebration, Cantú toasted her parents, who responded emotionally. Her father confessed that for him the best part of the event was the toast she had made to him and her mother. Later on, Cantú noted that some of the single women looked either bored or discontent sitting around while others danced. She found a solution and what she hopes will become a permanent tradition of future *cincuen-tañeras: danza de las madrinas*. She asked the band to play a long *cumbia* [cóom-bee-ah] (a shuffling, percussive rhythm of Afro-Colombian origin), and all the women danced around her in a circle. Then one by one she danced with each of them.

Cantú had requested no gifts and instead urged that donations be made to the Laredo branch of Literacy Volunteers of America. In spite of this, friends could not refrain from giving her personal presents much like the ones she had received at age fifteen, perfume and jewelry.

Why did she give herself this celebration? Cantú is one of eleven children (eight females), and she wanted to influence her younger sisters, to demonstrate that at fifty, life is not over. It's just the beginning.

CRONING

"We are the old women. We are the new women. We are the same women, wiser than before."

This chant embodies the spirit and purpose of croning ceremonies, to honor women's passage into old age. The Feminist Spiritual Community (FSC) of Portland, Maine (see "Looking for More Information?"/Organizations, Feminist Spiritual Community, p. 265), one of the leaders in croning ceremonies, defines cronehood as having two characteristics: the woman has entered menopause and has reached her fifty-sixth birthday. While the word *crone* often elicits negative, witchlike images, women who have participated in croning ceremonies have chosen to stress the magical wisewoman aspects instead.

No standardized ritual exists (see "Looking for More Information?"/Videotapes, p. 266). Individuals and groups have evolved their own variations, including parodies such as the one performed by the Women's Section of the 1997 American Folklore Society Meeting in Austin, Texas. First the elders were invited to cross the great divide (of the room) separating them from the younger crowd. They chanted, "Bleed no more," and later, "Eggs no more," while smashing *cascarónes* [kos-kah-rów-nes] (eggshells filled with confetti) over each other's head. Leaders literally toppled the symbols of fertility—a fish, rabbit, and cow perched on top of pedestals—then relit the initiates' fires by igniting the tips of cone-shaped party hats taped over their breasts.

In spite of the playfulness at this particular event, the sustaining element found at all croning ceremonies is honoring rather than denying age. The ceremony celebrates the latter stage of life and prepares one for the next stage, including death. It is a time of empowerment, of dedication, of embracing all facets of life, the dark nights, bright mornings, and evenings that lie ahead. It acknowledges the importance of the stories women have to share.

As with most rites of passage, the element of fire is significant, hence the burning of candles. At the FSC, other ritual objects include flowers, herbs, plants, stoles, crystals, food. As each woman enters the room, two greeters welcome her by name and with hugs. All the women form a circle and begin chanting, "We are women giving birth to ourselves." Then, in a chain, the women walk through a simulated birth canal, afterward lighting three candles, one for those attending for the first time, one for those unable to attend, the third for all present.

One of the highlights of the ceremony is "The Decades." Standing in a circle, they first announce the decade from age ten to nineteen. Each woman says a few words describing something that occurred to her during that decade, and when finished, those over twenty step forward toward the center, leaving behind those who are not old enough. They repeat this process for each decade until they finish the fifties. While sharing the decades, the women reveal their sorrows, pain, joys, achievements, and aspirations.

After the decade of the fifties, the crones and initiate step into an inner circle. The initiate sits in the center; the crones sit around her and everyone else forms a circle around them. The old crones bestow affirmations on the new one such as "You are an honored and beloved woman." "You have a wealth of stories and ideas to share." Then the old crones talk about what it is like being a crone and ask the new one questions about her feelings, fears, hopes, and plans for the future.

The new crone receives two gifts. One is a stole made from braided ribbons symbolizing the weaving together of the strands of her life. She wears this at all subsequent ceremonies. The other gift is an amethyst crystal to help in her ongoing transformation.

Following this, the initiate receives more affirmations and gifts. Dancing, feasting, and singing take place with a benediction and opening of the circle. At the FSC, they close by chanting the following:

The circle is open but unbroken.
May the peace of the goddess go in your hearts,
Merry meet and merry part,
And merry meet again.

❂ *Gifts:* Amethyst is the jewel that represents croning, so any piece of jewelry containing this stone is meaningful. Other jewelry as well as flowers, fruit, sentimental objects. A wand, a shawl, a crown if she does not have one. Gifts should be individualized as they were for Connie Spittler, whose family gave her a glass egg containing messages of love and appreciation for what she had taught them.

Avoid all jokey gift remedies for old age, such as

references to dentures, wrinkles, hemorrhoids, unless you know that the particular crone would find it amusing. Above all, personalize the gift.

❂ *Words:* These should be from the heart and refer to wisdom, respect for age, the pricelessness of memories.

❂ *Clothing:* Purple preferred, since it is the crone's color. Often participants wear long dresses and happy, celebratory types of garments.

4   MARRYING

"I do. I do."

Feminists may cringe, but the intent of most traditional wedding celebrations is to incorporate the bride into the family of the groom; the ceremony marks a transfer of property. Indeed, prior to my own wedding in 1951, my about-to-be father-in-law likened me to an empty lot he was about to purchase but whose title was unclear. This motivated his desire to meet my parents.

Just as most couples are unaware of property exchange as the root of the wedding ceremony, they frequently don't know the reasons behind the myriad wedding customs most feel compelled to follow. For example, few newlyweds know that the wedding veil was meant to fool the evil eye as to the true identity of the bride, thus keeping her from harm before tying the knot. And what does "tying the knot" mean? In ancient times, knots offered protection against evil spirits, which was crucial during wedding preparations. In addition, the knot symbolizes interwoven affection. As for throwing rice at the couple, rice represents fertility, as do corn and birdseed or the old shoes tied to the back bumper of the couple's getaway car.

TRADITIONAL RITUALS AND BELIEFS

AFGHANI [AF-GÁH-NEE]

What follows are descriptions of Afghani engagement and wedding parties taking place in the San Francisco Bay area in 1994. These are typical of traditional Afghani weddings occurring in this country.

Engagement Party

The elegantly dressed engagement couple stepped out of a limo decorated like a wedding car with bows, streamers, and flowers. She wore a fancy pink weddinglike gown and carried a bridal-like bouquet. He wore a dark suit.

Once inside the reception hall, the family displayed wrapped gift packages on a table covered with a veil and decorated with pink and white balloons. The festive mood heightened as family members approached the bride-to-be and removed her old jewelry, replacing it with beautiful new rings and bracelets covering her fingers and wrists. Afterward, the groom-to-be placed an engagement ring on her third finger, left hand. Meanwhile, same-sex couples danced to the live music. When the future bride and groom stepped onto the dance floor, young women, clapping their hands, danced around the bride-to-be while the men danced around the bridegroom-to-be. Food was served buffet style, and dancing continued until past midnight.

FOLK WISDOM

Before the ceremony, the groom should not see the bride in her wedding dress.

The bride should wear something old, something new, something borrowed, something blue.

If a bride breaks the heel of her shoe, she will die in less than six months.

If you see a bride in your dream, there will be sickness in your family.

If you pull the wedding ring off your finger, your partner will become untrue.

It is bad luck to give a sharp object as a wedding gift.

The girl who catches the bridal bouquet will be the next one married.

If you place a piece of wedding cake under your pillow, you will dream of your future husband.

It is bad luck for a bride to participate in the wedding rehearsal. She should use a stand-in.

It is bad luck to be late for your own wedding.

A bride must cry on her wedding day, or she'll cry later.

It is good luck for the groom to carry the

bride over the threshold of the first room they share.

To see a white horse on your wedding day means your wedding has been blessed.

Always a bridesmaid, never a bride.

Married in white, you have chosen all right; Married in red, you'd better be dead.

Married in yellow, ashamed of the fellow; Married in blue, your lover is true.

Married in green, ashamed to be seen; Married in black, you'll ride in a hack.

Married in pearl, you'll live in a whirl; Married in brown, you'll live out of town.

If it thunders during the ceremony, the couple will be barren.

If the bride bakes her own wedding cake or makes her own gown, she will have an unhappy marriage.

If the bride wears a coin in her shoe, she will become wealthy.

If the bride carries a lump of sugar in her glove, she'll have a sweet married life.

WEDDING ANNIVERSARY GIFTS

1st	Paper
2nd	Cotton
3rd	Leather
4th	Linen
5th	Wood
6th	Iron
7th	Wool or copper
8th	Bronze or pottery
9th	Pottery (china)
10th	Tin or aluminum
11th	Steel
12th	Silk
13th	Lace
14th	Ivory
15th	Crystal
20th	China
25th	Silver
30th	Pearl
35th	Coral
40th	Ruby
45th	Sapphire
50th	Gold
55th	Emerald
60th	Diamond

○ *Gifts:* Jewelry, housewares. Avoid giving money, considered disrespectful.

○ *Clothing:* Best and latest-fashion clothing. Elaborate dresses with sparkle and sequins for women, dark suits for men.

○ *Body Language:* Because they are Muslim, they allow no public body contact between men and women. Men dance with men. Women dance with women. These rules are relaxed between close family members.

The Wedding

A white limo carrying the groom picked up the bride from the beauty salon and brought the couple to the wedding hall. She wore a long, dark green dress with a green silk veil head covering and carried no floral bouquet; he wore a black suit and wore no boutonniere. Every time they walked together, an older female family member held a green-fabric-covered Koran (their holy book) over her head as a gesture of protection.

In the lobby of the reception hall, a male representing the bride and another representing the groom plus witnesses gathered with the imam [ee-mom] (priest), dressed in a suit. The groom was present; the bride was not. The men discussed the wedding contract, which made material provisions for the bride in the event the marriage dissolved. Then two witnesses from each side went to the bride to ask if she was willing to marry the groom. The first two times, she gave no answer; after the third request, she agreed. (See "Marrying"/Iranian, p. 122.)

The representatives and the imam signed the contract; the imam gave a speech, which the others applauded, and the men hugged one another in celebration. Afterward, they passed among the men a tray filled with Jordan almonds, which was later passed to all the guests waiting in the other room. The men threw flower petals over the groom's head, and in turn, he kissed their palms.

Later, in the main room, everyone rose as the bride and the groom entered the hall and stood in front of two fancy thronelike chairs on a platform. The couple posed for photographs and greeted their guests, who kissed each of them on the cheek three times. In front on them on a low table lay the Koran, two burning candles, a pitcher of juice, and two fancy goblets.

In small groups, guests came up to the seated couple to greet them. The others dined on Afghani food served buffet style, this time more formally presented than at the betrothal party. Rice dishes abounded. Although music played, few people danced. Before long, the bride and the groom disappeared.

A change of mood occurred when two costumed dancers entered the room and swung baskets filled with burning incense. Then two eight-year-olds entered dressed like a miniature bride and groom. The wedding couple followed, the groom in a black suit with boutonniere, the bride in a traditional Western, white gown with train. She wore a veil over her face and carried a bridal bouquet. Again, an older female relative held the Koran over her head. When the couple reached their throne chairs, guests applauded and took turns taking photographs with them. The bride received more jewelry. Then someone placed spoonfuls of henna into the couple's right hands, temporarily wrapped together with cloth.

After the couple cut the wedding cake, they fed one another one bite and sipped juice from each other's glass. Then some women held an elegant scarf over the couple's heads to allow them privacy as they looked into a brand-new mirror and for the first time saw themselves as a married couple. They opened the Koran at random, read a few lines from the opened pages, and removed the scarf. The train was removed from the bride's gown, and the newly-weds danced together alone on the dance floor. Some male guests dropped paper money over them, which children scrambled to retrieve. Subsequently, other guests danced with the wedding couple.

Costumed dancers wearing white tunics over white pants, decorated vests, and sashes tied around their waists performed while everyone gave them their rapt attention. Then the bridal couple came onto the dance floor and the performers danced around them.

At the evening's conclusion, the couple left the wedding in a limo to travel to the groom's home. Family members joined them as they entered with an older female relative holding the Koran over their heads as they stepped into their new life.

✪ *Gifts:* Housewares. Avoid giving money.

✪ *Words:* "*Mubarak*" [moo-ba-rock]. "Congratulations."

✪ *Clothing:* This is a more serious event than the engagement, so dress less ostentatiously.

AFRICAN-AMERICAN

Most African-American weddings are no different from any other American weddings, affected by the rules and traditions of the churches where the rites occur. In a new trend, some couples are incorporating African traditions of their ancestors. For music, they may emphasize African drumming or perhaps vocals sung by Miriam Makeba; the bride may trim her gown with cowrie shells and wear her hair braided; the groom may wear a cummerbund in colorful Kente cloth.

Queh-queh [kway-kway], a prewedding custom from West Africa, is an example of an adopted African tradition.

Queh-queh is a ritualized song-and-dance party. On the night prior to the wedding, friends and family dance and sing songs telling the future bride and groom what to expect when they get married. In song, they introduce all of the relatives and guests who circle the couple. It is a highly joyous event filled with double entendres, especially in the songs. Often they serve black-eyed peas for prosperity, sometimes prepared in a dish called cookup rice.

Jumping the Broom (See "Marrying"/Anglo-American, Jumping the Broom, p. 103)

First brought to public attention by the televised miniseries based on Alex Haley's novel *Roots,* this custom was commonly used by slaves in the United States desiring to legitimize their unions when no clergyman was available. Slave reports describe someone holding each end of the broom and the couple jumping over it, or the broom being held across the doorway inside the house and the couple standing outside the house jumping over it into the house. Other times, they simply placed the broom on the ground and the couple stepped over it. Newlyweds sometimes stepped over it together or one after the other.

Today, when African-American couples jump over the broom, it may symbolize a positive recognition of their African heritage. It may also represent a bitter reminder of slavery. The custom seems to have antecedents among British Gypsies and the Welsh, as well. However, regardless of origin, the symbolism of the broom, which can represent the hearth and the sweeping away of an old life, is becoming a popular wedding tradition across ethnic borders. The Imperial Broom Company of Richmond, Virginia, has been making and selling ceremonial brooms for nearly ninety years. Some customizations have been made, such as Jewish couples requesting that brooms be tied with a bag of sugar to ensure a clean, sweet marriage.

New Orleans

Two different kinds of wedding cakes distinguish the event. The groom's cake is generally chocolate and shaped according to his occupation. If he is a physician, the cake may look like a doctor's satchel; a teacher's cake might resemble a book; if the groom drives an eighteen-wheeler, the cake might be shaped like a big truck.

The other cake resembles a traditional wedding cake except ten ribbons extend from it. The ribbons are attached to trinkets buried within the cake. The bride invites each single girlfriend up to the cake. Each girl warily selects a ribbon, then pulls on it to remove an attached symbol to learn her fate. The worst trinkets to extract are the button and the thimble, both signs of spinsterhood. A penny means poverty; a clover, horseshoe, and wishbone signify good luck. The anchor symbolizes hope. The heart reveals that "love will come," and the fleur-de-lis foretells that "love will flower." The luckiest of all is the young woman who retrieves the wedding-ring charm. She will become the next bride.

The reception comes to a rousing close with the second-line dance, a tradition borrowed from New Orleans funerals (see "Dying"/African-American New Orleans or Jazz Funerals, p. 196). The band plays a second-line song, such as "Little Liza Jane," and the father of the bride holds a specially decorated parasol, usually with white lace, flowers, and streamers. He, or another person chosen as leader, struts and moves around the dance floor performing the special steps of toe, whole foot, knee flex, and twist. The other guests follow, twirling and snapping their white hankies or table napkins in the air. The dance lasts as long as the guests have energy, and the band changes melodies to keep it going. The second line furnishes an exhilarating finale to the wedding reception and any New Orleans dance where it has become a commonplace ending.

AMISH

Amish weddings exemplify the no-frills Amish life. There are no rings, no flowers, and no vocal solos. The bride makes her own wedding dress and after the wedding continues to use it as her Sunday-best church outfit. She may be dressed in it for the last time at her burial. The dress is in shades of blue or purple, unadorned, of plain design, mid-calf in length and without a train. She has on black, high-topped shoes and a black head covering instead of a veil. She and her attendants wear white capes and aprons over their dresses.

The groom and his attendants are attired in black suits, white shirts with bow ties, black stockings and shoes. As with other non-work-related attire, coats and vests fasten with hooks and eyes. The groom wears high-topped shoes and a black hat with a three-and-a-half-inch brim.

Weddings take place at home in November and part of December after the harvest season. The short wedding season causes some Amish to attend several on the same day, accomplished by staggering times of their arrival, for example, during the morning part or for the noon or evening meals. They hold weddings during the week, most frequently on Tuesdays and Thursdays, and not on weekends. From two hundred to four hundred celebrate the occasion with helpers arriving as early as 6:30 A.M.

The three-hour service begins at eight-thirty with congregational hymn singing while the bride and groom receive instruction from the minister in another room. Later, in front of the congregation, the minister has the couple step forward to ask them questions akin to marriage vows. He blesses them, after which ordained men and fathers of the couple give testimony about marriage. The ceremony closes with a final prayer.

Immediately afterward, women prepare dinner while

men set up tables in a U shape in the living room. A special corner, the "eck," is an honored place set aside for the bride and the groom, where the bride sits on the groom's left. Single women sit on the same side as the bride, and the single men assemble on the groom's side. Because of the large numbers of guests, they may have two sittings for the meal, which frequently consists of stuffed roast chicken, mashed potatoes, gravy, creamed celery, coleslaw, applesauce, cherry pie, doughnuts, fruit salad, tapioca pudding, and bread, butter, and jelly. The prepared chickens come from several dozen decapitated by the groom the prior day.

Following an afternoon of visiting, games, and matchmaking, the guests gather for the evening meal, which begins at 5 P.M. and may consist of macaroni and cheese, fried sweet potatoes, stewed chicken, cold cuts, pumpkin and lemon-sponge pies, and cookies. The wedding day ends at 10:30 P.M.

There is no honeymoon. Instead, newlyweds visit family members at prearranged times on weekends, generally spending one night or one meal with each host family. They collect wedding gifts on these visits.

The above description applies to typical nuptials taking place in Lancaster County, Pennsylvania. As with all groups, variations occur in other locations and among the many other branches of the Amish and related groups of Plain People, including the Old Order Mennonites.

It is considered a great honor when the Amish invite non-Amish (called English) to their weddings. Few are included. If you are fortunate enough to be invited, be respectful in your demeanor.

❂ *Gifts:* Avoid giving anything requiring electricity. Generally, they do not bring gifts to the wedding but send them ahead or give them when the couple comes to visit. The newlyweds display gifts sent beforehand on a table with a piece of paper identifying the donor.

They welcome practical household items such as cookware, dishware, kitchen tools, pots and pans, canned food, and tools for the groom.

❂ *Clothing:* Subdued colors. Women wear dresses that cover the arms with hemlines below the knees, and modest necklines. Men wear jackets and ties.

ANGLO-AMERICAN

Jumping the Broom (See "Marrying"/African-American, Jumping the Broom, p. 99)

Since 1883, jumping the broom has been a wedding tradition in the extended Shippen family of New Jersey. According to one family legend, an Irish maid overheard Grandpa Shippen grumbling about costs and fuss over the marriage of his daughter Kate to Hilbourne Roosevelt taking place the next day on February 1. The maid offered the following commentary: "In my country, when people can't wait for the priest, they get married by the broom."

After the maid explained that jumping the broom legitimized the marriage and implied fidelity as strongly as any church vow, Grandpa Shippen requested that a broom be brought from the kitchen. He asked the betrothed couple to jump over it, and since that time, married couples descending from the Anna Shippen and Howland Davis families who so desire have a broom-jumping ceremony at their wedding receptions. Surnames of second generations include Howe, Steinway, Harvey, and Davis. To date, over one hundred couples have jumped over the very same 1883 broom.

An important aspect of this family's tradition is that the wedding couple embroider their initials and wedding date on a ribbon that is tied to the broomstick. Most of the ribbons or their remnants remain in place, the oldest pressed between clear plastic. Those that haven't held up are from the early 1940s, perhaps due to the unavailability of quality fabric during World War II.

Preceding or following the broom-jumping ceremony, the wedding couple reads some "bad poetry" they have written for the occasion that explains the custom and names persons who have participated. Rhyming and humor are the only requirements.

Through time, descendants of the original Shippen extended family have embellished the broom-jumping tradition. In addition to the newlyweds, other couples attending the wedding who had jumped it at their own ceremonies can rejump like a renewal of vows. A newer twist is to invite any married couples at the reception to jump.

Sam Chapin, of Hingham, Massachusetts, is the official family keeper of the original broom. He claims the old corn-bristle broom has held up well for 115 years. He keeps it well-protected, and when couples desire to use it, he ships it to them in a Styrofoam-lined metal box.

ARMENIAN

Weddings are their most significant rite of passage. When children are born, a common expression of congratulations to their parents is "I hope that you will see your son or your daughter on their wedding day." They repeat this sentiment at birthdays, graduations, and all other major life events.

The bride's family pays for an elaborate betrothal ritual; the groom's side pays for the wedding. At the engagement party, a silver tray holds sweets, which include Jordan almonds, the rings, flowers, perfume, and cognac, representing the sweet things of life. The priest blesses the rings at this time and places the ring on the bride's right hand. At the wedding it is changed to the left hand. The future groom's family presents the future bride with jewelry.

On the wedding day, the family dresses the bride and brings her to church. The groom comes with his father and best man. Armenians from Iran have an additional custom. Prior to the wedding ceremony, a traditional Armenian band accompanies the groom and his family to the bride's home. Each member bears a gift: candy, decorated candles, bouquets of flowers. The groom brings the bride's gown, shoes, and veil, which he has purchased. He dances with the gown; men drink vodka, and then the bride dons the dress, but the groom's brother puts on her shoes. The groom's family bedecks her with new expensive rings, bracelets, watches, and necklaces, and she wears all of them. The best man brings the car to take them to church, but when the couple attempts to leave the house, the brothers block the door until the groom gives them money to let the couple pass.

For the ceremony, the wedding couple selects godparents, generally relatives. The godparents are important to the couple and stay involved as counselors throughout the newlyweds' lives. To demonstrate their role, they stand closest to the couple during the ceremony, the godmother next to the bride. The godfather, holding a cross, stands next to the groom. During the ritual, the couple wear crowns of gold or silver, which are exchanged during the ceremony. At this time, they touch their foreheads together and hold right hands. The godfather touches the heads of the couple with the cross, after which the couple and the godparents drink wine.

Surreptitiously, while still at the altar, the bride or the groom may step on the other one's foot, signifying that he or she will be the boss of the family. Generally, the groom is the aggressor. Upon return from the honeymoon, the couple places a plate outside the door of their new home, and the groom has to step on the plate and break it to demonstrate once more that he will be the boss.

The newlyweds arrive last at the reception, and they enter dancing. After the first dance, family and friends present gold jewelry, which they put on the bride. Since most gifts are not sent ahead, the guests present them to the couple during the reception. Russian Armenians, in particular, bring jewelry and gifts of money.

Musicians play drum and horn music and sing special songs about the bride and groom. Guests dance to Armenian circle and line dances as well as Western music. While dancing, the groom's father throws dollar bills over the bride's head, and the bride's father throws money over the groom's head. Others throw money as well, all of which is collected and given as a tip to the band.

At the reception, they serve traditional foods: shish kebab, stuffed grape leaves, rice pilaf. Frequently, the groom's family makes flowery toasts about the bride: "She is ours now." "This is a flower in a garden which we came to pick." Other kinds of toasts are "I hope you will have a long, happy life together, as many children as you want, a warm family, and that you grow old together on one pillow."

✪ *Gifts:* Money or housewares brought to the reception.

✪ *Words:* Any kind of felicitation.

✪ *Clothing:* Black is popular and considered elegant. These are formal affairs that call for fancy clothing including sequins and sparkle. Men wear dark suits and ties.

CAJUN

At the reception, the bride and groom walk around the dance floor to a traditional Cajun tune "Marche de Mariés" [marrsh day mah-reese] (march of the newlyweds). Behind them in twos march their parents, grandparents, godparents, brothers and sisters, aunts and uncles. After the newlyweds dance a waltz, they invite the entourage to join them, which becomes the official wedding dance, *le bal de noce* [lay bol day noss] (the wedding dance). Later, guests take turns danc-

ing with the bride or kissing her in exchange for pinning
money on her veil, which soon becomes a mass of green bills.
A recent embellishment extends to the groom, who dances
with guests in exchange for their pinning money to his suit
jacket.

An unusual feature is the mop or broom dance. An older,
unmarried brother or sister of the bride or groom dances
alone with a mop or broom on the dance floor. This is a
form of teasing for being passed in the marrying line of suc-
cession by a younger sibling. The dancer is usually barefoot, and if the dancer is a man, he must dance with his
pants legs rolled up a few inches. Bare feet and too-short
pants symbolize the poverty of life without a mate. Underlying is the warning against becoming a spinster or bache-
lor. The single's dance encourages the dancer to find a life
partner and avoid repeating the embarrassment.

A variation of this custom has an older unmarried sibling dancing barefoot, often in a tub, to remind him of the
poverty of old age if he does not begin a family of his own.
This dance may take place simultaneously with the wedding dance.

✪ *Gifts:* Household gifts brought to the reception,
but many gifts are given ahead of time at bridal showers. Prepare to pin money to the bride's veil or the
groom's suit.

✪ *Words:* "Congratulations."

✪ *Clothing:* Avoid black, associated with mourning.
Men wear coats and ties; women wear nice dresses.

Charivari [sha-ree-vah-ree] (also called shivaree or chivaree)

Charivari is a French word referring to a noisy serenade for
newlyweds made by beating on metal objects: kettles, pans,
tea trays. After the wedding couple goes home, the *shivaree*
band disrupts them until they offer the noisemakers money

or invite them into the house for food and drink. A popular practice of eighteenth-century France, it was brought to the New World and popularized in Canada as well as in the United States. Other European immigrants brought variations of this custom, too.

In Cajun territory, any wedding merits a *charivari*. During the couple's wedding night, friends and relatives congregate outside the couple's bedroom window. They bang pots and pans and make loud, irritating noises and do not leave until the bride and groom invite them inside to serve them food: cake and coffee or a full meal. Additionally, this practice is observed for widows and widowers who remarry and estranged couples that reunite.

CAMBODIAN

To set the wedding date, parents of the engaged couple consult a fortune-teller to discover if the union will be fortuitous and to request the best date for the ceremony. Fortune-tellers make their prognostications based upon the ages and birth dates of the couple and correlate the calculations with lunar calendar symbols such as the year of the rat, year of the ram, year of the monkey. The fortune-teller draws upon special knowledge gleaned from many years of studying the relationships of the sun, the moon, and the stars.

The wedding ceremony takes place at the home of the girl and begins about 8 A.M. and lasts until early afternoon. The groom and his family arrive in a procession with offerings of fruit presented in pairs: pineapples, oranges, apples. The groom's party also presents a Cambodian cake and jewelry to the bride: rings, bracelets, necklaces, sometimes a sword to chase away evil spirits. They place offerings of incense, candles, flowers, and a small plate of fruit on an altar in front of a statue or a picture of Buddha. The bride is attired in an ornate brocade, wraparound skirt with many bracelets, anklets, necklaces. The groom may wear baggy pantaloons and jacket or a Western-style suit. During the ceremony and reception, the couple may change their outfits three to four times.

A Buddhist monk cuts a lock of hair from both the bride and the groom and mixes the locks together in a bowl to symbolize the sharing of their lives. As a blessing, elders may tie knots in a white string bracelet for each of them. (See "Marrying"/Lao, p. 133; "Marrying"/Thai, p. 139.)

If the Cambodians have access to a Cambodian restaurant, they hold their receptions there. If not, they go to a Chinese restaurant. At the reception, the bride and groom frequently change into a traditional Western, white wedding dress and tuxedo or dark suit. At the end of the meal, the couple visits each table. As they approach, all guests at that particular table rise, and a representative of the table, usually the oldest or most respected, hands envelopes of money he has collected from his tablemates to the bride and groom. He blesses the couple at this time.

Sometimes if younger people are at the table, they will tease the couple, coaxing them to kiss each other or playfully encouraging them to eat from the same banana. Although they serve Cambodian food, they always have an American-style wedding cake—in appearance only. Although it looks the same, it tastes less sweet and has a coconut flavoring. Festivities continue with dancing to Cambodian and Western music.

✪ *Gifts:* Hand a money-filled envelope of any color to your table representative. Write your name on the envelope.

✪ *Words:* Praise or bless the couple.

✪ *Clothing:* Avoid black, associated with death. A wedding party is joyful; colors should be joyful, too.

✪ *Body Language:* Use the *wai* [why] form of greeting. With hands pressed together in a prayerlike position, bring them up to just below the chin and nod slightly. Avoid male/female body contact.

CHINESE

Red invitations with gold lettering are sent in red envelopes. The Chinese wrap gifts in red, as well. If the couple is Christian, the ceremony follows the rules of the particular church. If they are Buddhists, the ceremony may take place in a temple or in the bride's home. Regardless of religion, they hold reception banquets in Chinese restaurants, where the bride changes from a Western-style, white gown into a red *cheong-san* [chong-san] ceremonial gown. Sometimes she will have more than one change of costume.

Family and close friends frequently give gold or jade jewelry, and the bride wears all of it, even if it means many rings on every finger and bracelets up to her elbows. This demonstrates how affluent and generous the new family is. The new mother-in-law provides a red comforter for the bridal bed.

An ornamental centerpiece, perhaps a silk flower with a poem, embellishes each table. The family and close friends make many speeches, then they serve the banquet food. Desserts may consist of dates and fruit, connoting fertility, and lotus petals, representing harmony for the new couple.

Before dinner, the bride's first duty is to kowtow to her in-laws. She serves them tea and in return receives jewelry and red envelopes filled with money. She later visits the guests' tables to serve them tea. Sometimes, the guests rap on their water glasses with chopsticks until the couple kisses.

✪ *Gifts:* Avoid giving clocks, a death omen, or scissors, a symbol of separation. During the reception, when the bride comes to each table to serve tea, leave a red envelope containing money on the tea tray. These envelopes can be purchased in Chinese gift shops. If you do not have access to these envelopes, avoid leaving money in a white envelope, associated with death.

✪ *Words:* Avoid talking about illness, death, or sadness of any kind. Focus conversations on happiness.

✪ *Clothing:* Females avoid wearing black or white, associated with death. Men have no apparent color restrictions.

EGYPTIAN (COPTIC)

Engagement

Since parents prohibit their daughters from dating, the only acceptable form of courting follows an official engagement ceremony officiated by a priest and performed either in church or at the bride's home. Girls may be as young as sixteen years old, but more often are between the ages of eighteen and twenty-two. After the engagement ceremony, which is financed by the girl's family, the girls may go out with their intended husbands.

At the ceremony, the bride wears a colorful dress, never white. She also does not wear any headdress. If they hold the ceremony in church, the choir sings and prayers are said. Whether in church or at home, the priest places wedding rings on the ring fingers of the couple's right hands. At the party held afterward, the intended groom presents his future bride with more jewelry. In the event that he later breaks the engagement, she keeps the jewelry and all gifts. If she breaks it, she must return everything.

✪ *Gifts:* Only close friends present gifts. The future husband is the only one to give jewelry to his future bride.

Wedding

The bride wears a traditional, Western-style gown and veil at the church ceremony. The groom has on a regal gold robe over his suit or tuxedo and a red sash *(zinnar)*, which represents his covenant with God. The couple walk in procession from the door of the church up to the altar.

During the forty-five- to sixty-minute ceremony, the choir sings, and the only musical accompaniment comes from cymbals and a triangle. The priest offers prayers and anoints the couple with oil, and the bride and the groom exchange vows. During the latter part of the ceremony, the priest places gilded crowns decorated with jewels on the couple's heads. From their right hands, the couple remove the rings they have been wearing since their engagement ceremony and give them to the priest, who ties three knots around them. Later, the priest unties the rings and toward the conclusion of the ceremony places the bride's ring halfway down on her ring finger, left hand. The groom then pushes the ring into place. In turn, the priest places the other ring halfway on the groom's ring finger, left hand, which the bride then pushes into place. There is no drinking of wine; there is no bridal kiss.

The groom's family holds the reception in a hall where they have a wedding feast, which includes lamb, grape leaves stuffed with rice and meat, turkey, chicken, and Egyptian pastries. They dance to both Western and Egyptian music.

✿ *Gifts:* At the reception, place household gifts on a designated table. They welcome money, too.

✿ *Words:* In English, "Congratulations." In Egyptian, *"Mabarouk"* [mah-bah-rock] (blessings).

✿ *Clothing:* Dressy clothes for both men and women. Women avoid wearing pants.

✿ *Body Language:* Men and women sit separately in church.

ETHIOPIAN

Wedding festivities consist of three separate events. First, the religious ceremony takes place in a Coptic church. Right after the ceremony is an intimate reception in a park. A large evening reception in a hall or hotel follows.

A distinguishing characteristic of the wedding ceremony is the *caba* (mantle), an ornate, often gold-trimmed robe worn by the bride and the groom over their wedding clothes whether traditional or Western style. His robe is gold and hers is white. If they choose to wear traditional Ethiopian attire, their head coverings are close-fitted, gold-colored, jewel-trimmed hats. Frequently, they display the Ethiopian flag in the back of the church behind the priest. The ceremony consists of vows, songs, prayers, blessings, and an exchange of rings. During the ceremony, the couple each kiss their holy book, but they do not kiss each other inside the church.

Only close friends and family attend the park reception amid many flowers. They serve special drinks, *teje* [tedj], a mead, made of honey and hops, and *tela* [tell-lah], a kind of beer made from fermented barley, corn, and hops. Ethiopian music enlivens the scene. After a few hours, guests leave and change into more formal clothes to wear at the elaborate, large open reception held in either a hall or hotel, depending upon the financial resources of the groom. The bride and the groom greet each guest upon entry, and they always serve Ethiopian food, even in hotels that cater only American food. In such situations, the Ethiopian community members bring in the food.

✪ *Gifts:* Household gifts brought to the reception. Giving money is not an Ethiopian custom.

✪ *Words:* All forms of congratulatory expressions. Wish them the best.

✪ *Clothing:* Dressy. Too casual clothing is considered disrespectful.

✪ *Body Language:* Inside the church, men sit separately from the women, but if space is limited, they disregard this rule.

FILIPINO

Listed on the formal wedding invitation may be the headings of *ninong* [nee-nong] and *ninang* [nee-nang] (or *nino* [nee-no] and *nina* [nee-na]). This refers to sponsors, usually affluent family friends who provide gifts, generally money to cover the cost of the wedding, honeymoon, or setting up housekeeping. These sponsors guide and encourage the couple throughout their married lives. The invitation also lists the names of the entourage as well as the parents.

Generally held in a Roman Catholic church during a full Mass, the ceremony lasts about one hour. Each of two candle sponsors lights and places one small candle on opposite sides of a unity candle located near the priest. Together, the bride and the groom proceed to the unity candle. Each takes a light from the smaller candle, and jointly they light the unity candle.

Later, a white veil physically links the couple and symbolically unites their families. One end is pinned to the shoulder of the groom that is farthest from the bride, and the other end is draped over the bride's head. The veil encloses the two of them as one of the steps toward union. Afterward, the priest links the couple once more by placing a *yugal* (an eight-shaped, white cotton cord) over them. This cord represents a lifetime union.

✪ *Gifts:* For the reception, be sure to have folding money, $1 to $100, ready to pin on the bride because men line up for a two-minute dance with the bride, and women do the same for a dance with the groom.

Pin it anywhere. This money is expected in addition to wedding gifts, which may be brought to the reception.

⊛ *Words:* Any words of congratulations.

⊛ *Clothing:* Avoid black, associated with funerals. Women avoid wearing white, which competes with the bride.

GREEK ORTHODOX

The priest blesses the rings, and the best man exchanges the rings three times, taking the bride's ring and placing it on the groom's finger and vice versa. The exchange signifies that in married life the weaknesses of one partner will be compensated for by the strength of the other, the imperfections of one by the perfections of the other. Alone, each of the couple is incomplete. Together they are made perfect.

Throughout the service the bride and the groom hold candles and join right hands. The crowning is the climax of the wedding ceremony. The maid of honor and best man hold crowns tied with a common ribbon above the bride and bridegroom's heads. This symbolizes unity. During the ceremony, the best man picks up the crowns and crisscrosses them three times over the couple's heads.

After the couple drink from a common cup of wine, denoting the sharing of joy and sorrow, the priest leads the bride and the groom in a circle around a table on which sits the Gospel and the cross. These symbols represent the husband and the wife taking their first steps as a married couple, and the Church, represented by the priest, who leads them on their path.

⊛ *Gifts:* Household items. Money in envelopes.

⊛ *Words:* "Congratulations."

⊛ *Clothing:* Dressy clothing for women. Suits and ties for men.

HAWAIIAN

Hawaiians may be of varied faiths, and religious ceremonies follow the dictates of either the church or temple. In any case, they incorporate Hawaiian elements. For example, before the ceremony, a chanter dressed in a coverlet *(kilui* [kee-loo-ee]*)*, which is like a sheet tied over one shoulder with a traditional Hawaiian design on it, welcomes the guests and calls on *ke akua* (God), for His blessings. The groom wears a formal white aloha shirt with lei maile [mah-ee-lay] intertwined with white jasmine and pikake blooms. The bride has on a white gown or white *huloku,* a more fitted long dress with a train. Her bouquet may include floral leis worn during the reception. Over their tuxedos, the groom and his ushers may have pikake garlands, stolelike leis of maile, a fragrant leafy vine, intertwined with jasmine or stephanotis, worn only on special occasions. Instead of a traditional veil, the bride may wear a *lei haku* (a crown of braided leaves and flowers).

At the reception they serve foods for the gods, which when eaten bring the spirits to the people. The menu varies with the ethnicity of the wedding couple. Frequently they serve Chinese, Japanese, and Korean dishes along with the roast pig. They serve poi (taro paste), roast pig, *lomi* (salted salmon), sweet potato, chicken long rice with green onions (a kind of chicken noodle soup), and coconut pudding.

Wedding reception locations depend on the affluence of the families. They may take place in posh hotels, recreation centers, or in backyards. Regardless of location, entertainment is a highlight. The family brings their instruments to play and accompany singing. Then to honor the wedding couple, each person gets up and does a hula. All hulas are individualized, and over time people develop their own signature dance. One hula dance teacher explained that

Hawaiians express all that is within them when they dance the hula. She calls it "aloha in motion" and explained that when one dances as a gift, one's love and emotions for the family pours forth. "All of it comes up and enhances your dance."

✪ *Gifts:* Nowadays, young Hawaiians register at department stores and have bridal showers. If you have nothing material to give, the finest tribute would be to pick flowers from your own backyard and string them into a lei to adorn the couple. This advice applies to all other Hawaiian occasions, as well.

✪ *Clothing:* Aloha attire, colorful floral prints for muumuus and shirts, which can be worn in church and temple. Shorts are unacceptable at formal events.

✪ *Body Language:* At all occasions, acknowledge elders with a kiss. Hawaiians kiss on one cheek. Kiss the couple, the parents, and the grandparents. Avoid handshakes, considered offensive. In ancient times, Hawaiians greeted one another by going up close and pressing nose to nose and inhaling each other's essence. When the first Caucasians landed, the Hawaiians called them haole [hah-oh-lay], which means "not of the same breath." Caucasians smelled different. Kissing has replaced the inhalation form of greeting.

HMONG [MONG]

The Hmong have several acceptable forms of marriage, and in all forms, the girl lives with and becomes a part of the boy's family. The first, called *zij poj niam* [jhee-paw-niah], means bride capture, where a young man of nineteen or twenty takes a girl as young as thirteen to his home and consummates the marriage. Before entering his home with the girl, the boy kneels before his parents and asks for their help in proving his decency. The parents bring a rooster and circle it over the couple's heads to bless their union. Afterward the young man sends two male representatives to the girl's family home. They present $100 to the father and $100 to the mother, give each one a cigarette, and kneel twice in front of each parent.

If the girl's family is unhappy with the union, they will try to get her back, but if the girl doesn't want to go home, she will stay in spite of her parents' opposition. Sometimes the boy's family gives the girl's family extra money to appease them, and sometimes the girl's parents complain about the young man merely as a form of bargaining. For the first three days at her new home, the girl does nothing. If she is shy, she stays in her room and people come to visit her there. After three days, her husband's family expects her to participate in household chores. The bride capture custom is waning because many young women now wish to pursue their educations and careers rather than being tied down to raising families at such a young age.

Elopement is another form of marriage. Parents may also arrange marriages when their sons are between fifteen and eighteen and daughters are thirteen to fifteen. Both sides agree on the bride price, which symbolizes that the wife will be highly valued and treated well when she moves in with her husband's family.

The Hmong also practice a form of mutual-consent marriage where the bride may not know in advance that a marriage proposal is going to occur, and her parents are completely unknowing. The young man consults with his family about the most propitious time for marriage to the young woman of his choice. Family members choose a date that falls on an even number and is close to the new moon. Hmong avoid marrying on rainy days.

In the late afternoon or evening, the groom-to-be meets with two wedding specialists and a third man, who serves as their porter. They bring the equivalent of bamboo backpacks to carry to the girl's home. One is filled with blankets, the other with food. They also bring along a bridesmaid and a large black umbrella.

The girl's parents are completely surprised, as may be the future bride, when outside the front door one of the wedding specialists sings a song to announce their presence. They ask the parents to open the door. Once the entourage enters, the specialist sings another song and hangs the closed umbrella on the wall. The umbrella signifies that the boy's family will protect the bride.

The boy's representative makes a monetary offer for the girl. Generally, there is a $500 variance in negotiation, and families of brides today generally receive about $6,000 to allow their daughters to marry. The groom's side gives cash only, which is immediately counted and carefully examined. If the girl's family agrees to make a wedding party, which often takes place the next day, the boy's side gives an extra $500 to $600. In addition, the boy's side must set aside extra money for the girl's special relatives, such as uncles.

Once the financial arrangements are settled, the bride leaves her home with the groom and his representatives and travels to her husband's home. On her way, she must not look back at her former home. To welcome the couple at the groom's home, his family sets out a plate with offerings of two freshly killed chickens, a boiled egg, a lit candle, and cooked rice.

The wedding party takes place at the bride's house. She wears a traditional Hmong dress and headdress, one typifying her homeland region. Family members give her jewelry, costumes, money in envelopes, pillows, blankets, other household items. At the party, someone collects the money and keeps a list of donors. During the party, a long table is filled with food for the men, who drink beer and make ritual toasts. Following this, wedding specialists from the bride's side sing songs. Afterward, her family gives blessings and presents gifts of money, jewelry, and costumes.

One year later, if the bride is caught in an affair or if she is lazy or does not fulfill her household chores, or if the in-laws dislike her, the boy's family will send her back to her family with $300. They call this "washing the parents' door." In contrast, if the girl runs away or she doesn't want her husband anymore, she must return to her family, who must repay the marriage money. The Hmong have a low divorce rate.

❂ *Gifts:* Money in an envelope. Avoid giving anything red, such as red towels or blankets, or wrapping anything in red paper. Red is a taboo color symbolizing blood and foretelling danger (see "Dying"/Hmong, p. 206). If someone dreams of red before leaving on a trip, the person cancels the trip.

❂ *Words:* "Congratulations."

❂ *Clothing:* No restrictions.

❂ *Body Language:* Although it is appropriate for Hmong males to shake hands with non-Hmong females, Hmong married women may not shake hands with any men. They must also avoid smiling at other men, considered an insult to their husbands. Unlike other Southeast Asians, the Hmong use no physical greeting gesture. They do not sit on the floor, and they use spoons instead of chopsticks.

INDIAN

Mehndi [men-dee] (also spelled mehendi) (Prenuptial Ceremony)

This custom of drawing henna designs on the hands and feet of the bride-to-be is found with variations throughout South Asia, the Middle East, and parts of North Africa, practiced by Hindus, Muslims, and Sephardic Jews. (See "Marrying"/Jewish, Sephardic Variations, p. 130.) It takes place at a prewedding ceremony where female relatives gather to anoint and beautify the bride.

They make a thick, smooth mixture of ground henna leaves mixed with water, lime juice, and oil, which becomes a paste after being left to sit overnight. Applying it like paint, they create designs on the skin and leave it to set. When washed off, the henna leaves a stain that varies from pale orange to a rich brown. The longer the paste is left on, the deeper the color and the longer it will last.

Specialists paint patterns on brides' palms, fingers, backs of hands, and sometimes the bottoms of their feet, extending up to the ankles. They can be lotus flowers, intricate lacy, or bold geometric designs. Frequently, they draw fertility symbols or configurations to ward off the evil eye.

During arranged marriages of the past, the bride and the groom never saw each other until their hands were symbolically joined over the ceremonial wedding fire. The bride's face was veiled, and the only glimpse of her was her ornamented hands. Although in the United States brides and grooms are generally not strangers to one another, the *mehndi* tradition persists and is spreading outside of traditional ceremonies to become a fashion statement.

BRAHMAN

Brides from South India wear red, except those from Andhra Pradesh, who wear white and gold. The bride's sari is made of nine yards of silk, three more yards than used for standard saris. For the wedding, it must be tied in a particular way, and after the wedding the bride may wear it only for ceremonies in front of a ritual fire, for example at her child's first-birthday celebration. The groom is bare-chested and wears a dhoti [doe-tee], a single length of cloth wrapped to form pants with a pleat in front. Neither wears shoes or socks.

The wedding couple sits together before a burning fire, considered the witness. They pour ghee (clarified butter) on the fire to keep it burning strongly. This means the fire god is listening to them. Those in charge make certain that the fire remains burning until the ceremony is over. Meanwhile, the priest recites the mantras. In Sanskrit, the bridegroom promises to protect his wife and children and provide for their material needs. Often, these promises are translated afterward into English. Similarly, the bride must promise to care for their home and children.

After the couple walks around the fire three times, the bride sits in her father's lap as her husband winds a yellow thread smeared with turmeric paste around her neck and ties it with three knots. This is the moment when they are officially united, when he literally "ties the knots." Later, the string is often replaced by a gold chain, and the bride wears it throughout her life to safeguard her husband. She discards it only when she becomes a widow.

Guests throw flower petals at the couple after the knot-tying, and the petals must come from fragrant flowers, never nonfragrant ones. They frequently use carnations, roses, and jasmine. A reception follows, but not necessarily on the same day.

○ *Gifts:* General household gifts or merchandise gift certificates brought to the reception.

○ *Words:* Any felicitations.

○ *Clothing:* Best clothing, and avoid black. Females also avoid white, a mourning color.

○ *Body Language:* People greet one another with the *namaste* [nah-mah-stay], a sign of respect. With hands pressed together in a prayerlike position, bring them up to just below the chin and nod slightly.

IRANIAN

As a part of the ceremony, the person officiating, a mullah or civil official, asks the bride if she will agree to all the provisions in the marriage commitment. According to tradition, she is not supposed to say yes the first time. She keeps quiet and smiles. After the third time, she agrees. (See "Marrying"/Afghani, p. 92.)

The event takes place in the largest room in the bride's home or in a reception hall. If the latter, the wedding couple sits on a bench, preferably on a platform area. In front of them on the floor are pieces of a handwoven, Persian, multicolored cloth *(termeh)*. A stand-up mirror sits upright on it, one large enough for the wedding couple to see themselves. On either side is a candelabrum. On a colorfully painted wooden tray rests rue *(esfand* [es-von]*)*, an herb used to keep away the evil eye. Another tray holds a long, thin flatbread alongside feta cheese, and a plate filled with washed mint, chives, tarragon, and basil.

While a ceremonial speech takes place, two young women hold a piece of cloth over the heads of the bride and the groom. Then a happily married young woman takes two large cones of sugar (approximately one to one and a half feet) from the cloth on the floor. The cones are decorated with ribbons or flowers. The woman comes up behind the bride and the groom and runs the flat ends of the sugar cones together so that granules fall onto the cloth above the couple's head. While doing this, she blesses the couple.

After all the married women have taken turns grinding sugar over the newlyweds' heads, the remainders of the cones are returned to the floor, and the couple holding the sugar-filled cloth shakes it so that the granules fall on the bridal couple, who attempt to get away without a sugar shower. The ground sugar symbolizes wishes for a sweet future.

✪ *Gifts:* The Iranian community has now adopted American ways, and they have bridal showers and register at department-store wedding-gift departments to guide you. Generally, the groom's family pays all wedding expenses, and the bride's family provides most of the household items.

◉ *Words:* *"Tabrik arz mikonam"* [tah-bréek-arz-mée-ko-nam] ("I congratulate you").

◉ *Clothing:* Dressy apparel for women. Suits and ties for men.

ITALIAN

Incorporating ethnic roots into contemporary wedding receptions, Italian Americans are dancing the tarantella and hiring musicians to play Neapolitan love songs strummed on mandolins. *Confetti,* white-sugar-coated almonds, are a hallmark of the reception. Formerly, guests threw them at the bride and groom as a wish for fertility, but that became dangerous. Now, instead, the candy-covered nuts are wrapped in little net bundles and presented at each place setting at the reception meal. The candy comes from Sulmona, *confetti* capital of Italy.

The newlyweds give *bomboniere,* small party favors, to their guests as a thank-you for attending, and more extravagant gifts to each member of the wedding party—for example, silver or crystal dishes, often running $25 to $30 each. Add to this the cost of dinners, which may be $120 per person, and Italian parents spend a lot on weddings. However, the tradition of *la busta* [boo-stah] (the envelope) helps defray those expenses. After leaving the reception line, guests place money-filled envelopes into a decorated container: a box, mailbox, or birdcage placed on a special table.

Some wedding couples have eliminated the receiving line. Instead, the bride and the groom visit each table to greet their guests. This becomes an opportune time to accept money-filled envelopes, as is commonly done at Chinese and Vietnamese weddings. (See "Marrying"/Chinese, p. 110; "Marrying"/Vietnamese, p. 143.) However, some Italian couples have now adapted *la busta* to match the famous opening wedding scene in the film *The Godfather.*

In that film, wearing a silk money purse hung from her shoulder, Connie, Don Vito Corleone's daughter, moved from table to table collecting envelopes from those in debt to her father. To emulate this, some brides are ordering large (ten-by-ten-inch) silk shoulder purses to stash the cash-filled envelopes when greeting their seated guests. Designers at Saks Fifth Avenue in Manhattan make *le buste* in fabric matching the wedding gowns.

Other Italian Americans look askance at this. "Too gauche." Old-timers comment, "Why, we used to do that during the Depression." In those times of financial hardship, while going through the receiving line, guests commonly handed the bride and groom an envelope with money for living expenses. What makes *la busta* new is having the bride collect with a specially made purse, à la Connie Corleone.

❂ *Gifts:* One wedding coordinator at an Italian Catholic church advises that at her church, close friends of the bride and groom never give anything under $100. That would be looked upon unfavorably. They are expected to give $300 to $400 per couple, family members even more. Other guests can figure out proportionate amounts depending on their relationship to the couple.

❂ *Words:* Old-timers say, *"Tanti auguri"* ("Best wishes"). They may also express wishes for a male child, *"E figli maschi"* [eh féeg-lee móss-key].

❂ *Clothing:* Dressy.

❂ *Body Language:* Lots of hugging and kissing.

JAPANESE (BUDDHIST)

During the ceremony, the priest pours sake [sah-kay] (rice wine) into two small sake cups, and the bride and the groom sip from each other's sake cup in three sets of three sips totaling nine. Note that the number of times they drink the wine is an odd number. Even numbers indicate that a set is complete, that it is over. That is why they often use even numbers at funerals.

At the reception both Christians and Buddhists display one thousand origami [oh-ree-gah-mee] (folded paper) cranes that bridesmaids have helped to make. These are strung together and often hung from a tree. They are good-luck symbols, generally gold in color, and sometimes marked with a Chinese character that bodes well for the couple's future.

An older person often reads poetry. The bride's parents give a token gift to guests such as souvenir matches or origami birds, especially folded cranes.

✿ *Gifts:* Money, given in special envelopes with appropriate designs and characters and marked for the occasion by *mizuhiki* [mee-zoo-hee-key] (colored ties). (See "Giving Birth"/Japanese, p. 31; "Dying"/Japanese, p. 210.) These ties may be attached to the envelope or merely printed on the envelope. For weddings, the ties are gold. At the reception, someone receives these envelopes and logs in the amounts of money with the names of the donors. If you do not wish to give money, standard wedding gifts are also appreciated. Avoid giving a matched set to the couple. When giving a husband/wife gift, there should be a slight difference between his and hers, either in color, size, or design. Avoid giving an even number of objects. Traditional Japanese believe that one should not give something that can be divided. That explains why Japanese sets of dishes come in odd numbers and why gifts for the wedding guests are odd-numbered.

✪ *Words:* During the reception, the best man makes a toast by saying, *"Banzai!"* (one thousand wishes). However, because of the word's negative connotations associated with World War II, they may substitute *"Kampai!"* (good luck). The best man says the word three times, then takes a drink. Well-wishers join in.

JEWISH

ORTHODOX

Shortly before her wedding day, the bride visits a *mikvah* [mick-vah] (ritual bath) and undergoes ritual immersion. This represents a spiritual cleansing in preparation for the approaching marriage. Many bridegrooms also observe a ritual immersion in a *mikvah* but are not required to do so. On the day of the wedding, the couple fasts from morning until after the ceremony.

The bride wears a traditional white wedding gown, and the groom wears a long, white smock *(kittel)* over his regular clothing. Men wear the *kittel* at their weddings, on Yom Kippur (Day of Atonement), and at their funerals. Just prior to the ceremony, the bridegroom and other males gather in a separate room for the signing of the marriage contract, called the *ketubah* [keh-too-bah]. This is a legal contract in accordance with Jewish civil law where the husband guarantees to support his wife. Written in calligraphy in Aramaic, the document is dated according to the Hebrew calendar. *Ketubot* [keh-too-boat] range from simple pieces of paper to highly decorated parchments designed with flowers, vines, and lions.

The *ketubah* must be signed by two witnesses who are not related to either side. The groom formally accepts its terms by taking hold of a handkerchief handed to him by the rabbi on behalf of the bride. When finished, the men escort the groom in a singing procession toward the bride, who has been waiting in another room. Seated upon a thronelike chair, she blesses and greets family and friends who come to share in her joy, offer her blessings, and sample delicacies arrayed at the laden bride's table.

When the groom meets the bride on her throne, he partakes in a ceremony known as *badeken* (veiling). By placing the veil over her face he confirms that he is marrying the right person and avoids the possibility for deception that caused Jacob to marry Leah instead of Rachel as described in Genesis. The marriage ceremony follows and takes place under a *chuppah* [khu-pah, rhymes with book-a] (bridal canopy), which is supported by four poles. It is often made of velvet with embroidery and fringe, other times of flowers, or may be a tallit [tall-eét] (prayer shawl), a gift from the bride to the groom. *Chuppah* means covering or protection and symbolizes the wedding couple's new home together.

The bride's parents accompany her down the aisle. When she arrives at the *chuppah*, she walks around her bridegroom seven times. During the service, the couple shares a goblet of wine and receives seven blessings. Then the groom places a plain gold band on the bride's right index finger, considered the finger of intelligence because it points at the words when one reads the Torah. Next, the rabbi reads the wedding contract aloud and formally presents it to the bride.

At the conclusion of the ceremony, the groom breaks a glass with his foot. There are many different interpretations of this act, but traditionally it has been meant to keep the ceremony from being totally joyous by reminding that no joy can be complete since the destruction of the temple in

Jerusalem two thousand years ago, or it may serve as a reminder that at such a joyous time one must still be aware
of sadness and pain existing in the world.

The newlyweds leave the *chuppah* amid singing and
dancing and adjourn to a private room. Originally, this is
where they consummated the marriage. Today, it is a time
alone together to share a few private moments and break
their fast. Soon afterward, they rejoin their guests, who
have already begun the wedding feast.

Dancing occurs, but men and women dance in separate
circles, and a fabric screen may divide the dance floor for
this purpose. One of the highlights is the chair dance, where
the bride and the groom, seated in chairs, are hoisted into
the air and danced around. This is a highly joyous moment.
Because dancing with the opposite sex in public is considered immodest, the bride and the groom hold opposite ends
of a scarf or handkerchief.

To entertain and evoke laughter at the reception, some
people may don costumes, and women may wear silly hats
or rainbow wigs.

✪ *Gifts:* Household items and money placed in an envelope or greeting card are welcome.

✪ *Words:* During the ceremony, after the groom suc-
cessfully breaks the glass, people shout, *"Mazel tov!"*
(congratulations or good luck).

✪ *Clothing:* Suits for men, women in below-the-knee
dresses with modest sleeves and necklines. Men
should wear yarmulkes [yáhr-mull-kes], and a boxful
is usually available for those who do not own one.
Non-Orthodox married women cover their heads
with hats or scarves.

✪ *Body Language:* Depending on the level of obser-
vance, some Orthodox may not separate men from
the women, but more commonly males and females

sit separately from one another during the ceremony and at the reception. As a form of modesty, separation rules apply to the dance floor, as well.

SEPHARDIC VARIATIONS

A few days prior to the wedding, the women may have a henna party, where they paint symbolic designs on the hands of the bride. (See "Marrying"/Indian, *Mehndi,* p. 120.) These symbols offer protection from the evil eye. Depending on whether the bride's background is Moroccan, Syrian, or Judeo-Spanish, the bride alone will have her palms and feet decorated for joy and happiness, or she may have just the palms done or just the right hand. In some situations, all females in attendance will have their hands beautified by henna designs, as well. They may present the bride with a *hamsa* [khóm-zah] (a hand-shaped pendant) for further protection from the evil eye, to which brides are most vulnerable.

REFORM AND CONSERVATIVE CEREMONIES

Compared to Orthodox rituals, ceremonies are less complex. There is no separation of males and females. They emphasize gender equality rather than differences. For example, instead of the groom presenting the *ketubah* to his bride, the rabbi may hand it to the newly wedded couple, each holding a part of the usually framed document. Their mutual carrying of it symbolizes that each partner must uphold his/her part of the contract.

Often the bride and the groom express their love to each other by reciting poetry or personal variations of the wedding vows during the ceremony. At the reception, during the chair dance, brides and grooms may touch one another. Interpretations of the breaking of the glass may include a statement about the symbolic grinding out of violence, hatred, and evil.

KOREAN

Yak Kon Sik [yock-cone-sheik] (The Engagement)

This formal occasion is often the first time the groom's family meets the bride's family. An emcee introduces each side of the family, giving biographies and histories of each member of the family. Alone and together, the couple sing traditional songs without musical accompaniment.

An important feature is giving gifts to the future bride and groom. If wealthy, the family of the future groom presents the future bride with three sets of jewelry, each set containing a necklace, earrings, and bracelet, and each set made of a different semiprecious stone, such as sapphires or rubies. They are presented in a traditional wooden box *(ham* [hom]*)*. The bride's side presents the future son-in-law with a suit and an expensive watch. In Korea, the bride's family provides the groom with an apartment. Traditionally, the bride's family gives the future mother-in-law an expensive gift. In the United States it may be a fur coat. To not present expensive gifts on this occasion brings about a loss of face.

The Wedding

Frequently, they hold wedding ceremonies at commercial wedding halls, often located in the Korean business community, where they can have both a Western-style and a Korean-style wedding, one immediately following the other. At the Western-style wedding, the bride and the groom wear traditional Western garb, but afterward they often have a brief ceremony where the bride and groom have changed into traditional clothing. The bride wears a blouse with wide, rainbow-striped sleeves, flared skirt of lively colors and vivid embroidery, and a beaded hat, sometimes adorned with jewels. She wears two red dots, like stickers, on her cheeks, reminiscent of the painted rosy cheeks of the past. The groom wears an embroidered blue robe and a hat like those worn by scholar-officials—black with horizontal ears.

During this part of the ceremony, the bride and the groom stand in front of the groom's family, who are seated all around them. The bride and the groom bow to each other, share sake [sah-kay] (rice wine), and offer fruit and wine and bow to each member of the groom's family. Then they sit down and receive blessings from the groom's family. As a means of protecting the couple from evil influences, the groom's family throws nuts to the bride. How many she catches foretells how many children she will have.

Another prognosticator of future children is tied to the behavior of the bride and groom. Since a wedding is a serious occasion, the wedding couple is not supposed to smile. If the bride smiles, it means that her first child will be a girl.

✪ *Gifts:* Money in any color envelope with your name written on it. Frequently they set up two tables to collect monetary gifts, one for the bride's guests, the other for the groom's guests. A close and trusted relative guards the collection and tallies the amounts. Housewares are acceptable, but if you give knives, you must receive $1 from the couple to preserve rather than sever the relationship.

✪ *Words:* Any form of congratulations.

✪ *Clothing:* Dressy clothes show respect. Avoid wearing white, associated with funerals. Females avoid wearing white hair ribbons, also a mourning sign. If the couple has a traditional Korean ceremony, remove shoes before entering the room.

✪ *Body Language:* Nowadays, in most situations, it is acceptable to kiss the bride. Avoid hugging family members. The most respectful form of greetings and salutations is the bow. If you feel uncomfortable with this gesture, nod your head.

Sixtieth Anniversary

The entire traditional Korean wedding ceremony is reenacted in a restaurant, nightclub, or hall. The wedding couple enters through the main entrance of the room in full Korean wedding regalia, including the bride's rosy-cheek stickers. From afar, the couple may look just as they had sixty years earlier. However, age and arthritis betray them as they attempt to bow, sit down, and rise. It is both humorous and touching to witness.

All the events of the wedding are repeated: an emcee details their individual and couple histories; they display a formalized food table; each relative offers them rice wine; guests sing and dance.

✪ *Gifts:* Hand money in envelopes to someone in charge who collects, records, and tallies amounts.

✪ *Words:* "Congratulations."

✪ *Clothing:* Good clothing.

LAO

Prior to the wedding, the families consult in a temple with a priest as to the best date for the wedding based on astrological implications. The day before the wedding ceremony, close friends and relatives come to the bride's home for a preparty where they assist in preparations. During this time, they eat and drink with gusto. The major task, however, is to prepare food for the wedding and to build two identical towers of a flower and leaf arrangement used only at weddings, *pha kouane* [pah kwan]. These towers sit on the floor on a silver or aluminum tray base. From these bases, they build a tower about two and a half feet tall constructed of flowers of all colors and kinds except those that have thorns. In Laos, they use banana leaves in the construction, but away from Laos they substitute green, folded paper to which they attach the flowers. Depending on whether the family is from northern or southern Laos, they place different kinds of food offerings at the base of the flowers. These may be rice, whole chickens, eggs, candles, fruits, and sweets. These offerings feed the ancestor spirits.

Generally, the morning ceremony lasts two to three hours and most frequently takes place in the bride's home, where she awaits the groom, his family, and other guests. A shaman performs the ceremony. The bride wears a traditional Lao gown with a silk, gold-patterned skirt, while the groom wears a dark-colored sarong, often topped by a long-sleeved shirt or military-type jacket.

A striking feature of the Lao wedding is the bride's hairdo, *kao phom* [cow-pomm], a particular fashion created by a specialist, who spends up to three hours fixing it. The hairdresser pulls the hair up away from the face and ties it into a bun at a straight angle without one single strand of loose hair. Then the bun is decorated with gold chains and gold jewelry topped by a gold umbrella-type object resembling a flower that sits at the top of the bun, called *pak pin kao* [pock-pin-cow]. Sometimes these objects have been kept in families for generations. If a bride's family does not own one, they may borrow one from a friend.

During the ceremony, the shaman ties white strings around the wrists of the wedding couple and temporarily connects them to the two towers of flowers and himself. After receiving blessings from the shaman, the bridal couple present nicely wrapped gifts to their parents, such as a skirt for the mothers or some fabric for a shirt or blouse. Then the couple ask their parents for blessings or forgiveness for any wrongdoing in their pasts. In turn, the parents wish them good luck and bless the marriage. Afterward, all the guests tie white strings around the wrists of the wedding couple and offer their blessings in a *baci* [bai-see] or *soukhoanh* [sue-kwanh] ceremony. (See "Giving Birth"/Lao,

p. 37; "Marrying"/Cambodian, p.108; "Healing"/Hmong, p. 161; "Healing"/Lao, p. 165.)

They hold the reception in the evening either at home, in a restaurant, or in a hall. While guests are dining, the wedding couple visit each table with a bottle of liquor and a shot glass. The couple thank the guests for being there, serve the elderly first, then friends of the parents, then the rest of the guests, who all drink from the same glass. The bride and the groom drink, too.

Live music and dancing take place. The bride and groom dance first, traditional Lao style in a circle *(lam vong),* but they do not touch one another. Then the parents dance, after which everyone is invited to join in. The men dance inside an inner circle; the women dance outside. Only family members and close friends may dance with the bride, no one else.

When a man wishes to dance with a woman, he invites her by performing the *wai* [why] gesture by pressing his hands together in a prayerlike position and bringing them up to just below his chin and nodding slightly. When the dance is finished, the couple make the *wai* sign to one another as a thank-you and form of respect.

✪ *Gifts:* Household items, but avoid giving knives or anything sharp. Money may be enclosed in any color envelope. Write your name and address on the outside and deposit it in a slotted, decorated box sitting on a special table at the reception. If a box is not visible, present the envelope to the person who appears to be in charge.

✪ *Words:* All felicitations.

✪ *Clothing:* Guests should dress up. Lao women have certain skirts and scarves they wear only when going to temple or attending weddings. The skirts contain many gold threads. In the past, guests would not wear black to a wedding, and in some families this taboo persists. Women wear skirts rather than pants, but no miniskirts. At the home ceremony, remove shoes. If the reception is in a hall and people sit on mats on the floor, remove shoes.

✪ *Body Language:* Avoid kissing the bride. The groom won't kiss her either. There is no kissing at all. Avoid hugging or kissing family members. The respectful form for greeting elders or other honored persons is the *wai*. They will return the gesture.

MEXICAN (ROMAN CATHOLIC)

The priest performs the marriage in the middle of a Mass. After the exchange of vows and the rings, one of the *padrinos de arras* [pah-dreé-nose deh ár-rahs] (sponsors in charge of the money and rings), hands thirteen dimelike coins encased in a heart-shaped or pillbox-sized chest to the priest, who hands it to the groom, who in turn gives it to the bride. Symbolically he is saying, "I will always take care of your material needs." Her acceptance means that she will use the money to take care of their household.

In the nineteenth century, this custom meant that the groom would give the bride his future earnings, which would be plentiful. After the bride accepted the coins, which in those times were real and often of gold, she spilled them. They then became the property of the officiating priest, to be used for furnishing the church or distributing to the poor.

In modern services, after the vows, a lasso of silk and flowers or two cords or ribbons are placed over the couple as they kneel. This signifies that they will be together always.

✪ *Gifts:* Household items, money in wedding congratulations cards or plain envelopes. Gifts may be sent ahead or brought to the reception.

✪ *Words: "Felicidades"* [fay-lee-cee-dáh-dess]. "Congratulations." "May you have a long happy life together."

✪ *Clothing:* Suits and ties for men. Nice dresses for women. Dressy pants suits.

NIGERIAN (IBO [ÉE-BOW])

Following a typical Roman Catholic or Protestant church ceremony, the wedding party and friends move to a large hall for a reception that lasts about five hours. The breaking of kola nuts by a male elder is the most important part of the ritual. The elder takes the nut and begins a prayer consisting of a series of affirmations, such as "May the marriage last." "May they live in peace." "May they have children both male and female." "May they not bring shame to the family." After each statement, everyone responds in Ibo, *"Ise"* [ee-say] or *"Ofor"* [oh-for], both meaning "amen." At the end of the prayer, the kola nut is broken and everyone claps. Other guests make toasts, and everyone samples the bitter-tasting nut.

As an adaptation of the African dowry tradition, in the United States the bride's family participates in the custom "sending her home." The bride's family buys most of the items to help their daughter start a new household in her husband's home. Items may include furniture, cooking utensils, clothing, perhaps a car. The family displays the gifts outside the new home, but they do not bring them indoors until after the wedding ceremony. These items demonstrate the family's support for their daughter and publicly announce, "Thank you for being a good daughter."

Because as many as five thousand people may attend, a committee of friends organizes fund-raising to assist. If other Nigerians cannot afford to give money, they volunteer to bring food: baked chicken, pans of rice. Friends provide at least 80 percent of the food.

✪ *Gifts:* Since the bride's family provides most of the gift items, money is preferred.

✪ *Words:* "Long life." "Good Health." Give marital advice: "Don't go to bed mad." "Marriage is for better or for worse." "You must have good communication."

✪ *Clothing:* Dressy.

SAMOAN

Samoans are Christians, most belonging to Congregational churches. Therefore, wedding ceremonies take place in church and follow the customs of the particular denomination. Inside the church, the wedding couple looks like any other with the bride in a traditional white gown, groom in a tuxedo, and their attendants in coordinated outfits. Full-fledged Samoan traditions surface at the reception.

All Samoan rites of passage are noted for their joyousness and generosity, and wedding receptions are prime examples with the emphasis on singing, dancing, feasting, and having a good time. Immediately after the church ceremony, the bride and groom change into traditional outfits. Often the bride's dress is of natural-colored, woven fabric trimmed with brilliant red and yellow feathers around the neckline, waist, and midcalf hemline. She also wears a head ornament of red and white feathers.

The groom wears a lavalava (wraparound skirt) with a white long shirt over it and a white floral lei. If they hold the reception outdoors, he will be shirtless. Some of the female guests wear muumuus (loose, brightly colored dresses) and the men may wear lavalavas.

Reception activities include presenting the bridal couple with fine mats, traditional singing, and dancing by performers in native costumes accompanied by a Samoan band. In one of the highlights, the bride dances alone in the middle of the dance floor and guests attach dollar bills to her clothes or stick them to her body, which is easy to do if she has oiled herself with coconut oil. This not only makes the money adhere but makes her body shine, as well. The bride alone receives the money while she dances, but her husband dances close by as a sign of support.

Whole roasted pigs lying on wooden pallets and placed on the floor in front of the head table are another specialty. Roasted pigs presented in such a fashion are hallmarks of Samoan feasts. The pigs are prepared in underground, rock-lined ovens in backyards or at commercial bakeries that have sufficient-sized ovens to accommodate them. The higher the social status of the couple, the more roast pigs.

A tradition apt to surprise first-time guests is the appearance of cardboard boxes, the size that holds two dozen canned drinks. These sit at individual place settings and may contain a whole fish, a whole chicken, cooked yam, large slabs of corned beef, pork ribs with potato salad, cold noodle salad, fruit salad, and a canned soft drink. Guests are expected to sample the food but take most of it home to their families in the cardboard containers. This tradition reflects the strong Samoan emphasis on community sharing.

✪ *Gifts:* Bring paper money to put on the bride during her dollar dance. Place gifts on a table set aside to receive them. Give housewares or money tucked inside congratulatory cards or plain envelopes.

✪ *Words: "Talofa fa'amálo"* [tah-lów-fa-fa-ah-máh-low], "Congratulations."

✪ *Clothing:* Respectful church attire.

THAI

Thai customs vary according to region. In the northeast they resemble those of neighboring Laos. Outside, customs seem to mix. Prior to the temple ceremony, people tie white strings around one wrist of the wedding couple. Each guest takes a piece of precut string and ties a knot in the middle and then ties it to one wrist of the couple's hands. This is a form of blessing. The act is repeated at the wedding ceremony and later at the reception. (See "Healing"/Hmong, p. 161; "Healing"/Lao, p. 165; "Healing"/Thai, p. 169.)

The ceremony takes place at home or at the temple. In a one-hour ceremony, the monk blesses the couple, who are dressed in traditional Thai costumes. The monk talks about Buddha's teachings and gives five rules for married life, which include being honest with one another and advising the husband to provide for his wife according to his economic status.

A respected elder, one who has only been married once and has remained with his partner his whole life, blesses the couple. The couple kneels in front of him and he links them together by placing a loop of white thread on their heads. Then over their hands, he pours sacred water into bowls of flowers. Guests follow suit as a means of anointing the bride and groom. Before leaving the temple, the newlyweds offer food and money donations for the monks. Later, they celebrate at an evening wedding reception, generally held in a Thai restaurant, where, as a part of the festivities, they dance Western style.

✪ *Gifts:* Bring them to the reception. The bride receives jewelry from her husband's family. Give envelopes with money, and write your name on the outside and hand it to the person who seems to be in charge. If you give a household gift, avoid knives or anything sharp. Avoid giving handkerchiefs, representing future tears. Avoid giving matches, symbol of danger.

✪ *Words:* Wish them a successful, long life together.

✪ *Clothing:* Dressy clothes. Avoid black.

✪ *Body Language:* Traditional people use the *wai* gesture as a sign of respect. (See "Marrying"/Lao,

p. 133.) Younger, more Americanized Thai may be open to shaking hands, hugging, or kissing. Observe others before you act.

TIBETAN

A young man who wishes to marry sends two friends to the home of the young woman he has selected. They bring her parents tea and champagne or a rice wine called *chang* [rhymes with song]. The emissaries ask for the young woman's hand, but the parents never make a commitment. They say they must consult with their daughter.

Two to four weeks later, the friends return bringing more tea and *chang*. If the girl or her parents do not like the young man, her parents will say their daughter is not ready at this time. If the girl and her family are interested, parents make no commitment. However, lack of rejection signifies agreement.

The third visit is akin to an engagement ceremony. The groom sends four or five people with many gifts for the bride and her family. They present tea, expensive fabric, and white scarves to everyone. (See "Giving Birth"/Tibetan, p. 42; "Dying"/Tibetan, p. 231.) They give the bride's mother one or more trays holding small, white fabric bags filled with vertically placed rolls of paper money. Each bag is tied with a white scarf and looks like a flower. These bags are called *nureen* (payment for milk) and show gratitude to the mother for nurturing the bride-to-be.

The families set the wedding date according to astrological calculations, and the day before the nuptials, the bride's family hosts a party. Everyone dons colorful Tibetan clothing, hats, and shoes. The bride wears a *patu*, a black wig with two conelike rolls of hair standing upright on each side of her head. A Y-shaped, woven fabric strip, adorned with turquoise and coral, attaches to each cone, its tail reaching midway down the bride's back. The bride also wears elaborate, large turquoise earrings and a turquoise necklace that looks more like a breastplate.

During the evening, the groom takes five arrows that have been bound together with braided strips of silk in the five sacred colors of blue, green, red, yellow, and white and inserts them vertically down the back of the bride's dress. Their upper half is visible.

On the wedding day, at about 10 A.M., the groom's emissaries drive in cars decorated with colored ribbons to pick up the bride to take her to the groom's family's home. One of the escorts carries a painting of a deity. Another escort replaces the arrows into the back of the bride's dress. Meanwhile, at the groom's home, the bride's emissaries hang five colors of scarves on his front door and one scarf on the inside door leading to the home altar.

Before the bride enters her future home, a boy offers her *chima* [chi-máh], a mixture of roasted barley and wheat seed, which she flicks into the air three times. She then dips her ring finger into the rice wine *(chang)* three times and flicks it, too. Once inside, the bride joins her groom, who waits for her seated in front of the altar. Guests offer white scarves to the wedding party accompanied by envelopes filled with money. They make additional offerings of tea, rice wine, and the *chima*. At the late-night conclusion of the ceremony, as guests leave, they form a circle, sing, burn incense, and offer the *chima* to the gods three times. Upon leaving, each guest receives a white scarf.

✪ *Gifts:* Anything but shoes, which symbolize parting company.

✪ *Words:* "Have a long, good life together."

✪ *Clothing:* Dressy.

✪ *Body Language:* Avoid kissing the bride. Use the *namaste* for greetings (see "Marrying"/Indian, p. 120). The urbanized younger generation may shake hands.

Vietnamese

If they are Christian, the wedding ceremony takes place in church, and the bride wears a traditional Western, white wedding gown. If they are Buddhists, the ceremony takes place at the temple or at home in front of an altar. In both situations, they hold dinner receptions at a restaurant. The bride changes into a mandarin-style red gown embroidered on the front with an entwined dragon and phoenix and worn over baggy pants.

The bride may change into different-colored outfits at different stages of the event—during the ceremony, when greeting guests, when cutting the cake. Nowadays, she wears a white, Western-style bridal gown at the end of the reception. Bridesmaids, too, change outfits. All the men and women in the bridal party wear headpieces called *khan dong*. The men wear them lower on the forehead and the women wear them more like a crown.

In Buddhist families, the groom's family arrives in procession at the home of the bride with offerings of roast pig, red-dyed sticky rice, tea, red wine, brandy, and cakes covered with red cloths with gold fringe, and a black lacquer box holding the two wedding rings. Servings are double, everything in twos. They place the gifts on the altar inside the bride's home. The altar, decorated with gold-trimmed red covers, holds additional offerings of incense, flowers, fruit, and red candles.

The couple kneels and bows before the shrine to pay their respect to the bride's ancestors. After the bride thanks her parents and they advise that she live up to their expectations, the couple place the rings on their fingers and the groom's mother and sisters present the bride with gold jewelry. The couple eat some of the food, and then the groom and his family, taking some of the food they have brought to the bride's home, leave and repeat the ritual at the home of the groom.

When guests arrive at the reception, generally held in a Vietnamese or Chinese restaurant, they sign their names on a piece of red fabric. Later, one person from each of the round banquet tables for ten collects red envelopes containing money from each single guest or each couple. (See "Marrying"/Chinese, p. 110; "Marrying"/Italian, p. 124.) This money defrays the cost of the banquet. When the bride and groom visit the table, a self-appointed envelope-gatherer hands the envelopes to the bride, who in turn gives them to one of her bridesmaids for safekeeping. In exchange, the bride gives a small wedding token to each guest, for example, a miniature wedding shoe or flower or tiny wine cup.

The newlyweds live with the groom's family. They strongly believe that the bride and groom must be the first ones to sit on their wedding bed. Sometimes the mother-in-law prepares the wedding bed and locks the bedroom door so that no one accidentally breaks this taboo. If a pregnant woman were to sit on the bed, it would foretell of arguments between the bride and the groom.

✺ *Gifts:* The red money envelopes often hold $50 from a single person and $100 from a couple. In addition to money, other gifts may be given, but avoid giving handkerchiefs, which presage tears; clocks, which are omens of death; and scissors or knives, which symbolize the severing of a relationship.

Avoid giving anything white, such as towels, pillowcases, or candles, because white is associated with funeral rituals. Give pink linens, because pink and red are associated with good luck.

✺ *Words:* "Congratulations."

✺ *Clothing:* Good clothing.

EMERGING TRADITIONS

LAS VEGAS WEDDINGS

Las Vegas weddings are so popular that, according to the Las Vegas Convention and Visitors Authority, the number averages one hundred thousand per year. To accommodate the demand, the Clark County Marriage License Bureau remains open from 8 A.M. to midnight Monday through Thursday, and twenty-four hours a day Friday through Sunday and holidays. And if the couple change their minds afterward, it takes only forty-eight hours before the divorce comes through.

Although it covers only eighty-five square miles, Las Vegas boasts of forty-two wedding chapels with such appealing names as San Francisco Sally's Victorian Chapel, Lamour Wedding Chapel, Cupid's Wedding Chapel, and We've Only Just Begun Wedding Chapel.

The wedding trappings are appropriate to the chapel themes. At the Canterbury Wedding Chapel at the Hotel Excalibur, the bridal couple and their attendants wear medieval wedding attire. At the Graceland Wedding Chapel, an Elvis impersonator walks the bride down the aisle and sings "Viva Las Vegas." If the couple is too tired to walk, they can have a drive-through wedding, available twenty-four hours a day. At the Little White Chapel, a staff member videotapes the five-minute ceremony from the backseat, and if being on the ground holds no appeal, the city's Stratosphere Tower has wedding chapels nine hundred feet in the air.

The Divine Madness Fantasy Wedding Chapel advertises six theme chapels and costume ensembles, "from innocent lace to erotic leather." Couples can play Cleopatra and Marc Antony in the Egyptian Tomb or Calamity Jane and Buffalo Bill in the Western chapel. They have a Space Voyage chapel, a Renaissance chapel, and an S&M chapel in a dungeon complete with whips and chains.

For the more daring, Wedding Dreams wedding packagers arrange helicopter or hot-air-balloon weddings, even bungee jumping. For $725 the bride and groom can take the plunge, and if the maid of honor and best man want to jump in, the cost rises to $900. The chapel throws in six roses for the bride, a two-rose boutonniere for the groom, and two disposable wedding cameras.

Costs and risks rise considerably for a skydiving wedding, available beginning at $1,500. For the "From the Heavens Above" package, it skyrockets to $2,000. Included are jumping for the best man and the maid of honor, private use of a passenger jetliner, jump masters, minister, pictures, video, and a limousine for five hours.

If expenses seem steep, they are a bargain compared to traditional weddings, which can run into the tens of thousands of dollars. Anthropologist Young-Hoon Kim studied the Las Vegas wedding chapel phenomenon and claims that one of the great appeals of a Las Vegas wedding is its economy. For only $100 a couple can obtain a $35 cash-only license and get married. If they want flowers and a video, the cost escalates to $300. Not unexpectedly, there seems to be a relationship between Las Vegas and the Vegas wedding chapel industry. According to Kim, one invites you to gamble on money, the other invites you to gamble on love.

These weddings do not signal that Americans have lost faith in the institution of marriage. Kim believes that if that were true, there would be fewer marriages taking place. Instead, these marriages demonstrate that couples expect less of marriage. If it doesn't work out, they'll get out. If they have spent less, their investment is less and so is their loss.

SAME SEX WEDDINGS (ALSO KNOWN AS PARTNERSHIP-IN-LIFE VOWS OR COMMITMENT CEREMONIES)

In a mass wedding held in March 1996, Mayor Willie Brown of San Francisco enthusiastically officiated at a wedding ceremony for 165 gay and lesbian couples, who marched down the aisle to music from the fifteen-piece San Francisco Lesbian/Gay Freedom Band. The ceremony consisted of participants' names read aloud with short statements they had written. Frequently they told about the years they had shared together, some for as long as twenty-one years. Some referred to their pets; one couple announced the birth of their first mortgage.

The biggest difference in these weddings is the absence of traditional roles and use of the words *bride* and *groom*. Instead there are *partners, spouses,* or *newlyweds*. Accordingly, stags and bridal showers are simply labeled premarital celebrations.

Elsewhere, at an elegant private ceremony, Alexandra and Kathryn welcomed their guests with a description of their beliefs inscribed on their wedding program and an explanation of the multiple ritual motifs they had chosen. Like so many of the new and emerging rituals in this book, the celebrants blended customs and rites from many sources, taking what was to their liking and what seemed appropriate. They incorporated music by Barbra Streisand and Sade; a priest gave blessings and led them in a guided meditation and closing benediction; a friend performed a Native American smudging with burning sage to carry prayers to heaven and purify the energy and to bless the four directions in honor of the four spheres of their lives: physical, emotional, mental, spiritual. The couple lit a unity candle, and under an arch created by seven forty- to fifty-foot-long strands of helium-filled balloons, one for each color of the rainbow, they had a blessing of the rainbow wishes, a ritual of their own creation.

Before the ceremony, they requested that each guest go to a wishing table under the rainbow archway of balloons and select two beads of different colors. Each person made a separate wish with each bead, one for themselves, one for the newlyweds, then placed the beads into a Native American wedding vase, later blessed by the priest. The newlyweds took home the beads and strung them together and hung them over an indoor ficus tree to honor the day, their families, and their friends. Finally, during the recessional, guests blew bubbles at the couple.

When Jeanne and Lynn had their partnership ceremony, they, too, chose eclectic ritual elements. They played South African praise songs by Ladysmith Black Mambazo. They rang Tibetan bells and during the procession marched in to Pachelbel's Canon in D. Over traditional wedding outfits of gown and tuxedo, they donned ceremonial robes to symbolize their ethnic heritages. Lynn's robe had African motifs representing her South African birth, and Jeanne's robe had Guatemalan designs tied to her Latino paternal heritage.

As in Native American and Wiccan traditions, they blessed the elements and the four directions, then participated in a Celtic handfast rite where they clasped each other's hands to confirm their covenant of betrothal. Afterward, they tied a lovers' knot, spoke their vows, exchanged rings, and marched out to the recessional.

This wedding was an overt political statement about human and gender rights. An activist in the gay/lesbian movement, Jeanne's contributions were acknowledged by numerous guests including folksinger Holly Near, who sang in honor of the couple and their commitment to each other.

At the reception, replicas of the couple dressed in their robes topped the wedding cake. The miniature couple stood beneath trees, Lynn's metaphor for women. Trees, like women, nurture and reach to the heavens, their branches representing relationships. Each guest received a memento of the couple's commitment and love printed on a souvenir bookmark:

> *Now we stand at the center of the circle where all things meet their opposites. Energies of feminine and masculine, darkness and light, spirit and matter, God and Goddess, that which makes each whole and complete.*

✿ *Gifts:* The couple may be registered at local department stores. Prior to the event, ask which one. At bridal registry computers, don't automatically push the button for "Weddings." Try "Commitment" first, and if that doesn't work, then try "Weddings." However, many store computers require listing by either "bride" or "groom" even though both parties are of the same gender.

For lesbian weddings, since there will be no male to take care of handyman chores, they may appreciate power tools to help with home repairs.

✿ *Words:* Don't refer to a gay male or a female couple as *husband* and *wife*. Use the terms *mate, spouse,* or *partner,* rather than *bride* and *groom,* although some gay men may like to be referred to as "husbands." Avoid remarks like "Oh, this was just like a normal (or regular) wedding." While it may be intended as a compliment, it may be perceived as condescension. Avoid skepticism while congratulating the couple: "I sure hope it lasts." Think of the wedding as a different cultural experience, just as you might if you were attending a wedding of a couple from an ethnicity different from your own.

✿ *Clothing:* Whatever is appropriate to the venue. Invitations might also indicate what is expected or required.

VAMPIRE WEDDINGS

"Here comes the bride, all dressed in black." That's what happens at vampire weddings. An unforgettable one occurred in a small cemetery on Halloween night, 1992. The bride wore an elaborate satin wedding gown in black with purple accents that she herself had fashioned. She carried a purple floral bouquet with black ribbons. The groom and his attendants wore black leather jackets. The only member of the wedding party not dressed in black was the tearful flower ghoul, a five-year-old dressed in white. Even the six-tiered devil's-food wedding cake continued the theme, its chocolate frosting trimmed with black roses and spiderwebs. Atop the uppermost layer reigned a skeleton bride and groom.

Costumes and fangs were de rigueur for the over one hundred wedding guests, who had carefully followed the dress code noted in the black and purple wedding invitations along with the warning "Bring your own flashlight." The cemetery was alive with black capes and stand-ins for Dracula, Marie Antoinette, the Energizer rabbit, nuns, witches, cadavers, ghosts, and the grim reaper with scythe.

Members of a local hearse club added a macabre touch with eight parked hearses alongside the road next to the tombstones, some carrying open caskets and candelabra. Their president, Catrina Coffin, ensured that members left lasting impressions, such as the man costumed as a car-accident victim with blood, gore, and maggots oozing from his fake wounds.

At eleven-thirty a hearse carrying the bride and groom pulled into the eerily lit cemetery where carved, glittering jack-o'-lanterns set atop tall tombstones illuminated the

way to the makeshift altar in front of a tall tombstone with
a six-foot-high candelabrum holding purple candles and
decorated with a black floral wreath and purple ribbons.
Paper ghosts strung in trees and bats hanging from
branches added to the spooky atmosphere.

With a live violinist dressed as the Phantom of the Opera
playing the theme song from that musical, the bride and
groom slowly followed their attendants and flower ghoul
down an aisle created by luminarias [loo-mee-nár-ee-oz]
(paper bags placed on the ground holding flickering candles). They arrived in front of a minister from the Secular
Church of Humanistic Agnosticism, who wore a black top
hat, black tuxedo jacket, and white T-shirt. Following a
brief sermon, he asked the couple, "Do you promise to love
each other and be cool until doomsday?" They replied af-
firmatively, to which he responded, "Excellent, very excellent." When he pronounced the couple husband and wife,
an enthusiastic guest called out, "Bite her!" After the
crowd's cheers died down, the bride shouted, "Let them eat
cake!" And they did.

✪ *Gifts:* Candles, candlelabra, stake (steak) knives.

A more intimate vampire wedding occurred on October 31,
1995, when Susan Duncan and Del Howison, owners of
Dark Delicacies Horror Book Store in Burbank, California,
held a vampire wedding inside their shop. An elderly female
minister in a pink-and-white seersucker suit with black
stockings, who was a psychic but might have doubled for a
stand-up comedienne, officiated. The couple had found her
in the phone book by dialing 1-800-I-Marry-U. With music
from *Bram Stoker's Dracula* setting the mood, the couple
stood in the archway in the middle of the store and took
their vows flanked by gargoyles, vampires, masks, and horror memorabilia. Sue wore a long black velvet dress with a

bat veil and held a bouquet of black roses and white calla
lilies. Del wore black denim pants and a shirt with a skull
on the back. Thirty-five friends and family members wit-
nessed the brief ceremony. Since it was Halloween and most
guests were going to parties after the wedding, they were
appropriately costumed: vampires, London after midnight
with white face, top hat, and tux, and a witch-in-training
with shards of glass stuck to her clothing attesting to her
novice status.

Afterward, the newlyweds cut the chocolate-frosted
wedding cake shaped like a coffin and decorated with a single red rose down the center. When it was sliced, the cherry
filling oozed like blood. Red-colored champagne punch
added another morbid touch. The refreshments sat on a
table with a centerpiece vase of mummified hands holding
dried roses.

Since Halloween is one of the busiest seasons for the
bookstore, Del and Sue didn't have time to print wedding
invitations. Instead, they later sent out announcements
showing a ghoul with a girl draped in his arms and the caption "Del has carried away Susan in marriage."

✪ *Gifts:* Because many of their friends are part of the
Burbank entertainment industry, gifts reflected their
friends' talents and connections—even the wedding
cake, made by one of Marilyn Monroe's stand-ins.
They received many handmade items: a statue of Del
and Sue that through special effects had been altered
to make them look like a fifteen-inch-tall ghoulish
wedding couple, a velvet-covered scrapbook, handmade picture frame, an animation cel of Pinhead. A
former vampire bride presented them with a large
black wreath with a Dracula quote printed on its purple ribbon: "I bid you welcome."

REMARRYING

LATER-IN-LIFE WEDDINGS

While it may not be officially taboo, numerous ethnicities do not encourage later-in-life marriages, particularly when, in some cultures, widowed parents are expected to live with their adult children and grandchildren. Those most likely to remarry are persons who live independently or are active in social or religious groups, such as Pete, a free-spirited centenarian who outlived three of his four wives, all of whom he met at church. Retirement hotels, too, boast of weddings between residents. Other times seniors may be "fixed up" by a mutual friend, such as the eighty-eight-year-old bride who had a stock answer for those who asked why she bothered to get married again: "Why buy the cow when you can get the milk for free?"

Most of the bride's friends, also widows, were not enthusiastic about her taking on a third husband after outliving two previous ones. "What do you need it for?" They would have preferred that she continue her social activities with them rather than marry her intended, a ninety-three-year-old widower, but romance and tradition prevailed. The couple married in a formal but simple Jewish religious ceremony in front of their immediate family and closest friends. She wore a St. John suit in green, her favorite color. One of her daughters placed a garter on her still-shapely leg, and the newlyweds spent their honeymoon in Las Vegas.

Other later-in-life weddings may be more elaborate, such as the surprise nuptial celebration for one hundred guests who thought they were only invited to the couple's home for dinner. The about-to-be bride, who refused to give her age but who had first been married fifty years earlier, greeted her guests wearing a black crepe cocktail dress. Her eighty-

year-old about-to-be groom dressed in a brown cashmere
suit. After cocktails, he announced their engagement. Then
as all were drinking champagne, the couple disappeared
and changed clothes. She donned a blue chiffon dress, he a
tuxedo. To the guests' astonishment, the orchestra began
playing "Here Comes the Bride," heralding the arrival of
the wedding couple and the ensuing brief ceremony.

✪ *Gifts:* At this stage of life, most rewed couples need
nothing. Their gift desires, if they have any, might be
stated in the invitation, such as a contribution to a
favorite charity. If not, any traditional gift would be
appropriate, as well as theater tickets or a compli-
mentary dinner at an elegant restaurant.

✪ *Words:* Avoid making jokes or negative statements.
Instead, honor them with affirmations about their
ability to savor life and their spirit of adventure.

✪ *Clothing:* Laud the extraordinary event with dressy
clothing.

DIVORCING

Divorce rituals are nothing new, except that they are receiving more attention these days as a means of coping with the
trauma of marriage dissolution. Some traditional peoples
have mechanisms for dealing with this difficult event. For
example, a Lakota woman going through a divorce gives
away all her belongings in a cleansing ceremony. In return,
her friends and family give her new goods to begin afresh.

Here are other means of coping.

DIVORCE PARTY

After a three-and-a-half-year marriage and a three-year divorce ordeal where Kimberly (not her real name) became

the victim of credit loss, harassment, and financial defeat, friends, support-group members, and her attorney encouraged her to do something festive as an act of closure. "You need to have a party." While at first reluctant, she changed her mind to celebrate the finality of the ordeal that had seemed surrealistic, more like a TV movie of the week.

On the day of the party she sent herself roses and held an open house scheduled from 6 P.M. until midnight but which lasted until 4 A.M. Friends enjoyed the celebration, and the spirit of the event was "Thank God, it's over." She received bottles of champagne, a subscription to *Playgirl*, and new clothes. She served chicken, caviar, sushi, shrimp, champagne, margaritas. The cake bore the inscription "Congratulation, Woman, You're Free."

The mood was festive. The guests watched a Chris Rock comedy video and laughed. They made bad jokes about the ex-husband, too. Making jokes about the ex appears to be an important part of these types of events. Steve, whose ex received an extraordinarily large settlement, could not stop joking about his former wife at his divorce party. Most of the jokes centered on the money he had lost and about the shortcomings of her personality, of which everyone was aware. Although jokes about the ex sometimes make guests uncomfortable, this becomes a creative outlet for loss.

❂ *Gifts:* For women, a gift certificate for a pedicure, manicure, massage, anything she might have denied herself in the marriage or was not able to afford because of divorce expenses. For either men or women, a good book, flowers, objects to affirm them, a favorite cake or pie.

❂ *Words:* If the couple had no children, avoid saying, "Thank God you didn't have kids." This might have been a problem within the marriage and perhaps the celebrant wished very much that children had been born from this union. Don't say, "Didn't you know he/she was crazy when you met him/her?" or "We knew something was wrong with him/her?" Those statements make the celebrant wonder why good friends hadn't said anything before it was too late. Avoid saying, "Look how old you're getting." "Aren't you afraid you're going to end up alone?" "Haven't you met somebody yet?" These statements are never appreciated.

Emphasize positive statements: "No matter how hard it gets, remember this isn't going to last forever." "One thing for sure, this will never happen to you again." "You'll meet someone someday who will truly appreciate you."

DIVORCE CLEANSING CEREMONY

Some newly divorced people need more than frivolity in their divorce rituals. Jennifer (not her real name) is a good example. After the bitter legal battle for custody rights and a property settlement, she had difficulty living in the home she had once shared with her ex-husband. Everywhere she looked, unhappy associations sprang to mind. Powerful negative memories kept her from sleeping well at night. In desperation, she turned to a therapist, who suggested that either she move or have a house-cleansing ceremony. Jennifer chose the latter.

Determined to help, thirty-five of Jennifer's friends gathered to participate in the cleansing. Because memories can be ignited by aromas, they altered previous house odors by burning sage throughout her home. Each person moved from room to room distributing the sage smoke, and as they did, they articulated requests that new energy enter the room, that negative energy be removed, and that all occupants be healed. They went in and out of every door and blessed the entire house, indoors and outside, front and back.

After smoking out the negativity, Jennifer's friends reconvened in the living room and sat in a circle. They lit candles of all colors and acknowledged Jennifer's new status. They spoke of how far she had traveled on her spiritual journey to become an independent woman. They paid tribute to her strength at being able to stand on her own. They urged her to let go of the relationship with Jim, all that it was, the bad and the good.

Earlier, the therapist had told Jennifer that the hardest part would be letting go, that for the ritual to be effective, Jennifer herself had to announce to the world that she was on her own. At the same time, Jennifer had to hear herself make the announcement and acknowledge her anger, fears, and joy. By the end of the ritual, she was able to do this. Afterward, with appetites sharpened by the buoyant experience, Jennifer and her friends savored the food they had prepared to honor her new freedom. Ultimately, the sage smoking, blessings, announcements, and affirmations brought Jennifer relief, and since that time, she has lived comfortably in her home.

❂ *Gifts:* Food, personal indulgences such as gift certificates for facials, massage, tickets to the theater, items personalized for the honoree's interests.

❂ *Words:* Affirmations: "You are so courageous." "I admire your strength and conviction."

❂ *Clothing:* Some may choose to wear white as a symbol of purification. Others may choose vivid colors to represent new life. Avoid black.

5   HEALING

"Take two aspirin and call me in the morning."

Traditional people interpret healing as a rite of passage. For example, the Navajo organize ceremonies to create a bridge from the state of illness to a state of health or wholeness. Through elaborate ceremonials they rally the people and restore the sick person as a functioning member. This rebalances the community and restores harmony. The Navajo are not the only ones to do this. Mainstream society has begun exploring the value of healing rituals that have restoration of balance as their goal. Participants and some medical and spiritual counselors acknowledge that these celebrations impact positively on the mind/body connection. Dr. Lewis Mehl-Madrona, a half-Cherokee physician and Native American healer, explains that the power of ceremony comes from people joining in the same thought. The community concentrate their thoughts and send them back to the spiritual world requesting help for the sick person.

FOLK WISDOM

An apple a day keeps the doctor away.

Early to bed and early to rise makes a man healthy, wealthy, and wise.

Good medicine is bitter to the taste.

An ounce of prevention is worth a pound of cure.

While there's life, there's hope.

There is medicine for all things except death and taxes.

A man who is his own doctor has a fool for his patient.

If you lack health, you lack everything.

Step on a crack, break your mother's back.

After breakfast sit awhile; after supper walk a mile.

Sickness comes in haste and goes at leisure.

Feed a cold; starve a fever.

Some people's illness is their health.

A dry cough is the trumpet of death.

Without measure, medicine will become poison.

The doctor buries his mistakes in the cemetery.

Not all rituals must be community based. Individuals may create their own healing ceremonies to suit particular needs and talents. *Blue Jelly* author Debby Bull discovered canning food as a personal ritual for overcoming depression. The source of her sorrow was losing her boyfriend to someone else. For Bull, canning was better than suicide or Prozac; canning was more effective than the talk-based therapies she had tried: "When you're really depressed, you have to do something that takes you out of the drama, that makes you detach from the big world and become king of a tiny, controllable world, like one of berries and Ball jars."

Bull explains that when she was canning, she had to pay attention to the details of measuring, sterilizing, and temperatures. If not canned properly, some foods could become lethal, a notion that kept her on track. Through canning, Bull pulled her attention away from herself. Once she had amassed the lovingly prepared jars of food, she felt better after she gave them away to all her friends with broken hearts. By so doing, she divested herself of her problems and pain. A healing took place.

Her method, which she discovered intuitively, parallels the Japanese tradition of writing down one's troubles on a piece of paper, then tying the paper to a tree to have the wind whisk away the worries.

TRADITIONAL RITUALS AND BELIEFS

HMONG [MONG]

Hu Plig [who-plea]

The Hmong believe that illness is caused by soul loss, and *hu plig* ceremonies reinstall the wandering souls. Malevolent spirits cause soul loss. The shaman, *txiv neeb* [ceeneng] (person with a healing spirit), diagnoses the cause of illness, accidents, and misfortune and during treatments uses rattles, gongs, incense, and candles and chants himself into a trance state with severe shaking. This allows him to enter the spirit world and free the trapped soul.

Sometimes the shaman rides a winged horse simulated by a wooden bench supported by sawhorselike supports. Ceremonies take place in the early morning and include the sacrifice of animals, used as ransom for the fugitive souls. Depending on the seriousness of the situation, the Hmong may kill chickens, pigs, or cows, all of which they later eat.

In her powerful story *The Spirit Catches You and You Fall Down,* about an epileptic Hmong child living in Merced, California, Anne Fadiman details the variety of traditional rituals the desperate parents employed attempting to heal their severely afflicted daughter. In addition to hanging herb-filled amulets around her daughter's neck, the mother fed her homegrown-herb brews; she also inserted a silver coin into the yolk of a hard-boiled egg wrapped in cloth and rubbed it onto the body of her ailing child. She used cupping (heated, inverted cups placed on the back to create a suction to draw out the "poison") and pinching, a common dermal technique used throughout Southeast Asia. She wrapped spirit strings around the child's wrist (see "Healing"/Lao, p. 165; "Healing"/Thai, p. 169) and changed the child's name to fool the evil spirits. Shamans performed numerous *hu plig* ceremonies attempting to re-install her soul and free the child of her torment.

JEWISH (SEPHARDIC)

Prekante [pray-cón-tay]

Unlike most rituals described in this book, the *prekante,* a traditional Sephardic Jewish healing method used by Spanish Jews and brought from the island of Rhodes, seems doomed in the United States and abroad because most of its practitioners have died and the ritual has not been passed on. The two largest settlements of Rhodeslis Jews live in Seattle, Washington, and Los Angeles, California. In Seattle, at a synagogue with a large congregation of Rhodes immigrants, the *prekante* is already obsolete. One rabbi explained, "A couple of old women used to do it, and psychologically it did them [the patients] some good, but no one does it anymore."

Rebecca Amato Levy of Los Angeles, California, appears to be one of the last surviving practitioners of this healing ceremony, practiced only by women on both male and female patients. The ritual removes the effects of the evil eye, and in Judeo-Spanish, the language spoken by Rhodeslis, *prekante* means to cast a good spell.

Levy was born in Rhodes in 1912, where as a child she observed her grandmother, well known as a healer, cure many people. However, only many years after moving to Los Angeles, when she was in her fifties, did she first perform it herself. At that time, only one other local woman practiced it. Levy says that although she has taught many Rhodeslis customs to her children and grandchildren, none have been interested in learning this one. Consequently, when she passes on, the ritual will die here, too.

"If adults don't believe in the *prekante*, they can't be healed," Levy stated. The *prekante* ameliorates symptoms of the evil eye, which include fatigue, ennui, loss of appetite, sleeplessness, weakness, and a general "I just don't feel good." According to Levy, the person who casts the evil eye doesn't necessarily do it out of malice. It's just that the person has so much power, like electricity, and when that person looks at a weaker person, the look or stare affects them negatively. Because they are so weak, babies are frequently victims.

Levy's most recent patient, a woman in her eighties, had gone to the doctor several times feeling upset and depressed, but the doctor found nothing wrong with her. After Levy performed the *prekante,* a procedure that lasts fifteen to twenty minutes, the patient improved. Gratefully, she kisses Levy's hands whenever she sees her.

Words must precede the action because *prekante* means "incantation." The following is a translation of one used by Mrs. Levy:

> With the name of God, Abraham, Isaac, Jacob, Moshe, Aaron, David, Shelomo, I was walking through a narrow street and met the Prophet Elijah, and he asked me where I was going, kind Jewess. To see Miriam, daughter of Sara, to remove all her illness and depression and throw it to the bottom of the sea, and this child will be freed of all illness.

Traditionally, upon entering the home of the patient, the healer requests a fistful of salt, and when it is brought to her, in Judeo-Spanish she asks, *"Kualo es esto?"* (What is this?) The other person answers, *"Sal"* (salt). The healer then chants and promises that the salt will dissolve all the impurities of the body, go to the bottom of the sea, and restore the person to good health.

During the *prekante* the healer requests that the evil eye leave the patient alone, and placing her hand upon the patient, she says that through her, God will heal just as He did for Miriam, the prophetess. The healer asks that if the afflicted is a man, he should not lose his name, or if a woman, she should not lose her knowledge, and if a silent bird, God should help it. In a final plea, the healer asks that the stares and the pain be sent to the bottom of the sea freeing the afflicted from the evil eye.

The healer repeats the *prekante* seven times and, while chanting, passes her fist, holding salt, over the upper extremities of the patient. She also yawns in an attempt to make the patient yawn and symbolically allow the evil spirits to leave the patient's body. At the end of the chant, someone brings a pitcher of water and an empty pan. The healer pours the water into the pan and adds the fistful of salt she has been holding. Afterward, using the saltwater mixture, she washes the patient's face, arms, torso, and legs, always moving with downward strokes. Finally, she throws the water away outside the house, chanting, *"El Dio ke lo guarde de todo modo de mal"* (May God keep him from all evil).

LAO

Sou-Khoanh [sue-kwanh]

When a person returns home from the hospital or is recovering from a serious illness treated at home, family and friends may perform a *sou-khoanh* or *baci* [bai-see] ceremony. (See "Giving Birth"/Lao, p. 37; "Healing"/Hmong, p. 161; "Marrying"/Lao, p. 133.) Well-wishers come to the patient's home and wrap white strings around each wrist of the recovering person to ensure that the soul remains within. This act assures patients that their family and friends support them. After three days, they remove the strings.

If someone is going to be away from home for over a year, they perform the same ceremony before the person leaves.

✪ *Gifts:* For both the healing and going-away ceremony, give money in an envelope.

✪ *Body Language:* There is no body contact other than tying the strings onto the afflicted person's wrists. Use the *wai* [why] for greetings. With hands together in a prayerlike position, bring them up to just below the chin and nod slightly. After someone makes this gesture to you, return the gesture.

NATIVE AMERICAN

Native Americans have long recognized the value of ceremonials for cures. Through rituals they enlist the participation of the entire family and community. The patient feels
emotionally supported by the physical and financial participation of the tribe, for these events are costly. Generally,
they last more than one day, which means that regular
work must cease so that ritual demands may be met. Supplies must be gathered to feed those in attendance. The
healers must receive compensation.

Sick persons see evidence of nurturing by everyone
around them. The drama of the costumes, masks, and other
paraphernalia contrasts sharply with the mundane. It becomes an extraordinary experience. Affecting mind/body
relationships, these community endeavors have a positive
effect on the emotional health of the patient and assist in
the restoration of bodily health.

Of course, ceremonies vary with tribal groups. For example, members of the False Face Society of the Iroquois
use ornately carved masks in their ceremonies, and each patient cured then becomes a future False Face member to
cure others. Among the Midewiwin or Grand Medicine society of the Ojibwa, members throw sacred medicine bags
filled with special shells toward initiates. This causes the
initiates to collapse trancelike, but when they arise, they are
restored. In turn, they aim their own medicine bags at other
members.

Sweat Lodge

Across the country, almost every tribe uses a form of the
sweat lodge for purifying the body, mind, and spirit as well
as for petitioning for the health of others. It is a sacred
place where Native Americans reconnect with the spirit
world. Members sit inside an enclosed structure, frequently

made of bent willow branches, shaped like an igloo, and covered with blankets, matting, or a tarp. Participants sit on mats or blankets, and those in charge sprinkle cold water over hot rocks to form steam and make the bathers sweat. During the sweat they pray, drum, and sing. Sometimes during the sweat, they leave and reenter the structure four times to cool off.

In most tribes, men and women are separated, yet sometimes they may be together. Among the Lakota, women cannot enter the sweat lodge when they are "on their moon" (menstruating).

Nonmembers may be invited to participate in a sweat lodge ritual, but they must observe the rules.

✪ *Gifts:* Before the sweat lodge ritual begins, give tobacco to the sweat lodge leader and to each of his assistants. Purchase shredded tobacco such as the Native Spirit brand, available in most supermarkets, or obtain tobacco in leaf form from a tobacco or smoke shop and have them shred it. Freshly picked sage is also appreciated, particularly if the plant has been respectfully removed from the earth. If possible, wrap the tobacco and sage in red felt.

✪ *Words:* Upon entry into the structure, participants will be requested to intone words acknowledging ancestors in the particular tribe's dialect.

✪ *Clothing:* A Lakota woman lamented the influence of the film *Dances With Wolves,* which romanticized Native Americans, causing some nonmembers to falsely believe that one should be naked inside the sweat lodge. This is offensive to most Native Americans. According to the Lakota, "In the Creator's eyes, you must be modest and cover the body." Women wear loose-fitting garments like muumuus. Men wear shorts, swimming trunks, or wrap a beach towel around their waist. Sometimes, they place a towel around the neck, as well. Before entering, remove shoes and socks, all jewelry, and contact lenses.

✪ *Body Language:* Frequently, participants must enter the structure on all fours.

Navajo Curing Chants

These ceremonial events last from two to five nights depending upon several factors: cause of the illness, ascertained through a divining ceremony; ability of the family to pay; availability of the healer, called a singer. Anthropologists Clyde Kluckhohn and Dorothea Leighton have written the definitive description of this ceremony. The singer (healer) uses a rattle as well as a bull-roarer made from a piece of wood cut from a tree that has been struck by lightning. The bull-roarer is attached to a leather thong and twirled over the head until it sounds like thunder.

As a first step, the Navajo consecrate the hogan of the person to be healed. Then they burn incense, use pollen, gemstones, and shells for offerings, and drypainting substances made of minerals. Other elements of the curing ceremony include songs, prayers, use of the sweat bath, emetics, prayer stick, a ceremonial bath in yucca suds, and singing throughout the final night. Because curing ceremonies involve purification, the patient, singer, and all major participants have strict rules to maintain clean thinking, which includes sexual continence.

Drypaintings, sometimes called sandpaintings, are a significant part of the ceremony, especially on the last day. The background of the painting is a buckskin spread on the ground. They always use white, blue, yellow, and black, associated with the four directions and made from charcoal and crushed minerals. Designs, handed down through generations from singers and assistants, represent stories of the eight major figures of the Holy People, four sacred plants, animals of the mountains, and sacred arrows or flints. Selection of design is related to the purpose of the ceremony.

For curing ceremonies, drypaintings are created inside the consecrated hogan. The patient sits in the middle of the painting and drinks an herbal preparation. Then the singer touches the feet of a figure in the painting, afterward touching the patient's feet, and asks that the feet become restored to health. The singer follows suit with each part of the patient's body. The colored sands may also be applied to the sick person's body. Afterward, the patient steps outside the hogan, and the singer destroys the painting in the order in which it was made. Subsequently, the singer and his assistants sweep up the sand and carry it to the north of the hogan, where relatives ceremonially walk across the painting, so that they might have contact with the Holy People, too.

THAI

Like their Lao neighbors, the Thai wear white wrist strings for protection. (See "Giving Birth"/Hmong, p. 28; "Giving Birth"/Lao, p. 37; "Giving Birth"/Thai, p. 41; "Healing"/Hmong, p. 161; "Marrying"/Lao, p. 133; "Marrying"/Thai, p. 139.) When ill, people offer food to the monks, who pray for the ill person. Afterward, family members gather at home and tie white strings around the wrists of the sick person. Everyone participates. Strings remain until they look ugly. For removal, the strings are not cut, but rather pulled apart or untied.

The Thai use white wrist strings for other occasions, too: after recovery from illness, at farewell parties, when soldiers go to war and return home, and when welcoming visitors. In northeast Thailand, after an accident, family members return to the place where it happened to collect the soul and return it to the person. Then they tie on the white wrist strings to keep the soul in place.

PILGRIMAGES

Pilgrimages, well known in other parts of the world, occur in the United States, as well. Some take place within our borders; others attract people across the southern and northern U.S. borders. Shrines draw the faithful, who seek conversion from illness to wellness for themselves or on behalf of others. Pilgrimages are another kind of rite of passage found in Christianity, Islam, Judaism, Buddhism, and Hinduism.

Visiting a healing shrine transports and transforms. A successful journey is almost ensured when leaving one's home and normal routine to trek to a sacred site displaying symbols of others' successful journeys. En route, the pilgrim endures discomforts but meets like-minded individuals in a communal setting. The individuals return physically and/or emotionally uplifted.

In Quebec, Canada, Saint Anne de Beaupré beckons the infirm and hopeless. On the southern side of the Mexican-American border, devout Americans join other believers flocking to the tomb of El Niño Fidencio. Within the United States, other sites draw seekers—to Chimayó in New Mexico and to the tomb of Rabbi Schneerson in Queens, New York. For more abbreviated pilgrimages, the faithful find physical and spiritual comfort journeying on labyrinths only one-sixth of a mile.

EL SANTUARIO DE CHIMAYÓ—CHIMAYÓ, NEW MEXICO

"Whenever I feel that I have a spiritual need of some kind, we drive five hours to Chimayó, a place where I find inner peace." These words, spoken by a New Mexico resident, echo the sentiments of Fr. Casimiro Roca, the shrine's resident priest. "At the *santuario* people feel that God listens to them."

After being told that she could not conceive, a New Mexico resident unexpectedly became pregnant at age forty. When her doctor informed her about the high risk of Down's syndrome, she convinced her husband to drive her to Chimayó so that she might pray for the strength to handle whatever outcome awaited her.

Grateful that she bore a healthy son, she returned to say thank you and leave her baby's shoes there for the *niño*. Leaving shoes in the Church of the Santo Niño de Atocha is a tradition tied to one of many local legends. It refers to a statue of a *niño* (child) portrayed in a seated position holding a basket of food in one hand and a gourd of water on a staff in the other hand.

People believe that at night the *niño* steps out of his wooden niche to promote blessings and prosperity. While the guards sleep, he causes sickness to disappear, crops and livestock to increase. In the morning, the statue has muddy feet, and the faithful believe it is because the Santo Niño wears out his shoes in ministering to the needy. He must have new ones to carry out his divine mission, so pilgrims leave their shoes for the *niño*. If they do not bring them, they may purchase some from a small store next to the chapel.

Another legend tells how Chimayó, also known as the Lourdes of America, became a healing shrine. A long time ago when the land was just desert, a man named Bernardo Abeyta saw a bright shining light on the desert. He began to dig there and found a cross and took it the nearby village priest, who hung it next to the church altar. The next day the cross disappeared and returned to its original hole. Abeyta returned it to the church, but again it disappeared and was found once more at its original site. On a trip there another time, a gravely ill Abeyta encountered the cross, this time with the figure on it of Our Lord of Esquípulas. Abeyta fell on his knees and was instantly healed.

To the villagers this was a sign, and they built a church

where today the hole full of mud, *el pocito* [poe-ceé-tow] (little well), is enclosed in a small room, seven feet by seven feet, adjacent to the church. The mudhole is only about three feet in circumference and one to two feet in depth, but it is the site of many healings. Petitioners kneel, touch, and frequently eat the sacred earth. Because pilgrims are always removing the dirt either by eating it or taking some away, the sanctuary caretaker constantly replenishes it with dirt removed from the nearby hillside and blessed by the priest.

Adjacent to the mudhole, in the ex-voto room, pilgrims express their gratitude for healing. Suppliants hang their discarded canes, crutches, and braces on the wall along with before-and-after photographs. They leave eyeglasses, hundreds of religious pictures and pieces of statuary, notes of gratitude, petitions for the protection of loved ones, pleas for cures, notes of thanksgiving.

On an ordinary weekday during the spring or summer, five thousand to ten thousand may visit the shrine, with more on Sundays. However, during Holy Week, as many as twenty thousand believers make the pilgrimage. They pass through the shrine, eight to ten abreast. Local police must direct traffic because so many cars and pedestrians jam the highway from Santa Fe. Commonly, they begin walking at Santa Fe, twenty-seven miles away; others travel eighty miles from Albuquerque. Some have walked for forty-eight hours. It is a moving sight. Some people are so old and sick they have difficulty walking; heavy crosses burden others. The pilgrims may be either barefoot or crawl the last few yards on their knees through the courtyard and up to the church in this painful manner. Most are Latinos.

Like the New Mexico woman who was grateful for a healthy child, some come because they have made a vow to return if a loved one is spared from harm. According to writer Elizabeth Kay, a man from Grants, New Mexico, carried a six-foot cross 137 miles to Chimayó when his son returned alive and whole from Vietnam. The shrine draws tourists, too, who mostly come to spectate and take photographs. They are disinterested in removing the dirt and commonly ignore modesty customs required for church attendance.

⊗ *Clothing:* In respect, women should cover their heads with a scarf upon entering the church. Although informality prevails in this rural part of New Mexico, avoid wearing shorts into church.

SAINT ANNE DE BEAUPRÉ–QUEBEC, CANADA

The French brought their devotion to Saint Anne to Canada when they settled in Quebec. Saint Anne is believed to be the mother of the Blessed Virgin Mary and the grandmother of Jesus. The French built a first church to her in 1658, later replacing and then adding to it. The first miracle occurred during the original construction. In spite of his being severely disabled by rheumatism, Louis Guimond, out of devotion, laid stones in the foundation of the new building. No sooner had he laid three small stones in the chapel than he was suddenly completely healed. In those early days, others were instantly cured as well—of epilepsy, blindness, dropsy. By 1667, written accounts of miraculous healings began to circulate. Word spread throughout North America, drawing pilgrims to the Saint Anne Basilica. Their numbers have steadily increased, from 27,000 in 1857 to 135,000 in 1900, leaping to an average of 1.5 million annually during the 1980s and 1990s. Miraculous and documented cures continue for such afflictions as paralysis, kidney disease, cancer, multiple sclerosis, meningitis.

Most pilgrims arrive during the summer for the novena, the nine days before the feast day of Saint Anne, July 26, the most crowded day of the year. This is the pinnacle of the pilgrim experience. Not all are Roman Catholic or of one social class. The shrine draws everyone: Native Americans,

Rom (Gypsies), the wealthy, the poor, wheelchair patients, the blind, patients arriving in hospital beds. Harried tourists on tight travel schedules descend in busloads, but once there, may become transformed.

Réjean Bernier, lay pastoral worker at the shrine, claims that the typical tourist is touched in a special way. "We call that grace, nothing magical, but a discrete change in the heart . . . a little fire is burning. . . . They say: 'I can't put words on it but . . . there's something different.'"

Bernier interprets the impact of the shrine: "The atmosphere, the peacefulness of the place, the different cultures, the living and colorful celebrations, the beauty of the shrine, the presence of the sick or handicapped people, young and old . . . to see them smiling and happy, to see their perseverance . . . makes this place a 'sacred' place, a place which gives us the opportunity to examine our priorities."

Bernier believes that to dare to become a pilgrim means that a person comes in a special spirit. "The distance a pilgrim travels is not only between the place of departure and the shrine, but also the distance between the head and the heart."

Some come to give thanks for a favor granted; others come to ask Saint Anne to intercede in their behalf, especially for medical miracles. A high point occurs when pilgrims kneel at the foot of the pillar that holds the Miraculous Statue of Saint Anne. An unusual shrine feature is Saint Anne's Hospital, which provides medical care and nursing for those in need while on the premises.

Smaller rites contribute to the overall pilgrimage ritual. Petitioners light candles, purchase Saint Anne's oil for blessings, preventives, and petitions for cures; they drink from the fountain that brings water from Saint Anne's spring, or they rub the water on afflicted body parts or bring some home; the priests anoint them; petitioners take printed accounts of cures, called the *Annals,* and not only read them but place them directly onto a pain or injury. Finally, those who feel healed display their discarded wheelchairs, eyeglasses, crutches, corsets, orthopedic shoes, and braces, giving hope to others who are afflicted.

⊛ *Gifts:* Monetary offerings.

⊛ *Clothing:* Inside the church, respectful attire. No shorts.

TOMB OF EL NIÑO [NÉE-NYO] FIDENCIO—ESPINAZO, MEXICO

Twice a year, in October and March, tens of thousands of petitioners from both sides of the U.S.-Mexican border conduct pilgrimages to this town in northern Mexico. They come from as far away as Wisconsin, Idaho, Florida, and from Eagle Pass, Texas, where they have special pilgrimage buses. No matter the pilgrim's starting point, all come to El Niño's tomb to pay homage to his memory and receive miraculous healings through his agents on earth.

El Niño (the boy), José Fidencio Sintora Constantino, was born in 1898 in Guanajuato, Mexico, and came to Espinazo to work as a housekeeper when he was a young man. His supernatural powers and knowledge of herbs soon led to his becoming a powerful healer, and word of his miracles spread throughout the country. One story says that in 1928 he cured the president of Mexico, Plutarco Elías Calles, of a serious disease. Other legends about El Niño abound, including one about his death—that jealous doctors murdered him. By the time he died in 1938, he was considered Mexico's most famous healer *(curandero* [coo-ron-dáy-roe]*).*

Believers say that after his death, El Niño began channeling his powers through his emissaries on earth called *materias* [mah-téar-ee-ahs] (female healers) and *cajones* [caw-hóe-ness] (male healers), who dress in white as El

Niño did. These *materias* and *cajones* receive their powers through some spiritual sign that El Niño has appointed them, and age is no criterion; sometimes youngsters become healers, too.

During the pilgrimage, devotees carry flowers and incense and wend their way in a procession through the streets of Espinazo to the pepper tree where El Niño first received his healing powers. They circle the tree three times, then pass his tomb inside the *curandero*'s healing room, which used to serve as part of El Niño's hospital. Inside the tomb, people may drop to their knees or roll on the floor.

When the seekers work with the many *materias* and *cajones* who are present in Espinazo, healing takes place through methods such as the laying on of hands or by *limpias* [léem-pee-ahs] (cleansings). The healer holds a bunch of herbs or some pepper tree branches and sweeps them over the body, front and back, always moving in a downward motion. Pilgrims also claim they have been healed by wading in the nearby sacred muddy pond (El Charquito [char-kéy-toe]) where El Niño healed lepers and cancer patients. Testimonials include a woman who claimed El Niño helped her kick a cocaine and alcohol habit. Others claim healings of breast cancer and polio. In spite of the seriousness of the event, a carnival atmosphere prevails, with musicians, dancers, magicians, vendors, and fireworks.

✪ *Clothing:* Extremely casual. Some people wear their grungiest clothing or bathing suits if they intend to go into the muddy pond.

TOMB OF RABBI MENACHEM MENDEL SCHNEERSON— MONTEFIORE CEMETERY, CAMBRIA HEIGHTS, QUEENS, NEW YORK

You don't have to be Jewish to receive blessings at the tomb of the late rebbe (rabbi), who died in 1994 at the age of ninety-two. So exalted was this leader that his followers consider Schneerson to be the Messiah. A rumor circulates that a hidden video camera is focused on the rabbi's tomb to record his moment of return. At his Crown Heights, Brooklyn, synagogue, the chair he sat in to perform weekly healing sessions now faces the wall.

The rebbe's followers believe that he would not have left them alone, that spiritually he is still with them. They also believe that the channels to God are more open where a great person is buried. Consequently, at the rebbe's tomb, petitioners somberly line up daily, sometimes thousands on weekends or holidays, to ask him to intercede on their behalf.

The Jewish tradition of visiting the graves of holy men to receive miracles goes back thousands of years and is noted in the Talmud. In Queens, they arrive as early as 8 A.M. by car, bus, and limo, and they represent all walks of life. The lines of people comprise the same variety of seekers who came for blessings when the rebbe was still alive at his Brooklyn headquarters.

From the street, the pilgrims enter a building that contains a business office, a room where people may write their petitions to place on the rebbe's grave, another room showing nonstop videotapes of the rebbe, and another space with sinks to perform required hand washing after leaving the cemetery. Visitors exit this first structure to enter the cemetery grounds and into a prayer room containing a Torah [tow-rah], unlit and burning candles, and prayer books. The small room leads outdoors to the rebbe's grave. His tombstone stands next to his father-in-law's stone, and both are enclosed inside a three-foot-high concrete wall creating a kind of a pit layered with personal notes.

Here pilgrims lean against the wall, say prayers, tear the messages they have written into four pieces, then drop them on the grave: "I want to marry." "I want to be healthy." "I want to be a better person." "I want to do well in school."

Sometimes they leave brochures, articles they have written, or invitations to weddings. Technology has aided this tradition. People unable to visit in person send their requests by fax and mail to the Lubavitch headquarters in Brooklyn, New York. Each day a Chabad member brings boxes full of written requests to the rebbe's grave, rips the notes, and pours them onto the graves. These petitions, too, cover a wide range of human concerns: financial, medical, personal, reports of new achievements, birth announcements. Healings have been claimed as a result of these requests including recovery from cancer and stroke and overcoming childlessness. Once a week, Chabad representatives remove the messages, then burn them in incinerators behind the mausoleum.

Unlike at the tombs of famous rabbis in Israel, at Schneerson's grave they sell no goods or prayers. However, a charity box to receive donations stands near the entry of his tomb. In addition, on Sundays petitioners may go to the rebbe's home at 770 Eastern Parkway and obtain amulets to ward off the evil eye.

✪ *Gifts:* Avoid bringing flowers. Visitors leave pebbles on the tombstone or grave to let the deceased know they have been there. (See "Dying"/Jewish, p. 212.)

✪ *Clothing:* Men and married women cover their heads. Women should be modestly attired. Avoid wearing shorts. Remove shoes before entering the small structure leading to the tomb.

✪ *Body Language:* Men and women may visit the tomb together, but they stand on opposite sides of the grave.

✪ If you wish to have the spirit of the rebbe intercede on your behalf, you may fax your requests to Chabad Lubavitch Headquarters in Brooklyn, New York: 718-723-4545.

LABYRINTHS

Considered a sacred path, the labyrinth is a symbol found in ancient cultures around the world—in the never-ending circle of Celtic Christians, the cabala of Jewish mysticism, among the early Greeks and Minoans, the old Nazca in Peru, the Hopi. Unlike a maze, which is a puzzle designed to confuse, a labyrinth is a single path that leads the walker to the center and back out. While traveling this forty-two-foot circular pattern, the walker turns off reasoning powers and switches into a right-brain or imaginative mode. Retracing the pattern connects the seeker with God. It involves the body, mind, and heart. Walking the labyrinth becomes a form of meditation and a spiritual tool for transformation. Traversing the sinuous path brings centeredness and self-healing.

Many contemporary labyrinths are replications of the stone labyrinth found at Chartres Cathedral near Paris and in use since the thirteenth century. Grace Cathedral in San Francisco has re-created it, and the Reverend Lauren Artress, originator and director of Veriditas, the worldwide Labyrinth Project at Grace Cathedral (see "Looking for More Information?"/World Wide Web, p. 263), suggests ways in which walking the labyrinth brings benefits: "Perhaps you are at a stuck point in your life and cannot move forward. Perhaps you are looking for direction or guidance about your next step. You may be wondering how you are going to manifest your gifts and talents. The labyrinth is such a wonderful tool for all these concerns." For Artress, the winding path offers a blueprint for the psyche to meet the soul. Since 1991, over two hundred thousand people have walked the Grace Cathedral labyrinth.

Pilgrims along the labyrinth's winding path may walk slowly, clasping their hands in front of them. Some may dance along the path; others may sit and meditate when they reach the center. Still others may pause before entering and bow their heads at the end. There is no right or wrong way.

Burning incense, flickering candles, fragrant flowers, and lowered lighting create a spiritual environment. The female-voiced medieval chants of Hildegard von Bingen may play in the background. Sounds of Tibetan singing bowls, cymbals, and the bar chime, which walkers may strike as they enter or leave, sharpen the senses.

Some rediscover new levels of awareness. Putting one foot in front of another becomes profound. Those in transition may find a calmer perspective. Others may have creative fires rekindled, while those in mourning may find peace. When finished with the journey, some feel emotionally healed. One twelve-year-old remarked, "It's calming if you're a hyper child."

Linda Sewright, of the Northwest Labyrinth Project in Seattle (See "Looking for More Information?"/Organizations, p. 264), has worked with patients recovering from breast cancer. By walking the labyrinth, the women transform their illness from a death sentence into a part of their mythological journey. Signing a written testimonial, a Southern California breast-cancer patient claimed that her pain disappeared after walking the labyrinth. Tom Murdock, who has introduced this ancient prayer tool to a dozen Southern California churches, says that other walkers affirm that they feel noticeably calmer, more at peace, that their pulses slow. In the scrapbook at St. Cross by the Sea in Hermosa Beach, California, labyrinth pilgrims leave messages: "Turn, turn inward see your goal. Turn outward, inward see your soul. The path to God makes many changes. You meet yourself. You meet a stranger."

People are rediscovering the labyrinth as a spiritual and healing tool. Since 1990, five hundred newly crafted labyrinths have been created on floors, lawns, and canvas, used at churches, wellness centers, and religious retreats.

Believing in them as powerful transformation tools, Artress would like to see labyrinths in hospitals, schools, and parks of the future.

EMERGING TRADITIONS

CARIBBEAN/LATINO SANTERÍA [SAHN-TEH-RÉE-AH] OR ORISHA [OH-RÉE-SHA] WORSHIP

Santiguo [sahn-teé-goo-oh]

Unlike the *prekante,* which is a fading healing ritual, the *santiguo* is relatively new, first surfacing in Los Angeles between 1992 and 1995. Its roots are found in the spiritist traditions of Puerto Rico, whereas in the United States it has become associated with Orisha worship, also known as Santería.

Santiguo is a restorative healing ritual for women of all ages, performed by either a priest or priestess, used to remedy female complaints. Often younger women seek help for menstrual cramps, infertility, and frigidity. Older women want to resolve problems of irregular menstruation, dropped uteri, misalignments, and tumors.

With eyes closed, the patient lies on her back on a mat on the floor of a room containing sacred symbols related to the Orishas or saintlike lesser gods of the Santería pantheon. The practitioner places candles, plates, honey, a pyramid, a triangle, and a pumpkin by the patient's head. After lighting candles, she applies honey to the skin, sings songs, chants prayers, and gently places a pumpkin on the lower part of the patient's abdomen. The pumpkin is key to the ritual, its golden color associated with the Orisha Oshun [oh-shóon], patron of fresh water, fertility, and wealth. While it rests upon the woman's belly, the pumpkin slowly begins to pulsate in rhythm to the patient's heartbeat and healer's singing. When finished praying, the practitioner leaves the patient alone to relax and enjoy the quiet with the pumpkin still in place.

The entire ceremony takes only fifteen minutes, but the priestess most closely associated with this ritual believes that explaining the procedure beforehand and afterward allows her to bond with the patient and build her confidence. In spite of its popularity with patients and their desire to experience the ritual again, the priestess only allows the patient to have the ceremony once per ailment.

The priestess encourages patients to see their doctors, separating the two styles of healing and perceiving them as complementary and nonconflicting. She believes that medications given by physicians will often not work until after the patient has the healing ceremony. Her patients disagree. They give total healing credit to the priestess and the ceremony rather than the medical profession. Not surprisingly, in a questionnaire distributed to patients by folklorist Roberta J. Evanchuk, patients healed in this pumpkin ritual reported that none of them had elected to tell their physicians about the healing received through *santiguo*.

TEDDY BEAR MEDICINE

America's love affair with the teddy bear can be traced to a 1902 political cartoon. Clifford Berryman drew President Theodore (Teddy) Roosevelt refusing to shoot an innocent-looking bear cub held tightly on a rope by a mean-looking man. The caption read "Drawing the Line in Mississippi" and referred to Roosevelt's settling of a border dispute between Louisiana and Mississippi when he officially drew the line between the two states. Nonetheless, the public thought it meant that Roosevelt had sacrificed his personal hunting enjoyments to spare the young bear.

The cartoon grabbed the imagination of Morris Michtom, a Russian-immigrant candy-store owner in Brooklyn, New York, who with his wife also sold homemade toys. Inspired by the cartoon, Michtom created the prototype for teddy bears, named after the president mistaken as benevolent to bears. Michtom used brown plush to resemble real bear's fur and added movable arms and legs and button eyes. He placed the first one in his store window alongside a copy of the cartoon and quickly sold it. Before long, he was making more and more bears. An American enchantment with teddy bears had begun. Michtom's teddy bears eventually led to the founding of the Ideal Toy Corporation.

Since Michtom first placed his teddy bear in the candy-store window, the cuddly creature has become a major American symbol of comfort, and not just for children. Women in labor have been seen clutching them on the way to the delivery room, and they are a common sight at scenes of illness, disaster, and death. (See "Introduction," p. 4; "Dying"/Diana, Princess of Wales, pp. 240-241.)

Recognizing the power of the teddy bear to help the ailing and the aged, the Spinoza Bear Company of St. Paul, Minnesota, has developed the bear to a more concrete therapeutic level. Spinoza is a seventeen-inch-tall teddy bear who talks by means of a high-quality tape recorder hidden in his belly. His soothing, warm, friendly voice has tonalities that promote relaxation. Through singing a song, "Hold On to Me," he helps dying children. He tells them that it's normal to be afraid, that they are going away where others have gone, but they're going to be set free. Spinoza counsels that it's okay to cry, to be sad about missing all the friends they're leaving behind.

Spinoza also describes a final farewell ritual. When Beatrice the Butterfly dies, her friends gather in Beatrice's favorite spot. With each holding a different-colored balloon, they speak a few words about what Beatrice meant to them. Then they release the balloons into the heavens and tightly join hands in a circle and watch the balloons float away.

Some hospice patients have adopted this ritual, which appears to give closure to those remaining behind.

Spinoza tapes aim at particular afflictions. The Central Ohio Lung Association has worked with the company in developing tapes to assist asthma sufferers in deep breathing and relaxation. Other tapes deal with self-esteem, encouragement, and stress management.

Spinoza makes a difference in the lives of children who are burn victims, have terminal diseases, disabilities, profound retardation, or who have been sexually and physically abused. He becomes their constant companion, providing unconditional love while helping them cope with the fear and pain they face daily. When terminally ill, Valerie became hospitalized and slept next to Spinoza, her heart rate and respiration rate dropped, demonstrating Spinoza's calming effect on the terrified child.

Oldsters benefit, too. Seventy-five percent of the twelve thousand to thirteen thousand nursing homes in the United States use the bears. With his ability to relax and soothe, Spinoza has become an alternative to chemicals and physical restraint. He helps the elderly breathe and sleep easier. Some nursing home residents have become so attached, they have been buried with their Spinozas.

✪ The company has formed a Buddy Bear program to find corporate money to supply bears for children with life-threatening illnesses, chronic disease, organ failure, and psychosocial needs. For information, contact the Spinoza Bear Company, 1-800-CUB-BEAR.

VIBRATIONAL HEALING

Didgeridoo or Didjeridu [did-jury-doo]

When Tillie (not her real name) learned that she had cancer of the uterus that had spread to her lungs, she sprang to action. A registered nurse, she was well steeped in the Western medical model and followed her physician's recommendations, which included surgery and chemotherapy, to the letter. However, Tillie is a spiritual person and strongly believes in the power of prayer as well as healing modalities from different cultures. In her battle with cancer she employed acupuncture, Chinese herbs, and massage. She met with a shaman; participated in a drumming ceremony; listened to audiotapes equalizing both hemispheres of her brain before, during, and after surgery; and ventured on a healing journey.

Which of the treatments helped Tillie recover from cancer? "What makes a cake?" she retorted. "Is it the flavor? Is it the shortening? Is it the eggs? Is it the flour? Which ingredient makes it a cake? You need all the ingredients."

One of the essential ingredients Tillie incorporated on her healing journey was vibrational healing using the didgeridoo, an instrument that may be as old as eighty thousand years. For centuries, the Australian Aborigines have been blowing on these tools to create deep, resonating sounds for their sacred ceremonies. Termites create this unique wind instrument by eating out the insides of eucalyptus-tree branches, leaving a tube approximately two inches in diameter. Aborigines cut the hollowed-out branches into lengths of four to five feet and attach a beeswax mouthpiece. They decorate them by painting traditional designs from their mythological "dream time," such as the rainbow serpent, local animals, and other totemic elements.

Players use various breathing techniques to affect the instrument's tonality. They take a deep breath through the nose and mouth with the cheeks like a bellows, then press out the air by squeezing the cheeks. Tones are changed by altering the breath, tongue, lips, and pressure. For Tillie, who still employs the didgeridoo three times a day for meditation, "It is the sound of creation." For others, it has been likened to a giant alien mosquito. Its low, intense rumble penetrates the skin, spine, bones, and soft organs.

Rian McGonigal of Prescott, Arizona, is a didgeridoo healing practitioner and the director of the Therapeutic Sound and Music Program for the O. Carl Simonton Cancer Center in Santa Barbara. (See "Looking for More Information?"/Other Sources, p. 266.) A professional classical guitarist and cancer survivor, he was introduced while visiting Australia to the instrument's healing powers. There he learned how the Aborigines employed it in traditional healing rituals. After experiencing its powerful effect on his own body, he began using the didgeridoo for vibrational healing to help others.

How does it work? One interpretation is that the sounds emanating from the didgeridoo rotate the energy *chi* around the body and circulate energies that realign the chakras and restore balance to the body. Another interpretation is that every organ, bone, and tissue in the body has a resonating frequency at which it normally vibrates. When disease sets in, the vibrations in that part of the body become unbalanced. When the medicine man sings the didgeridoo over the afflicted part of the person's body, the powerful resonance of the instrument envelops the body and realigns it and balances the flow of energies, which is likened to a massage at the atomic and molecular level. This balanced vibration is transmitted into the vertebrae of the spine, which pick up the sound vibrations and transmit them along nerve pathways to all the organs and tissues, thus harmonizing the body back to its natural resonating frequency.

McGonigal finds the vibrational effects of the instrument to be most valuable in the alleviation of pain. He tells of a neighbor who, after ten years of chronic knee pain and lack of success from a variety of therapies, had her pain alleviated after only sixty seconds of treatment. He describes a patient suffering for over eight years from shingles pain, which disappeared after only three minutes of the vibrational treatment. He has had excellent responses with multiple sclerosis patients, who have reported that a few minutes of the didgeridoo produces feeling in previously "dead" areas of their bodies.

When people come to him for a one-and-a-half- to two-hour healing session, he creates an aesthetically pleasing environment. He fills the space with beautiful objects. Before he begins, he makes an invocation to the earth asking for assistance in the healing. Then he blows the instrument over the entire body, not just the affected area. The patient sits on a stool to allow greatest access to the head and torso. Dressed in white or light colors, McGonigal and his wife, Maria, play didgeridoos placed just a few inches from the patient's body to envelop it in sound. One blows toward the front of the body as the other blows toward the back, surrounding it like a cocoon. Sometimes they play the same tone to create the same vibration. Other times they play the two instruments slightly out of tune with one another to produce binaural beats that slow brain-wave activity into an alpha state, a state of deep rest. According to McGonigal, shamanic drummers use this same technique. Then patients lie down, as aboriginal patients do. After the didgeridoo, McGonigal plays other instruments to incorporate their vibrations, using Tibetan and crystal singing bowls, drums, and harmonic or overtone singing. At the end of the session, the McGonigals use burning sage to smoke the room and the patient.

The didgeridoo has become so popular that suppliers of Australian aboriginal didgeridoos cannot keep up with the demand. Consequently, practitioners have become resourceful in using other materials to create similar instruments: agave, aspen, cedar, glass, the century plant, bamboo—any tube long enough that has a one-and-two-thirds- to two-inch diameter. Surprisingly, McGonigal reports that PVC (polyvinyl chloride [plastic]) tubing works as well as the traditional termite-sculpted eucalyptus.

END-OF-THERAPY RITUALS

When Jane Goldberg, Ph.D., Orange County, California, therapist, begins working with patients, she asks them, what is their vision or what is their journey about? When they are finished, she wants them to be able to say, "I did it." "I found it." "I got there." Referring to Joseph Campbell, she points out that patients are heroes and have to travel the hero's journey. When they return, the community greets them to celebrate what they have accomplished. Based upon her dissertation in transformational psychology, Goldberg believes that therapy cannot be complete until, through a ritual, the patients announce to themselves and their communities that they have completed their self-exploration and are ready to move on.

The patients participate in the planning of the event. One patient, who had worked with Goldberg utilizing an art-therapy mode, felt she was ready to stop counseling. Together, they decided that for their final meeting, the patient would bring all the art pieces she had created during therapy, and Goldberg would bring all her notes about the patient. At their last session, they looked over the pieces the patient had created and recalled the significance of each work. Meanwhile, Goldberg correlated the pieces of art with her notes about the patient, highlighting the progress the patient had made. Together, they recalled the beginning of therapy. "Remember when you first started, how you . . . ?" "See how far you have progressed?" They acknowledged the distance the patient had traveled on her journey and how complete she now was.

This is but one form that a closure ritual can take. They are all individualized. For example, one client came to Goldberg because she felt lost, depressed, and scared.

Goldberg helped her find a safe place by imagining angels around her. Sometimes they would start their session by inviting angels in. During therapy, the patient began collecting pictures and stories about angels and becoming aware of angel prayers.

On their final day, which came as a surprise to the therapist, the client arrived with thirty-six angel cards she had created, each one representing a different positive quality, for example, healing, passion, energy. She presented Goldberg with an angel collage she had made. Then, in a final act, they did an angel reading. The client and therapist closed their eyes and each selected two cards from the set of angel cards. One represented where they were now in completing the journey, and the other, where they were going next. They each interpreted their own cards and in such a way created a satisfying end of the journey.

THE GODDESS OF HYSTERECTOMY

Desiring to avoid some of the terrible hysterectomy experiences of other friends and inspired by a friend's ceremony, Jean Tokuda Irwin, a Utah artist, seized upon a different approach in facing her hysterectomy. She confronted her feelings and anxieties through visual art.

Irwin decorated a glass mannequin head with objects she regularly collected for assemblages. She glued on one die showing the number three, representing the three children she had given birth to, now adults. In memory of their childhood, she attached tiny baby bottles, a miniature wooden baby carriage, a tiny Japanese doll, a plastic baby rattle, and a Nativity scene representing family and birth. Since cooking had been significant in her past mother/children relationship, she added a tiny ceramic Mexican mug and saucepan.

Irwin affixed a rock from Lopez Island, a favorite haunt in Puget Sound, a brass feather to represent a dear friend who had died of breast cancer, and one red bead fallen from red earrings associated with joyful retreats taken with fellow artists called the Border Broads. Near the mannequin's forehead, she affixed a miniature quartz penis surrounded by Mexican fabric flowers related to an inside joke among friends.

Tampons attached by their strings to the head of the goddess gave her a dreadlock look. On each cardboard tampon cover Jean wrote affirmations, such as "My surgery is going to go well." "I'm healthy and whole." "I will not experience a lot of pain." Then she solicited messages from friends and colleagues. From all over the country, affirmations arrived by fax and E-mail, some serious, some humorous. "Welcome to the Society of Poor Seamstresses" (women who don't menstruate [mend straight]). "Goodbye forever. You've [uterus] served well, but you won't be missed." "A physical part of giving life may be gone . . . but we all give life with our smiles and experiences, so continue to smile and embrace all those enriched." "May the gods of fertility be properly kept at bay." "My surgery was a beginning for me and it will be for you, too."

Most meaningful was the message from Irwin's daughter: "You cultivated my life within your walls. You gave me brothers in all their perfection. Nothing can compare to the magic you have. Now I have some magic of my own and look at the miracle it has given me. I will always be grateful for your gifts and I will not forget. With love and admiration, Amy."

Irwin transferred the messages onto the tampon cardboards and covered each one with different-colored Mylar tied with contrasting ribbon and cord. One fax from a Chinese friend requested that the tampon bearing her wishes be covered in red Mylar with gold streamers, traditional Chinese good-luck colors. Irwin's three-and-a-half-year-old grandson donated his Esmeralda doll to the goddess. He said his "Morchan" (his name for his grandmother) needed her because "Esmeralda was a strong girl!" Finally, Irwin glued on plastic rhinestones, Mylar stars and fabric roses, added ribbons, candles, and bows. The night before the surgery, her friends came over to make their own dreadlocks and put the last touches on the goddess and give additional moral support.

When it was finished, the goddess looked like a woman wearing an elaborate, exotic, two-foot-high headdress. The gaily covered tampons were now transformed into colorful objects like giant-sized party poppers or fat Shirley Temple curls, covered in Mylar in hues of purple, bright blues, and decorated with sparkly, contrasting trim of gold, red, and blue, and tied with varicolored ribbons. Bright-colored gems bedecked her face and headband.

On the day of surgery, Irwin brought the goddess with her and placed it on a chair in her room. Naturally, hospital staff were curious about her strange-looking companion, but after Irwin introduced them to the goddess of hysterectomy, word spread quickly through the hospital and nurses began popping in to tell their own hysterectomy stories. All of the tales were positive. Most women reported that they wished they had not waited so long before having the surgery because the operation had brought them dramatic relief from excessive bleeding and discomfort.

When the male surgeon came in to get Irwin, he, too, inquired about the awesome head, as did his head surgical nurse. They responded positively to the explanation, especially the doctor. When Irwin asked if the goddess might accompany her into the surgery, the physician agreed and placed the head on her abdomen as they wheeled her into the operating room. Once inside, they set the head on a nearby surgical tray to watch over the proceedings while an attendant swept off some of the gold sparkle that had fallen onto Irwin's sheet.

After the surgery, the doctor personally carried the goddess into the waiting room and gave it to family members and friends while his patient remained in the recovery room. When she woke up, the goddess was once more by her side.

During her four-day hospital stay, female staff continually visited to share hysterectomy stories with Irwin. One night in her darkened room, Irwin awakened to discover two graveyard-shift pediatric nurses holding penlights to examine the goddess. They had to see her for themselves.

At Irwin's three-week checkup, the surgeon commented on how quickly she had healed, "like a twenty-year-old." She told him it was due to the goddess. Surprisingly, the doctor concurred. He explained that before she went under the anesthetic, she had been laughing with the staff about the preposterous-looking head. He acknowledged the role of positive attitude on recovery. He cited studies about the importance of laughter in healing, as well as the support Irwin had received from her friends in the creation of the goddess and from the women who had shared their own stories about the benefits of the surgery.

Eventually, Irwin entered the goddess in an art show. She placed it on a pedestal surrounded by red lamé, three hundred twinkling Christmas lights, and colored rice and was amazed at the response. Viewers immediately began telling hysterectomy stories—about their own or others'. Since then Irwin has received calls from people wanting to borrow the goddess, but she has convinced them that to be effective, they must create one with their own talents and out of the needs of their own psyches.

✺ *Gifts:* Flowers, books, fragrances.

✺ *Words:* Affirmations about the benefits of the surgery: "How wonderful that you will now be pain free." Positive accounts about others who had the same surgery. Avoid all hysterectomy horror stories.

6 DYING

"Ashes to ashes and dust to dust"

We have control over most rites of passage. Even with birth, we have a pretty good idea when it will occur, so we have time to prepare. With death, we never know. Unless the deceased has left explicit instructions, planning for the ritual is hurried. Even if someone has been lingering near death, the final moment shocks us and that frequently prevents us from efficient organizing.

Because of its mystery, many beliefs shroud death. If mourners do not strictly conform to funeral rites and mourning customs, the deceased might be negatively affected in the afterlife. Even worse, spirits of the dead might linger on earth too long and interfere with the living.

Most immigrants from the early twentieth century and before now observe mainstream death rituals. These practices have become homogenized through time, traditional religions, and the standardizing influence of the mortuary

Folk Wisdom

Pregnant women should not attend funerals.

A clock stops when someone dies.

If someone sleeps in a dead person's bed before he or she is buried, it is bad luck.

Rocking an empty chair means the oldest member of the family will die.

One tea leaf in a cup means a hearse.

Don't sew on the Sabbath or the Lord will strike you dead.

To open an umbrella in the house means death to someone living there.

The hooting of an owl means a family member will die.

Death always comes in threes.

Hold your breath when passing a cemetery or you will have bad luck.

Always pull a few leaves of grass upon leaving a cemetery.

Whistle when you walk by a cemetery to keep away the evil spirits.

It is bad luck to take any flowers home from the graveyard.

Dead loved ones will return and can be seen by those close to them.

Friday funerals portend another death in the family during the year.

If a broom rests against a bed, the person who sleeps there will soon die.

Thunder following a funeral means the dead person's soul has reached heaven.

You will have bad luck if you do not stop the clock in the room where someone dies.

If a bird flies into your home, someone will die.

If someone is dying but his pet dies before him, the pet takes his place in the afterlife.

When a grave sinks early, another will follow soon.

A circular wreath hung on the front door or laid on the grave will prevent the spirit's return.

It is bad luck to wear gold jewelry when mourning.

If a mother dies in childbirth, her spirit will remain to watch over her child.

The widow should wear black and remain far from her husband's grave to prevent his spirit from pestering her.

industry. However, the heavy influx of late-twentieth-century immigrants has changed that. Funeral practices have become more complex, designed to meet the needs of these newest grieving families, who tend to cling to the traditions of their homelands, especially in times of sorrow. Some of these changes include larger-sized-family participation, more personal involvement in the preparation of the body, more days and nights of final farewells.

TRADITIONAL RITUALS AND BELIEFS

AFRICAN-AMERICAN NEW ORLEANS OR JAZZ FUNERAL

Spirited funerals with traditions rooted in West Africa and the West Indies are a local rite and tourist attraction of New Orleans. Famous jazz musicians, such as Louis Armstrong, Jelly Roll Morton, Bunk Johnson, and Kid Ory, developed their licks playing at these joyful processions. Until the 1960s, only jazz musicians received these heavenly send-offs. Since then, any New Orleans resident qualifies for this colorful burying ceremony.

In the past, slow-stepping, white-gloved pallbearers carried the casket from the mortuary to the hearse, and a marching brass band played hymns in a dirgelike tempo: "Just a Closer Walk with Me" or the "Old Rugged Cross." Somberly they placed the casket into one of New Orleans's aboveground graves, but as mourners marched away from the cemetery, melancholia transformed into jubilation when spectators joined in the parade and began their feverish "second line." (*Second line* refers to the group that marched behind the musicians.) The second line set up its own syncopation as a counterrhythm to the beat of the brass band.

Nowadays, second-line dancers may dance from the

church into the cemetery. Carrying an umbrella decorated with sequins, feathers, flowers, or fringe, the leader of the second line struts along the funeral route. Those who follow imitate his exaggerated motions until the line becomes a sinuous snake dance, bobbing, zigzagging, and gyrating through the streets. Sometimes a group of dancers circles a single dancer or duos who perform their own routines. The soloists dance free-form with myriad dance styles: cakewalking, stamping, jumping, crossing of feet and legs, but the second liners maintain their special steps: toe, whole foot, knee flex, and twist. (See "Marrying"/African-American, New Orleans, p. 100.)

Although not costumed, sometimes second liners roll up their trousers or add handkerchiefs around their necks or wear them as headbands. Some wear white aprons; others besides the leader carry decorated umbrellas, too. A dancer without an umbrella grasps an unfolded white handkerchief between thumb and index finger. As the second liners dance, they unfurl and snap the handkerchiefs overhead in time to the music.

Frequently, as the second line weaves around the city and excitement swells, they stop at a tavern to have a quick one or perhaps a free one at places that served as watering holes for the deceased.

No longer exclusively African-American, the second line is open to anyone to participate and sometimes grows to hundreds of dancers. All can join in the fun and wait with both anticipation and sadness for what is often the closing tune, "When the Saints Go Marching In."

AMISH

Like their weddings, Amish funerals take place at home, and customs vary according to particular branches of their religion. Most Amish communities now embalm the dead to give time for relatives to travel to the funeral. In Lancaster County, family members wash the body before the undertaker embalms it. The mortuary returns the body to the family home dressed in long underwear. Family members dress the men in a white shirt, white vest, and white pants, and women in their wedding-day white capes and aprons, sometimes the same dresses.

Generally, Amish woodworking shops produce the coffins, shaped wider at the shoulders than at the head and feet, with a simple white lining. They place the coffins inside the house and observe a wake or night watch for two days. The funeral takes place on the third day. Sometimes so many people attend, they hold two simultaneous services, one in the house and another in a barn for the overflow. After the closing prayer and benediction, the minister delivers a brief eulogy.

Graveside, the congregation may sing a hymn followed by silently saying the Lord's Prayer. Frequently the men remove their hats when the minister speaks. Often four pallbearers bear the coffin, usually neighbors and friends, but sometimes male kin. After the ceremony, they serve a simple funeral meal at home. One must be invited to attend an Amish funeral, and those few non-Amish who were close friends with the deceased will be included.

✪ *Gifts:* Prepared food for the family. A condolence card or note. Avoid giving flowers.

✪ *Words:* "My condolences to you and your family."

✪ *Clothing:* For women, dresses with arms covered, modest necklines, and hemlines below the knees. Avoid open-toed shoes and jewelry. Wear minimal or no makeup. For men, jackets, ties, and white shirts.

ARMENIAN

After the person dies, the family visits the home of the deceased to drink bitter coffee. They drink bitter coffee again after the funeral. Emotions are openly expressed; some may wail during the services. At the burial site, Russian Armenians drink vodka and toast the departed and help shovel the dirt on the lowered casket. When mourners return home, they immediately enter the bathroom to urinate and wash their hands.

The family holds a dinner immediately after the funeral, at forty days, and again at one year. Sometimes hundreds attend the dinner immediately following the funeral, served in either the church hall or a restaurant. They prepare shish kebab, rice, chicken. On the seventh day after the funeral, they hold a Mass at the cemetery and serve food afterward, especially Russian Armenians. On the fortieth day, the priest comes to the cemetery for Mass, and afterward the family rents a place to serve lunch or dinner. At the one-year anniversary of the death, they publish a notice in the Armenian newspapers inviting anyone who desires to attend a dinner for the soul of the deceased.

✪ *Gifts:* No gifts.

✪ *Words:* "I'm sorry" and other simple words of comfort.

✪ *Clothing:* Black.

BUDDHIST

General (See "Dying"/Cambodian, p. 200;
"Dying"/Chinese, p. 201; "Dying"/Japanese, p. 210;
"Dying"/Korean, p. 215; "Dying"/Lao, p. 217;
"Dying"/Thai, p. 229.)

The U.S. mortuary industry has made numerous adaptations to serve the needs of the growing Buddhist population. Some bury, others cremate. Often the funeral homes work in concurrence with religious astrologers, who determine which dates are the most auspicious for services. Some funeral homes allow twenty-four-hour tape-recorded chanting of Buddhist monks. They install ceiling fans and fire-resistant tile floors to allow for indoor incense burning. They supply tables for constructing temporary shrines, and some companies have installed kitchens for the preparation of ritual food. At the grave, family and friends often leave food, ranging from full plates to a solitary orange.

Additionally, outdoor incinerators may be provided so mourners can burn paper money, paper replicas of homes as large as six feet, cars—often Mercedes-Benz—clothing, and other items believed necessary for the journey to the next world and an easy life thereafter.

One funeral home in Orange County, California, built a separate chapel according to Vietnamese ritual needs, which included a large viewing room to allow the relatives and friends, sometimes numbering up to seventy, to watch the body entering the furnace.

Services may be held at the funeral home, and laypersons, with or without monks, chant appropriate prayers. They have a large photograph of the deceased on a stand or table near the casket, and at the temple they offer flowers and fruit and burn incense. As a sign of mourning, family members may wear white headbands and armbands.

They remember the dead each year in August on Buddhist All Souls' Day, when they hold special temple services. Memorial services are important observances.

CAMBODIAN

When a person dies, the family prepares a basket filled with the objects the deceased will need in the next life, such as new clothes, rice, medications, cooking and eating utensils. Families give these objects to a monk. If the person lies dying at home or in the hospital, to give him or her confidence the family shows the patient the basket full of objects. This lets the person know that his or her material needs for the next life will be met.

At the interment ceremony, the monk prays over the body before lowering it into the grave. Seven days after death, the family have a ceremony at home and dedicate everything to the spirit of the dead. A monk officiates to assist in steering the spirit toward a good place so he or she can be reborn again at a higher level.

✪ *Gifts:* Money, enclosed in an envelope of any color. If the deceased was a husband, give it to the widow. If the deceased was a widowed mother, give the envelope to the eldest or most responsible child.

✪ *Words:* Express your sadness. Praise the deceased. Tell the family that you share in their loss. Tell them you are sorry that they have lost such a fine person.

✪ *Clothing:* Mourners wear white or black. Guests wear black or dark colors.

✪ *Body Language:* Use the *wai* [why] as a respectful greeting. Press hands together in a prayerlike position and bring them up to just below the chin and nod slightly. Avoid male/female body contact.

CHINESE (BUDDHIST)

Sometimes a New Orleans–style jazz band parades through Chinatown. The procession usually passes by the deceased's home and place of business. Next comes an open car displaying a large photo of the deceased decorated with white flowers and sometimes carrying the sons or grandsons of the deceased. The hearse follows, trailed by other cars carrying family members. If the family is Buddhist or Taoist, the first son may walk in front of the hearse carrying an incense burner. The procession follows a zigzag course ensuring that the hearse not cross over its own path. To do so brings bad luck. At the funeral home, sometimes Christians will also burn incense as part of their Chinese past. The family may hire professional mourners to wail and shriek during the ceremony.

In front of the tombstone or stela, they burn three sticks of incense and place offerings on a red cloth sometimes holding a rice-wine bottle with two wine cups, and perhaps a bowl of uncooked rice or fresh fruit. Nowadays, after the ceremony, family and friends go to a Chinese restaurant for a special meal. In the late nineteenth century in California, as well as in some places in China today, they placed a whole barbecued pig, a whole parboiled chicken, a plate of dim sum, a bowl of rice, and sometimes fresh fruit in front of the tombstone. These are offerings to the spirit of the newly departed and the ancestors. In addition, they offer fake money called hell notes, symbolically used to help the deceased buy his or her way out of hell. This money is burned in an adjacent incinerator along with other paper replicas, clothing, houses, TVs, Mercedes-Benz, items thought to provide luxury in the afterlife.

In the past, when they did not go to a restaurant after the ceremony, those attending ate the graveside food offerings instead of burning them. Food offerings occur at the one-year memorial and at the subsequent annual feedings of the souls. The spring holiday *ching ming* is equivalent to a community memorial day with a general cleaning of the cemetery and graves followed by food and flower offerings.

Today at the restaurant following the service, they avoid having an even number of tables, for this might repeat the pattern of death. In addition, those paying for the funeral home services generally do not write checks because ultimately the checks return to the signers, and the death symbol would also return. Instead they prefer to pay in cash.

Some mourners refrain from visiting other people's homes until thirty days have passed.

❂ *Gifts:* At the ceremony, survivors of the deceased hand out red envelopes containing money to thank people who helped during the ceremony, such as the minister or priest, drivers, pallbearers, eulogizers, soloists, or musicians. In addition, as guests leave the service, they receive red envelopes containing a coin and a piece of candy. Flowers may be sent to the mortuary, not to the home. They should be white or yellow, never red. The family avoids bringing flowers home from the cemetery.

When making condolence calls, bring prepared food, pastries, and depending on financial need, a white envelope containing cash.

❂ *Words:* General expressions of condolence.

❂ *Clothing:* Nothing flowery or flashy.

EGYPTIAN (COPTIC)

Prior to the funeral, family members and close friends go to the home of the deceased to drink black coffee. The funeral generally takes place three days after death. Inside the church, they place the closed casket facing east. This is in accordance with the layout of the church, which is always built on an east/west axis. The congregation looks eastward; the priest looks westward. The coffin is placed parallel to the people, facing east, because they believe that the Lord will come from the east.

Although they no longer use professional mourners, the family cries and wails during the ceremony. Mourners wear black, and women in the immediate family may wear chapel veils. The graveside ceremony is brief, just a prayer or two. Family members do not shovel dirt over the casket.

❂ *Gifts:* Flowers, food for the family, or money placed inside a condolence card.

✪ *Words:* "May you not see sorrow again." "May the Lord console you." When a young person dies, they frequently say, "May the remainder of his expected years be added to your life."

✪ *Clothing:* Black. Men wear dark or black suits with black ties. Women wear black dresses, no pants. Women mourners and guests wear no makeup. Red is taboo.

✪ *Body Language:* Men and women sit on separate sides of the church.

ETHIOPIAN

Most Ethiopians prefer to be buried in Ethiopia, and if possible, the community raises money to ship the body home. If not, they hold the ceremony approximately two to three days after death. During the religious service they pray and have eulogies, and much crying takes place. They display a lot of emotion, including wailing. Commonly, friends openly weep.

Following the burial, they have a funeral meal, and everyone brings food for three days, during which time the family of the deceased stays at home in respect for the dead.

Forty days after death, the family goes to church to pray for the deceased, and close friends and relatives return home with the mourners. At this time, if the main mourner is a widow, she will be encouraged to discard her mourning clothes and return to a normal life. In spite of well-intentioned urging by friends and family, widows and widowers usually ignore the advice until one year has passed.

✪ *Gifts:* Money or food brought to the mourners' home. Those who bring food are expected to eat with the mourners.

✪ *Words:* Expressions of encouragement such as "Be

strong." "It is a matter of time." "Your pain is my pain." "If you need help, call on me."

✪ *Clothing:* Black for women and men, who must also wear black ties.

Hawaiian

The deceased wears traditional aloha clothing, a muumuu for a woman, preferably white or one of her favorite colors, and an aloha shirt for a man. The deceased may also wear traditional jewelry of gold, koa wood, or kukui nut. Sometimes they place a Bible or a Hawaiian hymnal in the casket. They may also use a Hawaiian-flag casket coverlet draped over the casket instead of an American flag. The immediate family may be dressed in white.

At the service, whether or not the deceased is Christian or Buddhist, an elder gives a blessing in Hawaiian, which may also be translated into English. This elder or *kahu* may be either male or female. If the deceased was of royalty or high status, they will post pairs of *kahili,* poles topped by colored feathers. Sometimes during the vigil, two women or men will maintain a twenty-four-hour watch, one at the head of the casket and the other at the foot.

In the old days, family members or professional mourners would wail. That tradition has been modified, and family members may still wail or some wailing may precede the eulogy or reading from the Twenty-third Psalm. In addition to prayers and readings from the Bible, they also chant. Often they have Hawaiian music—guitar, stand-up bass, and ukulele—playing favorite songs of the deceased.

During the church or temple service, attendees bring leis to place on the casket. They place a *hala* fruit lei at this time because it signifies separation, the end of one era and the start of another. They also wear the *hala* fruit lei at New

Year's and retirement celebrations. The *hala* fruit is a pod that is combined with either a ti leaf or a fern. If you give one of these leis to someone at New Year's or at a retirement celebration, you never place it over his or her head or else you might sever the relationship. Instead, you hand the lei to the other person, and the recipient places this special lei around his or her own neck.

A memorial feast follows at a luaulike celebration. It is not a somber event because they believe the deceased has joined his ancestors. When possible, prior to death, they may hold a celebration of life with the dying person present to hear the tributes that will be paid to him after he passes over.

✿ *Gifts:* Money in white envelopes. Guests also place leis over the casket as a sign of respect.

✿ *Clothing:* Subdued colors in Western or aloha wear.

✿ *Body Language:* As a message of condolence, guests must approach the elders of the family and give them a hug and a kiss on one cheek. Kisses and hugs for the rest of the mourners are signs of respect.

HMONG [MONG]

Hmong dread autopsies. They believe that an autopsy in this life causes the person to be mutilated in the next life. An autopsy also drives the soul to return and brings illness to family members and their descendants. Moreover, they believe that embalming may cause future misfortune.

Many of the complex Hmong traditional practices have been altered or eliminated by the Hmong living here. One major reason is that most deaths occur in the hospital, where family members have no access to the body. For example, they cannot wash and dress the deceased immediately following death. Later, however, they place *paj ntaub* [paw-dow] (hand-stitched fabric) inside the coffin to ensure the spirit's wealth and dress their dead in special shoes believed needed for the journey to the afterlife. Made of woven hemp, the shoes turn up at the toes, allowing the souls to safely walk on dangerous paths, step over valleys of snakes, and cross the big river on their way to the spirit world.

Another conflict arises because of the authority of mortuaries and their inflexibility of scheduling; Hmong prefer to bury in the afternoons because they believe the souls of the dead leave the body at sunset. If buried in the morning, the souls might return. Other problems arise with animal sacrifices, an important aspect of funeral rituals in Laos that conflicts with laws here. However, funeral directors allow Hmong mourners to bring in a live chicken, which must be immediately removed. The sustained loud playing of the *queej* [cane] (six reed pipes inserted into a wooden wind chamber) and funeral drums during visits in the mortuary causes other grieving families to complain, especially since the pipes and drums must play for at least three days. If there is no *queej* player at the funeral, the soul of the deceased won't be guided on its journey and will not be reborn. Not only that, it might make relatives sick. Some funeral homes request that the music not be played during concurrent services of non-Hmong.

The Hmong must have wooden caskets that are pegged and glued; they permit no metal or plastic. To allow the spirit to escape, the grave liner has no bottom. Sometimes they confer with a geomancer (a specialist who divines the best physical site) about the most propitious site for the grave; the best places are those with a view of mountains. They decorate the graves by placing stones in patterns over the grave. If the family has become Christian, they adorn it with a cross. At the burial, they engage in ceremonial wailing and ritual drumming, and following burial, they return to their homes for a ceremonial meal.

Thirteen days after burial they conduct a soul-releasing

ceremony to ascertain whether the deceased's soul has agreed to return to the spirit world. While it is difficult to carry out in this country, some are still able to do so. They create the replica of an upper body dressed in traditional Hmong clothing. To distinguish between male and female, they put a hat on the head for a man and a turban to represent a woman. Afterward, they place the mannequin on a large woven bamboo plate and an elder invites the soul of the deceased to return home to take residence inside the mannequin. In the late afternoon, they carry the mannequin to a small hill or slope in the road, remove the mannequin, and allow the plate to roll down the hill. It must roll three times and fall facedown or the action must be repeated. When the plate falls facedown after three complete rolls, it signifies that the soul has agreed to leave for the spirit world. Seeing the plate fall facedown is the major method of ensuring that the soul is departing for the spirit world. It calms anxieties of those left on earth. This marks the official end of the funeral.

✪ *Gifts:* Money enclosed in a white envelope and handed to the family representative in charge. If you are not sure who this is, ask. At the funeral, they publicly declare amounts given, and if the amount is generous, two or three family members may approach the donor and show respect for the generosity of the guest by bowing to that person. They do not send written acknowledgments.

✪ *Words:* A simple "I'm sorry."

✪ *Clothing:* Red is taboo. In Hmong culture, red represents blood and therefore is dangerous. This prohibition is so powerful that during the Vietnam War, if family members of a soldier dreamed of something red, they would ask their leader for permission for the soldier not to go to the front line. If they send a nasty note to someone and enclose a red tissue, it means, "We will be enemies forever." (See "Marrying"/Hmong, p. 117.)

⊗ *Body Language:* Older community members avoid body contact. They do not use any physical greeting gesture. If a married Hmong woman shakes a man's hand or smiles at another man, she disrespects her husband. Some of the younger generation may shake hands with non-Hmong.

INDIAN (BRAHMAN)

Brahman households possess sealed copper vessels containing Ganges River water. Therefore, if anyone is on his deathbed, they unseal the vessel and pour the holy water into the dying person's mouth, which is the equivalent of anointing them with Ganges holy water. Then they allow them to die.

Hindus believe that life deeds influence whether they will be reborn, but the words they speak prior to the moment of death have significance, too. If the dying persons chant the names of the gods at their last breath, they will go directly to heaven. Thus they will not have to be reborn, which is their greatest desire.

The priest invokes prayers within a few days of death. Often there is a delay to allow family members to gather. In this country, both men and women witness the cremation ceremony, and the eldest son pushes the button to set off the crematorium. After witnesses leave, they pour water on their heads. When they return to their homes, they take a bath, wash their hair, and wash their clothes. Through this purification act, they symbolically divest themselves of death.

They believe that the soul is still present for twelve days after death. During this time, they demonstrate their grief by crying. In India, they hire professional mourners to wail, but they do not observe this in the United States. During the twelve days of mourning, the family refrains from cooking in their home, so others bring food to them. On the thirteenth day, which is the day they believe the soul departs, crying ceases so as to release the soul. Mourners are not allowed to go to temple until this date, and if they miss this particular time, they can't enter the temple until after a year from the death.

On a weekend soon after the funeral, they hold a memorial service. In addition to chanting and singing, the priest gives a talk, or a friend may give a sermon. This is not a sad occasion because they believe that the soul has gone on to better things.

⊙ *Gifts:* Bring food to the mourners' home during the twelve days. During the twelve days, friends may also send flowers to their home. Avoid offering money.

⊙ *Words:* "I'm sorry."

⊙ *Clothing:* Solemn colors, black preferred.

JAPANESE (BUDDHIST)

Many funeral traditions have been eliminated. Mourners no longer wear white clothing nor do they use professional mourners. In addition, they do not burn paper houses or cars or money as funeral offerings.

The tolling of the bell signals the beginning of the temple service. They strike it in a particular funeral sequence. They strike it twice, followed by a crescendo and decrescendo, then five times, followed by another crescendo and decrescendo, then strike it a final three times. During this time, the guests rise and the pallbearers bring in the casket. The casket is usually open during the service.

The ceremony proceeds with chanting; incense offerings by family, relatives, pallbearers, and congregation; prayers; eulogies; and a sermon. The funeral ends with a family representative giving words of appreciation to those attending the funeral and those conducting it. Then they close the casket.

After the funeral, the family sometimes gives rice crackers to those who have attended. Generally, in urban centers where large numbers of people attend the service, there is no large gathering to eat following the funeral. Cremation or burial usually takes place the morning after the funeral. Memorial services take place on the seventh, thirtieth, and one hundredth day. During this time, mourners offer incense, plain white rice cakes, and white flowers. At the thirty-day and one-year ceremonies, the family shares a meal together following the service.

A special memorial service occurs at the *obon* [oh-bone] festival each summer at a *hatsubon* [hot-sue-bone], a ceremony to honor the return of the departed the first year after their death. Mourners go to the temple, burn incense, and send floating lanterns into the ocean. The lights guide the souls as they journey back to the spirit world.

⊛ *Gifts: Koden* [coe-den] is a monetary offering to the family of the deceased, originally used for incense, now used to cover other funeral expenses. If economic assistance is not needed, the family donates the money to charity. If you are not closely connected to the family, $20 would be an appropriate amount. Enclose the money in special envelopes marked by black and silver ties. (See "Marrying"/Japanese, p. 126.) Give the envelope to a family representative or receptionist. If you do not have access to these envelopes, a plain white envelope will do. The money should be clean, preferably new bills, and wrapped in white paper before being placed inside the envelope. The receptionist collects the *koden* and marks down the amount given and the name of the donor. This information is given to the widow (if the deceased was a married man), who then logs the information into a *koden* book. She uses this book as reference for giving an equal amount when someone in the donor's family dies. In acknowledgment of the donation, the family may send a card or token gift in return, frequently a book of stamps because it is practical and easy to mail. However, in urban centers, this custom is beginning to fade. As an alternative, the family may send notification that a donation has been made to some charity.

✪ *Words:* "*Sabishiku narimashita desho*" [sah-bee-she-coo nah-ree-mah-she-tah deh-show] (You must be terribly lonely). Avoid saying, "He or she has gone to a better place."

✪ *Clothing:* Somber colors, not necessarily white or black.

––––––––

JEWISH

ORTHODOX

At the funeral chapel they employ a *shomer* [show-mare], someone who guards the dead until burial and prays over the bodies as a sign of respect. The *shomrim* [shom-reem] are observant Jews, often students or semiretired people. Shifts last twelve to twenty-four hours, and the *shomer* is supposed to remain awake the entire time continuously reciting psalms and other religious texts to uplift the deceased's soul. Some *shomrim* receive pay for their work, while others volunteer.

The body must be buried as soon as possible without embalming. They place it in a wooden casket, which remains closed. Caskets must be kosher, which means that rabbis supervise construction; they are not built on the Sabbath; they use only vegetable glue, wooden dowels, and no metal, including screws. Kosher caskets have holes on the bottom to promote the biblical process "ashes to ashes and dust to dust."

At services they read from the psalms, and one to three persons may give brief eulogies. Men and women sit separately.

After the body has been lowered into the grave, everyone helps shovel dirt over the grave. They do not leave until it is almost completely covered to ensure that the body has been properly buried. Regardless of the branch of Judaism, before leaving the cemetery the rabbi tears the black ribbons affixed to the lapels of the immediate family. This simulates the rending of clothing, an ancient symbol of mourning.

Following interment, people wash their hands as they leave the cemetery or before entering the home of the mourners. At the home, they eat a religious, formal meal of boiled eggs, representing life, and bagels, which, through their roundness, symbolize the life cycle.

Mourners observe a seven-day period called shivah. They sit on low stools to signify that their station in life has been lowered. Likewise, they cover mirrors to demonstrate their lack of concern with their appearance. An older explanation for covering mirrors was that whoever looked into the mirror and saw himself might become the next to die.

Visitors come during the shivah to bring comfort to the mourners. They may bring food to the house but not take food away from it. A minyan (ten male Jews over bar mitzvah age) gather during the morning and the night to say the appropriate prayers.

Mourners burn a memorial candle for seven days following the funeral. On the one-year anniversary of the death, as reckoned by the Hebrew calendar, family members light a twenty-four-hour memorial candle. At the one-year death anniversary or earlier, they have a brief ceremony to unveil a grave marker. All branches of Judaism observe this custom. On subsequent cemetery calls, mourners may leave a pebble on the gravestone as a token of their visit.

✪ *Gifts:* Avoid sending flowers, either to the cemetery or to the home. Food may be brought to the house. For the Orthodox, anything cooked must be kosher and sealed. Fresh fruit is always appropriate. They sometimes request donations to charity in the deceased's name.

✪ *Words:* Avoid references to the afterlife. "I'm sorry" is acceptable. Since the departed can no longer speak, one should observe silence in their presence. If speech (other than prayer and eulogy) is unavoidable, it should be in undertones.

✪ *Clothing:* For women, long-sleeved clothes in somber colors with hemlines midcalf or longer. Necklines must be modest. Suits and ties for men. They must wear a yarmulke [yáhr-mull-keh] during the service and graveside. Extras are available for those not owning any. Married women cover their heads with either a scarf or hat.

✪ *Body Language:* During the service, men and women sit separate.

SEPHARDIC VARIATIONS

Children and pregnant women should not come to the cemetery. In the old days, no women came to the cemetery. The first postfuneral meal is called the *huevo* [oo-éh-vo] (egg), where each person eats a hard-boiled egg to symbolize the circle of life. The meal takes place in the synagogue or at the mourners' home and includes kashkaval cheese, Greek olives, and bread. They conclude with a blessing, after which they eat raisins for sweetness to compensate for the bitterness of the loss and as a hopeful sign for the future.

KOREAN

Three days before the funeral, guests visit and pay their respects to the deceased. This may take place at the family's home, a rented hall, or at a mortuary. At the entry, someone seated at a table receives donations placed in white envelopes and offers a guest book to sign. They display a black-and-white, framed photograph of the deceased, a floral arrangement, and incense on a table. Female family members of the deceased may wear white, traditional Korean dresses. Male family members may wear black suits with white handkerchiefs around their arms.

Guests approach the table, and if the family and visitors are Buddhists, they light an incense stick, kneel, then bow to the photograph. If they are Christian, there will be no incense or bowing. Instead, guests approach and acknowledge the photograph or say a silent prayer to the deceased. Food and drink are served during this preburial mourning period.

Most Christians prefer burial. Each family member throws dirt on the coffin, beginning with the closest family member and on to the furthest. At Buddhist funerals they burn imitation money for the deceased to take into the afterlife. Often they place a complete meal in front of the casket to offer nourishment to the departed soul. Funerals take place on odd-numbered days because even numbers are unlucky. They loudly express their grief and prefer to pay in cash rather than by check so that death won't return with the canceled check.

Buddhists prefer cremation. Ashes may be sprinkled at a lake or ocean. Korean Buddhist temples have a special room with photos of the deceased, many burning candles, burning incense, and a Buddha image in the center of the room. They make food offerings there, as well.

As a sign of mourning, some wives and daughters of the deceased wear, for approximately two weeks to one month, white, flat ribbons attached to barrettes.

Both Christian and Buddhist families hold memorial services on the forty-ninth day after death, and at one and at two years. At Buddhist temples, they place vegetarian food and many kinds of fruits on the altar. During the ceremony, the monks chant and a Zen master gives a sermon. Someone approaches the altar and takes a small piece of each kind of fruit, places it on a plate, and takes it outdoors to feed the hungry ghosts. After the ceremony, they burn an article of the deceased's clothing outdoors to symbolize that the deceased is truly dead. At the conclusion of the ceremony, the family and close friends go to a restaurant, frequently a Chinese restaurant, for a special meal.

At the one-year memorial, *jesa* [jay-sah], mourners gather at the cemetery for an ancestral-worship ceremony. They create an ancestor-worship table that includes piles of apples, Korean rice cakes, oranges, and other fruits. This small, low table holds a framed picture of the deceased. Family members bow to their ancestors, males twice, females twice, sometimes four times. Afterward, at nearby picnic areas, they eat the food they have placed on the table.

✪ *Gifts:* Flowers may be sent during the three-day preburial rites. Give money in envelopes only at this time. Names of donors should be written on the outside of the envelope. Families receiving guests at home appreciate food.

✪ *Words:* "I'm sorry for your loss," and any other sincere expressions of sympathy.

✪ *Clothing:* Black or somber colors, nothing floral. If the three-day period is held at home, remove shoes before entering. At the forty-ninth-day ceremony, men wear suits and ties. Women wear clothing comfortable for sitting cross-legged on the floor. Pants suits are acceptable.

❂ *Body Language:* When entering the temple, step over, not on, the threshold.

LAO

From the day of death until the funeral ceremony, the monks visit the house of the bereaved every day to pray for the dead and give comfort to the family. On the morning of the funeral and prior to the mortuary service, the monks come to the house to participate in a custom called *het boun* [het boon] (make offerings) for the deceased. Family and friends bring fresh fruit, cookies, and other sweets. The family provides food for the monks and the guests. The monks eat what they want first, then give the rest to those who wish to take home the leftovers. This food is considered blessed. The family presents new yellow robes to the monks. In addition, sons of the deceased don yellow robes and shave their heads to become Buddhist monks for the day. (See "Dying"/Thai, p. 229.) When the ceremony is over, the sons remove their robes and become laypersons once again. Close female friends dress in all white as part of this ceremony. Afterward, the Lao go to the mortuary, where the monks chant and burn incense for the dead. The funeral service ends at the mortuary.

Most Lao cremate their dead. Those who can afford it, prefer to take the ashes back to Laos, where they place them inside family tombs—memorial towers made of brick and cement that sit alongside the walls of temple grounds.

❂ *Gifts:* If invited to the home ceremony, bring fresh-fruit offerings or prepare some special food the family enjoys. Prior to the funeral, enclose money in an envelope and place it on the family's home altar.

⊛ *Words:* Any expression of condolence.

⊛ *Clothing:* Black or somber colors. Avoid brightly colored clothing or floral prints.

⊛ *Body Language:* Avoid hugging, kissing, or shaking hands with the mourners. Instead, they will appreciate it if you perform the *wai* [why]. With hands pressed together in a prayerlike position, bring them up to just below the chin and nod slightly. They will return the gesture.

MEXICAN

Customs vary according to church denomination. Generally, they have an open casket, and cremation is uncommon. Viewing of the body is important, and it must be dressed in the best or new clothing. The family usually requests all-night visitations, and the funeral service itself is generally quiet and solemn. Large numbers of family members attend the service. They commonly have a weeklong recitation of rosaries and observe anniversary rosaries.

Día de los Muertos [dée-ah day los moo-áir-toes] (Day of the Dead)

In addition to rituals dictated by the varieties of religions to which Mexicans belong, some may observe the folk custom of Day of the Dead, memorializing deceased family members. This occurs during the two-day period of November 1, All Saints' Day, and November 2, All Souls' Day. On All Saints' Day, families go to the cemetery and clean and beautify the graves of the deceased. For All Souls' Day they prepare an *ofrenda* [oh-frén-dah] (altar) at home, displaying a photo of the deceased with memorabilia and favorite foods of that person as well as seasonal treats such as Day of the Dead bread, shaped like corpses or round with crossbones on them, and spun-sugar candy skulls. They believe the dead do not go directly to their final resting place but once a year come home for a brief visit. The altar welcomes them. These rituals are more common in U.S./Mexican border states.

Sister Karen Boccalero, of the Sisters of St. Francis, founder and driving force behind Self-Help Graphics, a community-based art gallery located in East Los Angeles, was instrumental in reintroducing the Aztec-based Day of the Dead back into the U.S. Latino community. In the 1970s, Self-Help Graphics became a showplace for the spectacular altars they created. Fittingly, when Sister Karen suddenly died on June 24, 1997, in gratitude and love the Latino community constructed a huge altar to honor her.

Friends and artists adorned it with bunches of marigolds, the traditional Day of the Dead flower. A large photo of Sister Karen framed by bramble branches became the centerpiece. The altar was packed with artwork from her protégés, fruit offerings, incense, and her signature items of a box of Marlboro cigarettes with a box of matches next to her favorite brown, ceramic Mexican ashtray. Other items included plants from her magnificent gardens in which she took pride, Aztec figurines, statues of Catholic praying women, pieces of tapestry woven in Mexico, etchings, and words that were reproduced on her rosary card from Mahatma Gandhi's "Seven Sins in the World": wealth without work; pleasure without conscience; knowledge without character; commerce without morality; science without humanity; worship without sacrifice; politics without principle. Sister Karen spent her life fighting these evils.

On the Day of the Dead following her death, friends and artists created another altar for her. Franciscan nuns led prayers at her grave, then led a procession of forty on a one-and-a-quarter-mile trek from the cemetery to Self-Help Graphics. They gathered at Sister Karen's altar, still covered with mementos to lure her spirit's return.

MUSLIM

Surprising as it may seem, some American Muslims living in cities where they do not have their own mortuaries use Jewish funeral homes because many customs are the same. For example, they oppose embalming, forbid cremation, and must bury the dead within twenty-four hours after death. In a small Muslim community outside of Minneapolis, they have imported special waters to bathe the deceased and a special cotton used for wrapping the corpse in order to comply with Saudi Arabian burial traditions.

Frequently, family members prepare the body with oils and fragrances. Husbands may prepare their wives, wives prepare husbands, and children are prepared by either. For the unmarried, widowed, or divorced, only women prepare women, and men prepare men. Before the burial, they wash and shroud the body. The funeral service generally takes place in a mosque, but may also be held in a funeral chapel or at the cemetery away from the grave. They generally request closed caskets.

The leader at the funeral is an imam [ee-mam] (priest), who leads a prayer and asks God for forgiveness. The body is laid on the ground or a table. The imam stands in front and faces Mecca, while others stand behind him in rows. No bowing or prostrating occurs during the service.

Before lowering the body into the grave, they turn it slightly so that it rests on its right side. In the final resting position, the body faces Mecca. If Mecca is to the north, they dig the grave in an east-west direction and place the head side of the body on the east. They say prayers as they lower the casket. Crying is acceptable but wailing is not.

Among Iranian Muslims, the funeral home prepares the body, which is interred in a cemetery among other Muslims. The deceased wears a white shroud and is placed in the simplest wooden coffin. The ceremony primarily takes place graveside. Good friends recite from the Koran and they say a special prayer for the dead called *namazeh mayet* [nah-mah-zéh mah-yét]. Once the body is in the ground, mourners and guests may throw in three handfuls of dirt to help fill the grave. With the first handful they say, "From the earth did we create you." With the second they say, "And into it shall we return you." With the third they say, "And from it shall we bring you out once again."

After the ceremony, Muslims meet at a home or in a hall where they serve tea, coffee, and a special sweet, halvah. For the first week of mourning, some people have memorial ceremonies at home or in the mosque where they recite from the Koran. On the fortieth day in the evening, they hold a ceremony with a big dinner, almost like a wedding dinner. They recite from the Koran and talk about the deceased. This event is repeated at the one-year anniversary with an even bigger meal.

For some Muslims, for forty days after the funeral female relatives visit the grave every Friday, their Sabbath. They place a palm branch on the grave and distribute cakes to the poor. Sometimes widows wear black for an entire year.

✪ *Gifts:* Avoid giving material gifts. Respect for the deceased and the survivors is the greatest gift.

✪ *Words:* "My condolences." "May God give you patience." "I hope that this will be your last sorrow."

✪ *Clothing:* Men in dark suits with black ties, women in black. Avoid wearing light colors. Avoid wearing red. Avoid open displays of jewelry containing non-Muslim religious symbols, such as Stars of David, crosses, and signs of the zodiac.

NATIVE AMERICAN

As with most groups in this book, there are many variations, but generally, outsiders have to be invited to a funeral, which ordinarily takes place on the burial ground on a reservation or allotted land shortly after death. Depending on the status of the person, the ceremony may last from one day up to two weeks. Most people are buried horizontally, but medicine men may be buried in a sitting position with many artifacts. Sometimes, those considered "bad people" are placed facedown. Singing and dancing take place at nighttime only. Mourning lasts for one year. During this time family members refrain from singing or going to celebrations, powwows, or sweat lodges. A common sign of mourning is for immediate and extended family to cut their hair.

✪ *Gifts:* Water, because they consider it sacred, and it is especially appropriate when burial ceremonies last over a day. Food and money.

✪ *Words:* They prefer silence. Avoid words of condolence. Avoid offering them your prayers.

✪ *Clothing:* Respectful attire, nothing colorful. If you are a non–Native American, avoid wearing anything that might be construed as Native American clothing or jewelry. This is highly offensive.

✪ *Taboos:* Do not record the event on video or audio recorders, with cameras of any kind. Their songs and dances must stay within the family and are not to be shared with outsiders.

HOPI

They cover the face of the deceased with a cotton mask, which symbolizes the rain cloud. Mourners silently lower the body into a grave located in an obscure place and surround it with prayer sticks. After they cover the grave, they leave a bowl of food to feed the soul on its journey to the spirit world. Four days later, women mourners return to the grave and place another bowl of food there. After that, they believe the soul has safely returned to the spirit world, and normal activities resume.

Rededicating Disturbed Burial Sites

When Native American burial sites have been disturbed, steps must be taken to ask for forgiveness from the affected spirits. Tribal representatives must have a ceremony to ease the disturbance of the dead. Medicine people and spiritual leaders pray over the physical remains and make offerings. Commonly, they leave handmade tribal gifts such as baskets as well as clothing, tobacco, food, and sage, which they place on top of the grave. If bones have been disturbed, they must rebury them. Usually, the ceremony is attended by spiritual leaders and descendants of the particular tribal group. Ceremonial details vary according to tribe.

On May 10, 1997, tribal leaders of the Miwok and Pomo tribes and hundreds of other Native Americans and local residents gathered before sunset at the Mission San Francisco Solano in Sonoma, California, for a memorial service to bless the nine hundred tribal members buried under First Street.

They blessed the ground and those prohibited from burial in the nearby cemetery designated for Christians only. "We don't want them to think they're forgotten," explained one tribal member. The Native Americans didn't want angry spirits to return. They could counteract this possibility through the rededication ceremony, demonstrating that they protected their dead.

After the blessing and prayers, tribal leaders burned sweet grass, and afterward, traditional Pomo dancers performed. In addition to blessing the site, they raised money for a future monument that will be erected containing the Christian names of those buried. To cover its cost, the local tribes prepared and sold dinners to the locals, who enthusiastically supported the cause.

Reburial: Chief Long Wolf

In 1992, when Elizabeth Knight, of Worcestershire, England, first read a lament on the tragic life of Chief Long Wolf, she became captivated by his plight. An Oglala Sioux warrior, he had lain forgotten in a London cemetery since 1892, stranded from his native people in South Dakota. Knight vowed to return him to his ancestral burial grounds at Wounded Knee, and after five years of detective work and diligence, she fulfilled her promise.

Chief Long Wolf had been wounded at the brutal Battle of the Little Bighorn and joined Buffalo Bill Cody's Wild West Show rather than stay in South Dakota and live as a member of a vanquished people. He spent the rest of his life performing in Cody's troupe touring the United States and Europe. In 1892, at age fifty-nine, Chief Long Wolf died in London of respiratory complications. Cody purchased a grave for him at Bromptom Cemetery, later shared with Star, the seventeen-month-old daughter of another Sioux troupe member, Ghost Dog. The child had died after falling from a horse.

Elizabeth Knight's pledge became a reality when, on September 26, 1997, the chief's coffin was removed from the cemetery, 105 years after its original burial. A horse-drawn black carriage slowly carried the buffalo-hide-wrapped remains of the chief and Star. To the accompaniment of Indian drums, relatives and tribal members in native dress marched behind.

The reburial service commenced in London's St. Luke's Parish Church combining Native American and British church traditions: Indian drums and organ music; Sioux prayers and biblical verse; Native American headdress and Anglican robes; Indian medicine men and English clergy.

A descendant of the author whose story had impassioned Knight read from the Bible. An English quartet sang a Lakotan memorial song, and two of the chief's descendants intoned hymns in Lakota and English. A tribal spiritual chief prayed over the coffin, and after a final hymn, the bodies were carried from the church by four men in morning coats. A hearse transported the chief's flag-draped coffin to an airplane for the final lap of its journey.

Wilmer Mesteth, an Oglala Sioux tribal spiritual leader in attendance, proclaimed, "It [return of the body] means he's set free. He'll be among his own people. His bones will remain with us. The spirit remains with the bones, and the bones will finally be at rest among his own."

Two days later, the ceremony resumed at Wolf Creek, South Dakota. At first, the coffin remained inside a tepee surrounded by flowers. Then nine pallbearers bore it up a steep hill to a grave at Wolf Creek Church Cemetery. Seven of the nine were powwow dancers in traditional dance regalia; the other two were chiefs in feather bonnets. Mourners followed, and en route to the cemetery the entourage stopped four times to honor the four directions. At the burial site, traditional Lakota songs and prayers preceded the interment. Rather than feeling sad at this reburial ceremony, Chief Long Wolf's people rejoiced. He was finally home.

ROM (GYPSY)

Ordinarily the Rom prefer to die outdoors, but if they die in the hospital, all traces of blood must be removed from the room. Family members place the corpse next to an open window with a lit candle under the bed. This provides a lighted way for the spirit to travel to heaven.

At the funeral home, they hold a boisterous three-day feast. Large groups gather, and feasting takes place the night before and the morning of the burial. They bring huge amounts of food and drink to the mortuary and sometimes set up barbecues outside the building. During the night, mourners bring food to the deceased and place familiar

items into the casket such as telephones, toothbrushes, lipstick, cigarettes, whiskey, and cash. An elder presides at the
funeral service.

During the six weeks after the death, the family gathers
the deceased's belongings and clothing, everything but the
jewelry, and tosses them into a body of moving water for
the deceased to wear in the spirit world. The most honored man in the group says a prayer over the objects and
clothing.

A unique custom called the *pomana* [poe-máh-nah]
(black feast or table) takes place at three days, six weeks,
and one year after death. For the six-week feast, the family
rents a hall or banquet room in a hotel to accommodate
hundreds of guests for an elaborate ceremony. At one end
of the banquet table they provide a place setting for the deceased so ornate that it may consist of gold dishes, gold
utensils, and the finest linens.

Next, they place personalized objects at the place setting.
For example, if the deceased was a male smoker, they may
leave the finest cigars. If the deceased was a female who
loved Entenmann's cookies, they stack boxes of Entenmann's cookies for her pleasure. An elder stands near the
place setting, says prayers in Romany, and burns incense
over it and the gifts displayed in a different corner of the
room. Here family and friends exhibit extravagant items
for the deceased to use in the next world: fine luggage, a
certificate for a vacation, jewelry, envelopes containing
money. Offering these gifts sends a message that the spirit
of the deceased is still among them and receiving these lux-
urious presents. Later they distribute the gifts to the family
of the deceased.

The gifts are for people to enjoy here as a symbol of
what the deceased's spirit could or would enjoy if it were
still embodied. The people eat the cakes and say, "I'm eating this for you."

"Wearing the suit" is another significant custom of the

pomana. Rom believe that the spirit of the deceased is on earth until the one-year feast. At the six-week *pomana,* they outfit a surrogate for the deceased in an expensive suit of clothing, including hat, undergarments, and shoes. If the deceased was a female, her outfit includes underclothing, even makeup. It is an honor to be chosen for this role, but before giving the outfit to the chosen person, the elders may burn incense over it for purification. The person who wears the suit is symbolically saying, "I'm wearing it here; she [the deceased] is wearing it there [in the spirit world]."

At the *pomana,* some Rom may go up to the person wearing the suit and speak to him/her just as they might interact if the deceased were truly among the living. They may even apologize for past wrongdoings. This custom has variations because other Romany families believe that to talk to the dead person you have to go to the cemetery. Through the ritual of the wearing of the suit, the deceased is given a little more time on earth to enjoy life and be remembered. All of these acts demonstrate the Rom's strong belief that the spirit of the dead person stays among the living for a year before moving on to the next state of being. The Romany goal is for the deceased to be happy and not wander the earth.

After the six-week feast, the person who wears the suit and accoutrements is supposed to wear it to parties and special occasions until the year is over. This is a great honor, and everyone who sees the person in the outfit then remembers the deceased and talks favorably about him or her. At the one-year celebration, the person wears the suit again but afterward sends it to an unknown destination. The suit-wearer may hang the suit on a tree or shrub where someone unknown can take it, throw it into a body of moving water, or bring it to the dry cleaners and never pick it up.

One must be invited to attend any Rom event, including a funeral. Usually this occurs because the person is a good or helpful connection, such as an attorney.

✪ *Gifts:* Only family and other Rom give gifts. To give a gift would seem presumptuous.

✪ *Words:* Anything sincere is appreciated, or positive words including remembrances of what made the person unique: "He sure did love those cigars."

✪ *Clothing:* For the three-day or six-week tables, guests wear dressy, dark, formal clothing. Avoid pastel colors or white. Avoid wearing casual clothing, short pants, or casual dresses.

Note: The Rom view the lower half of the body as sacred and dangerous, so it must be covered. However, they also understand that outsiders don't know their customs. They expect that outsiders have their own rules to obey and watch closely to see if they observe them or not. If not, they ask, "Why would you give up your traditions?" or "Does he think he's a Gypsy?"

SAMOAN

Typically there is a lag of from one week to ten days between the time of death and the burial. They need that time to gather the family, many of whom fly in from the islands.

The women dress the bodies, frequently in white. Women may be buried in white wedding dresses; men may be buried in white suits, sometimes black. They cover the body with a veil, just as they might do to keep insects off the body if the service were being conducted in Samoa, but in the United States, they frequently substitute lace for veiling. They cover the coffin with lace, as well.

Customs vary with the status of the deceased. Sometimes they have an open coffin for a grandmother. If her children know she loves flowers, they give her lots of flowers. "You want to do your best for the grandmother," explained one

Samoan, "but it's always according to status." If the deceased is a chief, he has to have a fine mat unwrapped and on top. Women mostly have lace.

A small choir sings and the Samoans drape the casket and surround it with fine mats of handwoven grass or leaves. These mats circulate among families and appear at all rites of passage. They place dollar bills on the body and place highly valued family possessions in the casket as well, such as a watch or other jewelry.

Before closing the casket, the spouse or oldest child pours perfume over the body. The family gets together, sometimes while the person is still alive, and decides who will perform this act, called the last bath. It is a great honor to be chosen for this final loving task. During the interment, they sing and throw flowers, especially rose petals. The mood is not somber; a warm, lively atmosphere prevails.

✪ *Gifts:* Money enclosed in a card. In return, Samoans have a custom called *sua,* which is a thank-you for the gift. After some days have passed, members of the deceased's family may come to call bearing gifts of a can of soda, five yards of fabric, and turkey. These gifts substitute for the traditional island gifts of coconut, tapa, and pig. They also bring a tray holding chicken, crackers, and a fine mat.

✪ *Clothing:* Dress for church. In the past, everyone wore black, then later all white. Sometimes families request all white. Above all, respectful and comfortable clothing.

THAI

In Thailand, prefuneral rites take place at home from three to seven days before the funeral. People come to pay their respects and hosts serve them food. This custom is beginning to change, and in the United States the body may be taken directly to the temple. The most important day is the last day at the temple before the body is cremated. In front of the body they place a photo of the deceased, offerings of incense, oranges, and flowers. Generally, the family wears black, although those from northeast Thailand wear white.

Whether at home or at the temple, services only occur in the evening. At the ceremony, an even number of monks, preferably four, chant. Sons of the deceased become monks for the day; they shave their heads and don orange robes and participate in a monk's temple ceremony. (See "Dying"/Lao, p. 217.) By doing this, the sons ensure that their parent will more easily reach heaven. After the funeral, the body is most commonly cremated. Ashes may be kept at home, thrown into a river or ocean, or returned to Thailand. The Thai Buddhist temple contains a special room where people keep ashes in a pagoda-style container with a displayed photo of the deceased. They regularly place offerings there. Families observe one hundred days of mourning.

✿ *Gifts:* At home visitations, give money in envelopes and write your name on the outside. Someone is usually in charge of collecting them.

✿ *Words:* "I'm sorry." At the same time, you may hold their hands, but only if you see others doing the same. No joking. Do not talk too loud or laugh. Silence honors the dead.

✿ *Clothing:* Black or white clothing.

✿ *Body Language:* Avoid smiling. At the temple, guests should sit and refrain from talking. Temple members sit on the floor. If you are uncomfortable in this position, look for some chairs at the back of the room. The *wai* [why] is the most respectful form of greeting. (See "Dying"/Lao, p. 217.) When entering the temple, step over the threshold, not on it.

TIBETAN

Prior to death, friends offer the dying person sips of holy water. A monk or lama comes to the hospital or home to say prayers and to pour grains of colored sand from a sacred sand mandala over the crown of the dying person. This allows the person's spirit to exit from the top of the head.

The funeral takes place three to seven days after death and is determined by astrological calculations, but services do not take place on weekends, considered inauspicious times. During the ceremony and prior to cremation, monks chant and burn incense, and guests lay white scarves over the casket. (See "Giving Birth"/Tibetan, p. 42; "Marrying"/Tibetan, p. 140.) For seven days afterward, family members and friends make offerings to monks at monasteries. For forty-nine days following the death, the family prepares a dough of barley mixed with honey, milk, butter, sugar, and dried fruits. A small part of this mixture is offered into a flame three times daily to feed the spirit of the deceased. This ends on the forty-ninth day when they believe the deceased finds a way of reincarnating as a human or another life-form or goes directly to heaven.

✪ *Gifts:* The first few days, guests come to the mourners' home for lunch and to offer white scarves and envelopes with money. This recurs at the fourth- and seventh-week death anniversaries.

✪ *Words:* The Tibetans offer words of condolence while offering scarves placed around the mourner's neck. "Don't worry." If the deceased was elderly, they say, "She lived well. She led a long, good life."

✪ *Clothing:* Subdued colors.

✪ *Body Language: Namaste* [nah-mah-stay] is the most respectful form of greeting. (See "Marrying"/Indian, p. 120.)

Emerging Traditions

Lapel Ribbons

Transcending ethnic boundaries, other death rituals have evolved. One of the most popular of the 1980s and 1990s has been the wearing of red ribbons to remember those who have died of AIDS and to draw attention to AIDS and HIV charities. No doubt, the red ribbon tradition grew out of the custom of yellow ribbons worn by those awaiting the return of missing warriors, a symbol going back at least as far as the Civil War and popularly displayed during the 1979 hostage-taking in Iran and later during the 1992 Persian Gulf War.

Recent evolution of the memorial lapel ribbon occurred after July 17, 1996, when TWA Flight 800 exploded after takeoff from JFK Airport in New York. None of the 230 passengers and crew survived, and grieving families spent weeks at an airport hotel anxiously awaiting news of retrieved remains. In the lobby, TWA representatives distributed white lapel ribbons containing angel pins in the center. Families of victims, hotel staff, and any other hotel guests who desired wore them as well. The angel had been mounted on a small piece of cardboard containing this message: "May your guardian angel watch over and protect you."

The AIDS Memorial Quilt and NAMES Project

One of the most powerful contemporary death rituals is the memorialization of AIDS victims through a friend's or relative's creation of a cloth epitaph in the form of a colorful personalized panel. On plain or patterned fabric, panel makers paint, embroider, or appliqué their farewells. Each panel contains the name of the deceased with birth and/or death dates. Words may be added, such as "His eye is on the sparrow" or "We love you." Some panel makers have attached photos of the deceased or stuffed animals or car keys or wedding rings or bows. Others have visual representations through collage or needlework of pets, balloons, landscapes or moonscapes, and symbols meaningful to the person being memorialized—a piano keyboard or a chef's hat and a barbecue.

Genesis of the AIDS quilt occurred during a 1985 San Francisco candlelight march commemorating the city's one thousandth AIDS death. Gay rights advocate Cleve Jones noted that names of victims written on placards and taped to the side of a building resembled a patchwork quilt. This led to the establishment of the NAMES Project to celebrate the lives of those who had died of the disease.

The first part of the ritual is to create an individual quilt to memorialize a victim. The second part is the presentation of the visually moving massed quilts accompanied by the recitation of victims' names.

To display the massed quilts, a selected site is laid out like a big grid made up of walkways. Twelve-foot-by-twelve-foot folded sections of the quilt, composed of eight three-foot-by-six-foot panels stitched together, are placed in the center of each of the grid squares. Dressed in white, teams of eight unfolders move through the layout to their assigned positions around a folded quilt section. They join hands and stand in a tight circle around the folded section.

In choreographed movements, created in 1987 by Jack Caster, a NAMES Project volunteer, the unfolders begin a pattern called the lotus fold. Four unfolders reach in, take a corner of the folded quilt section, and pull it back. After the first four persons step back, the second four reach in and unfold the next layer. Simulating the unfolding of a lotus, they repeat this act four times until the twelve-foot-by-twelve-foot section is in full view. Then they lift the gloriously colored quilt section chest high as they make a quarter turn clockwise to set the fabric square in place on the ground. Unfolding teams are the only people allowed on the grounds until the quilts have been completely unfolded.

The introduction is read: "Welcome to the [name of location] display of the NAMES Project AIDS Memorial Quilt. The panels surrounding you were created by lovers, families, and friends to commemorate loved ones who have died of AIDS."

While listening to an appointed reader intone thirty-two names of victims, the viewers surround the edges of the grid and join hands as officials unfold the quilt. Names continue to be read by a series of speakers for however long it takes. Sometimes celebrities add their voices to the calling of names, such as actress Elizabeth Taylor, folk singer Arlo Guthrie, and Tipper Gore, wife of Vice President Al Gore. More frequently, the readers are heartbroken parents, lovers, siblings, and friends or panel makers, people with HIV and AIDS. When all the quilts have been unfolded, family, friends, and spectators mill slowly around the memorial banners to pay their respects and weep. At the closing of the display, visitors once more circle the quilt, stand along its edge, and join hands as the appointed persons in white ceremonially refold it.

The first display of the AIDS Memorial Quilt was in Washington, D.C., in 1987 when 1,920 panels were shown. In 1996, the number of panels had exploded to just under 40,000, large enough to cover twenty-four football fields. As of February 1997, 9 million people had visited it. (See "Looking for More Information?"/Videotapes, p. 266.) The quilt has become a jolting reminder of the death toll, estimated by the end of 1997 to have claimed 6 to 7 million lives worldwide.

⚙ If you are interested in becoming a participant in the NAMES Project by helping to create a quilt or becoming part of the display ceremony, contact the NAMES Project at 1-800-872-6263.

Project Blue Light

During the 1988 Christmas season, the mother-in-law of a slain Philadelphia police officer placed a single blue bulb in the front window of her home to mark the tragedy. Ever since sharing her idea with other victims' families, Concerns of Police Survivors (COPS) (see "Looking for More Information?"/Organizations, COPS, p. 265), a national nonprofit organization, has been promoting blue lights at holiday time as a way to pay tribute to law enforcement officers at all levels of government who have been killed in the line of duty. Approximately one officer is killed every fifty-two hours.

Families choose different ways to display lights. They may burn a single blue candle light in their window or, like one New Jersey family, place more than eight hundred blue bulbs on their front-yard pine tree to commemorate the death of a state trooper fatally shot during a traffic stop in 1981, three days before Christmas. Some families trim the outside of their homes in blue lights; police stations, too, may hang blue lights outside their buildings to pay tribute to slain officers and demonstrate support for those who wear law enforcement badges.

Children's Bell Tower

On September 19, 1994, bandits attacked the Maggie and Reginald Green family of Bodega Bay, California, while they were traveling on an Italian highway. Their seven-year-old son, Nicholas, was struck by a bullet and killed. Instead of expressing recriminations against the Italian criminals and resentment toward the Italian people, the Greens donated their son's organs to seven needy Italian patients.

Thunderstruck by such generosity in a country where organ donation is uncommon, the Italian people demonstrated their love for the Greens by running out of their homes whenever the Greens passed by to offer them bells that had been in their families for generations. In total, the Greens received 120 bells, with the largest donated by the Marinelli Foundry, the oldest foundry in the world. The pope blessed the large bell on which the foundry had engraved the names of Nicholas and the seven recipients of his life-giving organs.

Today, the bells hang on a tower on the north edge of the town of Bodega Bay, north of the intersection of Bay Hill Road and Highway 1. According to Reginald Green, Nicholas's father, "When a bell rings, you hear the sound, it fills the air, and then it is gone." The bells, responding to the slightest breeze, are like angel voices reminding us of the fragility of life.

The Green family hopes that the bell tower will become a site that brings people together as Nicholas's death has done. To continue making Nicholas's life meaningful, they have created the Nicholas Green Foundation to promote organ transplants. As the boy's father affirms, "When Nicholas died, he lit a spark in people all over the world. It's been an honor to tend that flame."

SURFER SERVICE

Hours after sixteen-year-old Joshua Dean Hall earned a place on the Huntington Beach (California) High School national championship surf team, he was knocked unconscious and drowned after colliding headfirst with a concrete pillar while surfing beneath the Huntington Beach Pier. A week later, his shocked teammates and friends participated in a farewell tribute to the fallen surfer.

Before sunrise, on September 10, 1997, the day after his tearful funeral service, two hundred surfers gathered at

Huntington Beach and said a predawn prayer led by the surf-team captain, Jason Robinette. Paddling out into the water, the surfers rode one more wave to catch Josh's spirit, then formed an enormous circle. In unison, they splashed their boards against the waves as if to castigate the waters for taking their friend. Afterward, they floated purple floral aloha wreaths on the choppy waves. Meanwhile, Joshua's grandparents and other family members and friends stood on the nearby pier and threw flowers into the sea.

Surfing memorials have their roots in Hawaii and take place whenever a famous surfer dies, when a former surfer who still identifies with the surfing culture dies, or when someone suffers a fatal surfing accident. Sometimes these farewell rituals are called paddle outs. That's how friends commemorated the surfing death of nineteen-year-old Beth Pitts of Santa Cruz, California. When the ritual was over, one surfing friend said, "With Beth now sleeping under the water, I will paddle more gently."

Generally, surfer friends gather at a favorite surfing spot of the deceased. They paddle out beyond the breakers, form a circle, and join hands. They tell stories about their departed surfer buddy and may become bawdy, even pass a bota bag, a leather container holding liquor. There are no set rules; ceremonies are individualized, such as the one where a participant threw a lobster into the middle of the circle to mark the death of his friend, a former diver.

The family may sit on the fantail of a boat that stays close to the circle, or they may paddle nearby in outrigger canoes. The mourners sometimes wear leis or lei crowns and at the end of the ceremony toss the flowers into the circle. If the deceased has been cremated, they toss the ashes into the middle of the circle. To signal the end of the ceremony, the surfers make a loud sound. They may strike their surfboards against the water, slap the water with their hands, shout, splash, hoot, or honk like seals. As one surfing enthusiast described, "It's a hear-me, see-me action. It's a way of adding presence. It's like the dropping of the curtain." It is the final act.

MEMORIAL WALLS

Graffiti murals painted on the sides of New York buildings act as death markers for those who have died due to accidents, arguments, fights, police killings, and drug-war violence. Sometimes these memorial walls become the rallying point for actions protesting drugs, police brutality, or substandard housing conditions. A spray-paint heart and cross mark the spot in a Lower East Side courtyard where Danny Sicard, age twenty-eight, fell to his death. This painting drew attention to Sicard's unsafe apartment building and its negligent landlord.

When an arson fire killed eighty-seven Latino immigrants at the Happy Land Social Club in the Bronx in 1990, graffiti artist Andre Charles paid tribute to their snuffed-out lives on the side of a Bronx building. Using prominent lettering, he painted " 'Rest In Peace' All 87 Innocent Victims." These words floated above clouds decorated with a cross and a cartoonlike angel with a halo. Charles captioned it "In the Lord's Hands."

Painted and signed memorial walls began appearing in Latino neighborhoods (barrios) in the 1960s and 1970s. The graffiti artists, primarily Latinos, come from a tradition of Catholic death markers popular in Puerto Rico and historically tied to European and New World Catholic mourning traditions. They utilize typical funeral motifs of flowers, candles, doves, tombstones, crosses, and angels.

Antonio "Chico" Garcia is considered one of the most prolific painters in this genre. His first wall was in memory of a woman brutally raped and killed in Brooklyn. In bold letters he painted "In Memory of Julissa" and included a cross, flowers, angels, and the prayer "Peace For Ever." His second wall surfaced in Manhattan, where he remembered JR, a childhood friend who had been gunned down in the street. It featured an oversize sentimental portrait of the young man wearing a thick gold-link necklace and in yellow, bleeding letters "The World Is Yours in Memory of JR."

In 1990, Garcia created "In Memory of All Who Have Died," memorializing the death of a state trooper killed in a police drug raid in the Lower East Side. The mural showed the trooper shaking hands with a youth in front of the slogan "Let's Work Together." Garcia added the flags of Puerto Rico and the Dominican Republic to represent local residents. Beneath the flags he editorialized, "The War on Drugs will be won in the home not in the street." Ordinarily, local police arrest graffiti artists. After this mural appeared, law enforcement officials instead commissioned Garcia to paint a memorial wall on one station house for officers killed in the line of duty.

SIDEWALK SHRINES

Bunches of flowers and collections of homemade cards at a busy intersection or in front of a convenience store signal sites of violence and death, often the result of shootings and car crashes. Frequently, they mark the spot where youngsters have died. Sidewalk shrines contain photos of the deceased, lit votive candles, religious statues, poems, and other messages. "I don't know you but I miss you. You will not be forgotten." Discovering these memorials in startling places is a jolting reminder of how precious life is.

Prayer Vigil Network

Every time another is senselessly slain in the urban warfare of the Indianapolis inner city, members of the Prayer Vigil Network gather at the site of the bloodshed. Begun in 1996 with only a handful of religious people, 250 participants from Indianapolis suburban churches and city congregations now meet at the site of slayings to sing, pray, and hug one another. They pour oil in the form of crosses to reconsecrate the ground and add the victim's name to a wooden peace pole: 129 names in 1996; 124 names in the first nine months of 1997. That someone would even venture into their dangerous neighborhoods to pray for them gives hope to victims' families. These vigils demonstrate that the families are not alone; someone cares about their losses. Each time the circle returns to the neighborhood, residents, formerly fearful of leaving their homes, become bolder about stepping outdoors to join them. The Prayer Vigil Network is a first step toward creating a positive sense of community.

Diana, Princess of Wales

"Good night, sweet Princess." "To the People's Queen." "The Queen of Hearts." These recurring messages were left at sidewalk shrines across the United States after the thirty-six-year-old, beautiful Diana, Princess of Wales, was tragically killed in a Paris auto accident on August 31, 1997. Her unexpected death touched millions of Americans, who, like their counterparts elsewhere in the world, expressed their sorrow for the slain princess by creating tributes of flowers and other sentimental offerings in public places. Flower tributes became a metaphor for this young woman who had blossomed in spite of problems that she had openly confronted.

Outside the British embassy in Washington, D.C., and in more than a dozen British consulate offices across the United States, the American public brought generous bouquets of roses, single flowers in vases, pots of cheerful daisies, stuffed animals, and touching handmade cards to create shrines to their beloved princess. Perfume from the mounds of flowers and the poignancy of the messages created waves of sorrowful emotions for onlookers. Tucked between the flowers, cards, and balloons, people left teddy bears. (See "Introduction," p. 4; "Healing"/Teddy Bear Medicine, p. 182.) Topping the Los Angeles sidewalk shrine in the heavens above, a skywriting airplane drew a large heart in smoke with "Di" written in the center of the heart.

In Los Angeles, above-ninety-degree temperatures wilted the flowers so badly they were unfit to send to hospital and rest-home patients, so the organic remains of thousands of bunches of wilted flowers were scattered from the deck of *La Ventura,* a fishing boat whose owner volunteered to toss the floral remains into the blue Pacific Ocean. As the faded bouquets drifted on the soft waves, a nearby boat shot a fountain of water into the air. Shortly thereafter, dolphins frolicked nearby, adding a fitting close to Diana's farewell. In the words of one of her mourners, "You came, you loved, you touched us all."

Starside Shrines

When a celebrity dies, film fans make pilgrimages to the movie star's star embedded in the sidewalk on Hollywood Boulevard to leave flowers and stirring words. Contributing to this ritual is the Hollywood Chamber of Commerce, which places a floral spray on a stand next to the celebrity's star. Jimmy Stewart, who died on July 2, 1997, inspired dozens to add their floral displays, but no other outpouring has been as great as that for Lucille Ball when she died on April 26, 1989.

Thousands of fans came to the boulevard to leave flowers and write touching messages on the rolled-out paper covering the sidewalk's entire block. One could not grasp the breadth of her comedic appeal until witnessing the public outpouring of grief—in English, Spanish, Portuguese, German, Japanese, and French. Crossing geographic and linguistic borders, Lucy had made everyone laugh. Her audience cherished her for this. One fan rationalized the loss, "Even God has a funny bone."

GANG MEMBERS' FUNERALS

In 1995, gang-related funerals in East Los Angeles accounted for one in ten funerals, but by the end of 1997, their deaths decreased to one in twenty-five. Regardless of frequency, 55 to 65 percent of the victims are usually under thirty years of age. Brothers of the deceased, whether by blood or gang affiliation, often seek revenge for the death. Consequently, law enforcement agencies in neighborhoods beset by gang activities ask mortuaries to inform police of the time and place of gang funerals. A police presence averts on-the-spot retaliation, providing safety for the mourners.

Fr. Thomas H. Smolich, SJ, executive director of Proyecto Pastoral and the associate pastor of Dolores Mission Church in Boyle Heights, East Los Angeles, describes a typical funeral ritual. To help the family with funeral expenses, homeboys use the church parking lot for a car wash, promoted through the posting of street-corner signs. Meanwhile, using coffee cans, pickle jars, and plastic pitchers, homegirls solicit funds door-to-door. This has become such a commonplace event, the girls simply tear off the name label of the previous victim and affix the name of the current one on the church-provided containers. Next, friends reproduce a photo of the deceased taken from an old snapshot and distribute hundreds of copies to announce the young man's death.

On the day of the funeral, friends distribute homemade booklets with a drawing on the cover paying tribute to the deceased, for example, "R.I.P. Rusty" displaying a heart enclosing a rose and praying hands. Frequently, the booklet includes a tearful good-bye from the victim's girlfriend, and page one usually contains a statement denouncing guns and gang violence. A homegirl reads the anti-gang-warfare statement at the service, but it is largely ignored.

At the evening service, the victim's homies wear new black T-shirts with their own names on the front and on the back "In Loving Memory of Rusty—R.I.P." Tears flow, the choir sings, and friends document the occasion by taking photos of the body, the homies, the flowers, the coffin.

They drive in procession to the morning burial, and afterward, the crowd lingers. Father Smolich laments, "There will be talk of getting the ones who did it, and in more private moments, of gang-banging no more. Then slowly but surely, we'll leave Rusty among the fallen homies and life will begin to return to normal—until another round of bullets finds its target some night."

✪ *Gifts:* Money for victims' families.

✪ *Clothing:* Gray, black, dark brown. Avoid wearing red or blue, common gang colors, which can set off further conflict.

Most rituals related to death deal with someone already deceased whose remains must be disposed of according to the precise dictates of a particular tradition. However, rites of passage taking place in a hospice help dying persons cross the threshold into death. In this challenging environment, new rituals are created for the staff to help them cope not only with dying patients and their grief-stricken families, but with their own feelings of anger and sadness.

HOSPICE RITUAL

At St. Peter's Hospice in Albany, New York, the chaplain, Sr. Jean Roche, has developed various weekly prayer-service rituals to meet the needs of patients and staff. She desires to create healing, affirmation, renewal, inspiration, and grace.

She recognizes that humans need concrete manifestations of spiritual realities. Therefore, in a typical ritual, patients, families, and staff sit around a table that may hold a bouquet of flowers, an incense burner, or a lighted candle. These elements become a multisensory focus. Sometimes they begin and end the service with the ringing of a chime, a Swiss gong, or a Tibetan cymbal. Then, using drums, rattles, cymbals, chimes, and a tubular lyre, participants may create music, which allows them to communicate nonverbally.

They bless each participant with incense and say a simple prayer to calm their minds and open their hearts. To give structure to the ritual, Sister Jean gives it a theme, such as peace, light, freedom, forgiveness, mercy. Then they follow it with music, a poem, prayer, or guided meditation to allow patients to tune into their own lives.

The hospice has borrowed from Native Americans' use of a "talking stick." While sitting in a circle, people pass a stick from person to person. The holder of the stick speaks from the heart while others listen. A variation occurs when each participant lights a candle and speaks a hope, wish, or prayer. A different adaptation has participants blessing one another with water. Other times, patients use puppets to facilitate communication with one another.

If patients are estranged from their families as death draws near, the hospice arranges a reconciliation ritual by creating a prayer service around the dying person's bed. In one situation, eight children and a mother encircled their dying father and husband, who, in his alcoholism, had caused great suffering to his family. Each family member expressed forgiveness, prayed for his peace, then all laid hands on him while listening to the song "Lay Your Hands." At the final note, the man serenely slipped away. Another patient had been estranged from her son, who was serving time in prison. The hospice arranged for the prisoner to visit his dying mother to say good-bye, bringing closure to both mother and son.

Continual loss of patients leads to anger of staff members, so the hospice employs a ritual to help them cope.

They begin with a recitation of the poem "A Just Anger," written by Marge Piercy and associated with Jesus' overturning the tables in the temple. Next, they reflect on which tables in the temple of their own lives they wish to overthrow. One by one, they stand up and overturn tables while shouting the names of things that make them angry, for example, "Feeling helpless!" "My divorce!" "Cancer!" Afterward, they are able to laugh and have become energized from the release of emotions.

Patients, too, feel anger and frustration, and Sister Jean has adapted the overturning of chairs for them, but without the physical exertion. For one patient, Sister Jean created a ritual to let her express her hidden rage. The patient lit several red candles, each one expressing a particular anger. Then Sister Jean had the patient blow them out, one at a time, to extinguish their power and relinquish their hold on her.

The following advice from Sister Jean applies to anyone visiting any kind of hospice.

◐ *Gifts:* Material items may be less important than bringing a patient something pertinent to the individual's life. In one situation, someone arranged for former students (one now a physician) to visit a dying woman who had been their teacher. If a patient loves nature, flowers might be in order. Animal lovers might enjoy a visit from a service dog (one licensed to visit patients in institutional settings) or their own pet. Someone brought a horse lover a live horse who visited her in her trailer. Still another patient who had struggled with alcoholism during her life and who valued her sobriety, as evidenced by the chip she clung to, received the meaningful gift of a visit from other AA members. (See "Giving Birth"/Alcoholics Anonymous, p. 60.)

⊙ *Words:* Listen rather than talk. Encourage patients to express themselves during your limited stay. "Tell me, what's going on with you?" or "What has given you consolation?" are the kinds of questions visitors should ask to elicit feelings and concerns of dying patients. Then take your cues from them. Avoid saying "I'm praying for you" unless you know that prayer is meaningful to them. Avoid phrases like "Cheer up. You're going to a better place." Don't tell the dying patient, "You look great!"

⊙ *Clothing:* At St. Peter's, the staff wears colorful outfits to brighten the environment. This has a positive effect on the patients. Visitors might want to do the same.

MISSOULA DEMONSTRATION PROJECT (See "Looking for More Information?"/Organizations, p. 264.)

The Quality of Life's End

The Missoula Demonstration Project is a fifteen-year study in Missoula, Montana, examining the ways that hospitals, doctors, residents, patients, family members, and services deal with death. Begun in 1996, they aim to improve the quality of life's end for dying persons and their families using rituals as key elements. These rituals encourage residents to confront death through reminiscences, artistic expression, and laughter.

Storytelling

Ira Byock, M.D., principal investigator of the project, believes that healing occurs when someone tells a story about a loved one's dying and listens to someone else's death story as well. Consequently, the project has created the Life Stories Task Force to conduct storytelling workshops for dying persons and their families, but the stories are not just about death. Dying persons record significant life incidents as a legacy for their children and grandchildren, so their descendants will know who they were and the wonderful things they did. This lessens the emotional discomfort of the dying and leaves a legacy for the living.

Shrine-Building

In 1997, the project sponsored twelve community workshops, "Images and Objects of Remembrance," facilitated by art therapists, who helped residents create temporary shrines for the deceased that they displayed either in their homes, at the art museum, or inside local churches. Participants included parents who had lost children, children who had lost parents or grandparents, a girl who had lost her horse. Using Day of the Dead as a model (see "Dying"/Mexican, p. 218), they built altars on which they placed objects to trigger memories of their loved ones incorporating photos, shells, fabric, mementos, poems, and magazine pictures.

Procession

Part of the project includes a Festival of the Dead procession held on All Souls' Day. In 1997, after a week of lectures and workshops dealing with the end of life, a thousand Missoulians watched with glee as two hundred marched in a macabre parade. Driven by Death, a car named *Sleeping Beauties* carried the Misses Limbo, Styx, Hades, Purgatory, and Inferno. The orange-and-black-striped Oldsmobile convertible was ornamented with cardboard human-skull hubcaps and a cattle-skull hood ornament. Other parade entries included a dancing dinosaur skeleton, a candlelit altar worn on top of a marcher's head, dead Shriners riding three-wheelers, drum groups playing cowbells and washboards, and a Barbie doll turning on a spit over briquettes and metal flames on a "Barbie-Q."

DO-IT-YOURSELF HOME FUNERALS

Natural Death Care Project (NDCP) (See "Looking for More Information?"/Organizations, p. 264)

When Carolyn Whiting unexpectedly died in Sonoma County in 1994, she astounded her friends by leaving instructions for the treatment of her body. Following Carolyn's directives, her friends moved her body from the hospital to lie in state at home. They washed and prepared her for a ceremony and, to honor her sense of humor, covered her body with fortunes from her fortune-cookie collection.

Touching the body enabled them to more easily deal with her death. "A lot of our fears of death seemed to dissolve," claimed Jerri Lyons, who because of this experience formed the NDCP. NDCP, now a program under the nonprofit Community Network for Appropriate Technologies (CNAT), advises those who would like to have a meaningful in-home, and financially reasonable, funeral. The NDCP educates people about their legal rights, responsibilities, and options for home funerals. It is dedicated to a compassionate and dignified alternative to traditional funeral practices and gives dying persons control over their final act.

When Michele Moser passed away on July 9, 1997, friends and family carried out her instructions, which she had developed with guidance from the NDCP. She wore black velvet, Shalimar perfume, and lay in state at home in a cardboard coffin with an Egyptian woman painted on the front according to her design. Her women friends bathed and dressed her, combed her hair, applied eye shadow and lipstick, and put on the necklace and other jewelry she had selected. When friends came to call, they lovingly added personal touches inside the open coffin: a purple lily, gold paper stars in her hair, a garland of purple asters, notes and pictures, rose petals strewn over her body.

Prior to her death, Michele had given her friends assignments: obtain the flower arrangements for the ceremony, held two days after her death in a redwood grove; clean house; arrange for food; purchase sixty pounds of dry ice to keep her body fresh; provide the van for the trip to the crematorium. Family and friends believe that active involvement in the planning and carrying out of funeral details according to Michele's wishes helped them deal more therapeutically with her death.

Since its inception, the NDCP has assisted with over sixty unique funeral rituals, including one where the dying woman painted her own pine coffin with flowers, trees, and birds.

WRITE-ON CASKETS

Responding to growing requests for caskets on which mourners might write farewell messages to the deceased, the York Group of Houston, Texas, has produced the York Expressions casket, an off-white casket with a pearlescent finish that absorbs mourners' marker-made messages. Children and adolescents have been the prime users.

While burying the deceased with meaningful possessions offers mourners some degree of consolation, it does not allow them to share and communicate their feelings. In contrast, by writing messages on the casket, they actively participate rather than passively observe. Grief counselors believe that active declaration of feelings is essential to mourners' spiritual and mental well-being.

In each of the following tragic situations, grief-stricken youngsters publicly and creatively expressed their anguish by writing on caskets at funeral services: students of a Columbus, Ohio, teacher who lost her life while saving twins from being run over; children at the Paducah, Kentucky, public school where three classmates were shot to death by a fellow student; classmates of high school sweethearts killed by a train in Rochester, New York.

The York Expressions casket comes with a memorial guide and a set of permanent markers.

Some changes in death rituals are rooted in economics. Because burial costs have become so exorbitant, cremation is becoming a more attractive alternative. This has caused new traditions—and disputes—to spring up over the sprinkling of ashes. Whether due to multigenerational families or sibling rivalry with everyone wanting particles of mom or dad, or conflict over where to sprinkle the ashes, people are now dividing cremated remains (cremains) among loved ones or resting places. A prime example is Allen Ginsberg, who, following cremation in April 1997, had his cremains divided into three parts and shipped to Buddhist centers in Colorado and Michigan and a Jewish cemetery in New Jersey.

HIGH TECH

Technology, too, impacts on funeral traditions. According to a study by the Wirthlin Group, attendance at funerals is down nationwide. In large part, distance is the cause. To compensate, speakerphone eulogies bring together family members physically unable to attend the service. One funeral parlor chain in Hackensack, New Jersey, has cell phones in hearses so clergy can speak long distance from the grave. Many funeral homes across the United States now sell videotape services for friends and relatives unable to attend.

CYBERSPACE

People may place obituaries of loved ones in cyberspace and with many options. Dial www.yahoo.com/Society__-

and__Culture/Death/Obituaries/Memorials/Web__Memorial__Providers. At this site you can select from at least seventeen different possibilities, such as Angels Online, Cemetery Gate, Garden of Remembrance, Virtual Heaven, and Virtual Memorial Garden, where persons can celebrate memories of their family, friends, and pets.

Most charge $10 to place an obituary on the Internet. This generally includes photographs of the deceased that they scan in, bios, and family trees. Best of all, you can send virtual flowers to appear on the screen of your loved one's memorial by contacting www.virtualflorist.com. Future developments in technology promise sound with images, and at one site already on the DeathNet, www.islandnet.com/-deathnet/gate.html, they recommend appropriate mournful background music on CDs to be played while simultaneously visiting their sites. Undoubtedly, electronic family crypts, cyberpyramids, and datasphinxes are already in development.

OUTER SPACE FUNERALS

The Celestis Project

In real space, a new trend has begun. The cremated remains of Timothy Leary, former Harvard professor well known in the 1960s for dropping acid and then dropping out, and of Gene Roddenberry, *Star Trek* creator, plus twenty-two others were rocketed into orbit on April 21, 1997, for the first commercial burial in outer space.

In this, the Celestis Project, they launched the rocket from underneath an L-1011 jet. The space capsule carried one-quarter ounce of ash from each person, encased in individual aluminum capsules the size of lipstick tubes. Remaining in low orbit from two to six years, the cremated will be recreated upon reentry into the atmosphere.

Looking for More Information?

Print

Allen, James P., and Eugene Turner. 1997. *Ethnic Quilt.* Northridge, Calif.: Center for Geographical Studies, California State University, Northridge.

Ancelet, Barry Jean; Jay Edwards; and Glen Pitre. 1991. *Cajun Country.* Jackson: University Press of Mississippi.

Andersen, Ruth E. 1999. *The Color of the Sun.* A forthcoming book.

Artress, Lauren. 1995. *Walking a Sacred Path: Rediscovering the Labyrinth as a Spiritual Tool.* New York: Riverhead Books.

Atwood, Mary Dean. 1991. *Spirit Healing: Native American Magic & Medicine.* New York: Sterling Publishing.

Bahti, Tom. 1982. *Southwestern Indian Ceremonials.* Las Vegas, Nev.: KC Publications.

Balz, Dan. 1997. "Chief Long Wolf's Last Journey." *Washington Post,* 26 September, A01.

Barton, David. 1996. "Wedding Reception." *Sacramento Bee,* 14 December, G1, 9.

Bates, Karen Grigsby, and Karen Elyse Hudson. 1996. *Basic*

Black: Home Training for Modern Times. New York: Doubleday.

"Bells Call to the Living: The Children's Bell Tower." 1997. *Coastal Navigator* (Northern California), Summer Guide.

Berry, Jason. 1995. *Spirit of Black Hawk.* Jackson: University Press of Mississippi.

Bertelsen, Cynthia, and Kathleen G. Auerbach. 1987. *Nutrition & Breastfeeding: The Cultural Connection.* Franklin Park, Ill.: La Leche League International.

Beyette, Beverly. 1996. "Public Devotions." *Los Angeles Times,* 6 December, E1, 8.

Bliatout, Bruce Thowpaou. 1993. "Hmong Death Customs: Traditional and Acculturated." In *Ethnic Variations in Dying, Death, and Grief: Diversity in Universality,* edited by Donald P. Irish, Kathleen F. Lundquist, and Vivian Jenkins Nelsen. Washington, D.C.: Taylor & Francis, 79–100.

Bonney, Philip. 1997. "Fond Farewell to Josh." *Independent* (Huntington Beach, Fountain Valley, Sunset Beach, Calif.), 11 September, 10–11.

———. 1997. "Young Surfer Died Just Hours After Making Surf Team." *Independent,* 11 September, 10.

Bruchac, Joseph. 1993. *The Native American Sweat Lodge: History and Legends.* Freedom, Calif.: Crossing Press.

Brunvand, Jan Harold, ed. 1996. *American Folklore: An Encyclopedia.* New York: Garland Publishing.

Bull, Debby. 1997. *Blue Jelly: Love Lost and the Lessons of Canning.* New York: Hyperion.

Bulow, Ernie. 1991. *Navajo Taboos.* Gallup, N.M.: Buffalo Medicine Books.

Burbank, James. 1997. "Catholics, Too, Venerate El Niño Fidencio." *National Catholic Reporter,* 7 February, 33:14, 3–4.

Butler, Becky. 1990. *Ceremonies of the Heart.* Seattle, Wash.: Seal Press.

Byock, Ira. 1997. *Dying Well: The Prospect for Growth at the End of Life.* New York: Riverhead Books.

Campanelli, Pauline. 1994. *Rites of Passage: The Pagan Wheel of Life*. St. Paul, Minn.: Llewellyn Publications.

Cantú, Norma E. 1996. "La Quinceañera: Towards an Ethnographic Analysis of a Life-Cycle Ritual." Unpublished monograph, Department of English, Texas A&M International University.

Chatam-Baker, Odette. 1991. *Baby Lore*. New York: Macmillan.

Chavez, Annette. 1996. "Queen for a Day." *Los Angeles Times*, Westside Weekly, 8 December, 1, 7.

Chin, Soo-Young. 1991. "Korean Birthday Rituals." *Journal of Cross-Cultural Gerontology* 6: 145–52.

———. 1989. "The Role of Ritual for Korean American Elderly." *Frontiers of Asian American Studies*. Pullman: Washington State University Press, 127–39.

Clark, Ann L. 1978. *Culture Childbearing Health Professionals*. Philadelphia, Pa.: F. A. Davis Company.

Clines, Francis X. 1994. "73,000 Times in 22 Tongues, Vow: 'I Do.' " *New York Times*, 30 October, 41.

Coffin, Margaret M. 1976. *Death in Early America: The History and Folklore of Customs and Superstitions of Early Medicine, Funerals, Burials and Mourning*. Nashville, Tenn.: Nelson Publishing Co.

Colker, David. 1997. "Final Flight." *Los Angeles Times*, 22 April, B1, 3.

Colton, Michael. 1995. "A Lasting Union." *Los Angeles Times*, 26 July, E1, 4.

Crissman, James K. 1994. *Death and Dying in Central Appalachia*. Urbana and Chicago: University of Illinois Press.

Daniels, Susan. 1989. "Funeral Customs of the New Americans." *The Director*, July, 10–16.

Desrochers, Gerard. 1990. "Healings Through Good Saint Anne." Quebec, Canada: Saint Anne de Beaupré.

Diamant, Anita. 1993. *The New Jewish Baby Book*. Woodstock, Vt.: Jewish Lights Publishing.

Dickison, Roland, ed. 1987. *Causes, Cures, Sense and Nonsense: Folklore Remedies*. Sacramento, Calif.: Bishop Publishing Co.

Dobrinsky, Herbert C. 1986. *Sephardic Laws and Customs.* Hoboken, N.J.: KTAV Publishing House.

Dockins, Metric. 1997. "Coast Episcopal Lays Out Labyrinth." *Sun Herald* (Biloxi, Miss.), 2 December, C1.

Doi, Mary L. 1991. "A Transformation of Ritual: The Nisei 60th Birthday." *Journal of Cross-Cultural Gerontology* 6: 153–63.

Dresser, Norine. 1994. *I Felt Like I Was from Another Planet.* Menlo Park, Calif.: Addison-Wesley.

———. 1991. "Marriage Customs in Early California." *The Californians,* November/December, 46–49.

———. 1996. *Multicultural Manners: New Rules of Etiquette for a Changing Society.* New York: John Wiley & Sons.

———. 1996. "Remaining Safe from the Remains." *Los Angeles Times,* 20 April, B7.

Dugger, Celia W. 1997. "Outward Bound From the Mosaic." *New York Times,* 28 October, B1, 3.

Dujardin, Richard C. 1997. "The Late Rabbi Schneerson Is Still a Presence to Many Around the World." *Providence Journal-Bulletin,* 26 February, 226.

Dundes, Alan. 1996. " 'Jumping the Broom': On the Origin and Meaning of an African American Wedding Custom." *Journal of American Folklore* 109: 433, 324–29.

Dunham, Carroll, and the Body Shop Team. 1992. *Mamatoto.* New York: Viking.

Evanchuk, Roberta J. 1998. "Bring Me a Pumpkin." In *Religion, Belief, and Spirituality in Later Life,* edited by Eugene Thomas and Susan Eisenhandler. New York: Springer Publications.

Fadiman, Anne. 1997. *The Spirit Catches You and You Fall Down: A Hmong Child, Her American Doctors, and the Collision of Two Cultures.* New York: Farrar, Straus and Giroux.

"The First American *Bat Mitzvah.*" 1997. From *Chapters in American Jewish History,* reprinted in *The Forward,* 7 November, 7.

Fleming, Mali. 1996. "Rites of Passage: Ceremonies Can Help Our Kids Cope with Today's Turbulent Times." *Essence* 26, no. 12 (April): 118–20.

"For Every Homicide, a Vigil Against Violence." 1997. *Los Angeles Times,* 11 October, B4–5.

Gardner, Dore. 1992. *Niño Fidencio: A Heart Thrown Open.* Santa Fe, N.M.: Museum of New Mexico Press.

Gatewood, Charles, and David Aaron Clark. 1997. *True Blood.* San Francisco, Calif.: Last Gasp Publishing.

Georges, Robert A., and Michael Owen Jones. 1995. *Folkloristics: An Introduction.* Bloomington and Indianapolis: Indiana University Press.

Gilanshah, Farah. 1993. "Islamic Customs Regarding Death." In *Ethnic Variations in Dying, Death, and Grief: Diversity in Universality,* edited by Donald P. Irish, Kathleen F. Lundquist, and Vivian Jenkins Nelsen. Washington, D.C.: Taylor & Francis, 137–45.

Gindick, Tia. 1983. "Ethnic Weddings Still Flaunt Their Roots." *Los Angeles Times,* 9 October, VII 1, 20–23.

Glover, Scott. 1997. "Blue Lights Keep Memories Alive." *Los Angeles Times,* 12 December, B1, 6.

Goldberg, Christine. 1994. "Choosing Their Futures, a Custom for Babies." *Western Folklore* 53 (April): 2, 178–89.

Gore, Karenna. 1997. "Superhighway to Heaven: The Eerie Stillness of Cemeteries in Cyberspace." *Slate* (Microsoft's on-line magazine), 3 June.

Gould, Lark Ellen. 1997. "Gambling on the Future." *Los Angeles Times,* 10 December, Las Vegas Winter Guide advertising supplement, 11, 15.

Gross, Jane. 1995. "All the Dead Young Men." *Los Angeles Times,* 5 December, B1, 3.

Guidelines for Display Committees. 1994. San Francisco, Calif.: NAMES Project Foundation.

Gutiérrez, Ramón. 1995. "El Santuario de Chimayó: A Syncretic Shrine in New Mexico." In *Feasts and Celebrations in North American Ethnic Communities,* edited by Ramón Gutiérrez and Geneviève Fabre. Albuquerque: University of New Mexico Press, 71–86.

Hall, Carla. 1997. "Diana's Floral Tributes Are Gently Moved." *Los Angeles Times,* 11 September, A1, 10.

Hand, Wayland D.; Anna Casetta; and Sondra B. Thiederman, eds. 1981. *Popular Beliefs and Superstitions: A Compendium of American Folklore from the Ohio Collection of Newbell Niles Puckett.* Boston, Mass.: G. K. Hall & Co.

Hansen, Barbara. 1995. "Quinceañera: Cinderella for a Night." *Los Angeles Times,* 9 February, H10.

Harlow, Ilana. 1997. *Beyond the Grave: Cultures of Queens Cemeteries.* Woodhaven, N.Y.: Queens Council on the Arts.

Hartman, Susan. 1997. "For Bar Mitzvahs, a Revival of Spirit." *New York Times,* 13 March, C1, 10.

Hazen-Hammond, Susan. 1995. "*Kinaaldá:* Coming of Age in the Navajo Nation." *Arizona Highways,* March, 14–19.

Hewitt, William W. 1996. *Astrology for Beginners.* St. Paul, Minn.: Llewellyn Publications.

Hikida, Kerri. 1997. "Medicine Man, M.D." *Whole Life Times,* October, 48–49, 77.

Holmes, Kristin. 1996. "Today's Funeral Directors Live Up to Diverse Customs." *Philadelphia Inquirer,* 2 January, B1–2.

Hopi: Following the Path of Peace from *Native American Wisdom.* 1994. San Francisco: Chronicle Books.

Hostetler, John. 1972. "The Amish in American Culture." *Historic Pennsylvania Leaflet,* no. 12.

Hufford, David. 1985. "St. Anne de Beaupré: Roman Catholic Pilgrimage and Healing." *Western Folklore* 44: 194–207.

Hur, Sonja Vegdahl, and Ben Seunghwa Hur. 1997. *Culture Shock!: Korea.* Portland, Oreg.: Graphic Arts Center Publishing Company.

Jones, Leslie. 1995. *Happy Is the Bride the Sun Shines On.* Chicago: Contemporary Books.

Jones, Rose Apodaca. 1997. "Vows for the Heart and for Vietnam." *Los Angeles Times,* 27 August, S4.

Katz, Jesse. 1997. "New Orleans Parade Tradition Advances Black Men's Image." *Los Angeles Times,* 4 September, A5.

Kay, Elizabeth. 1987. *Chimayó Valley Traditions.* Santa Fe, N.M.: Ancient City Press.

Kendall, Laurel. 1996. *Getting Married in Korea: Of Gender, Morality, and Modernity.* Berkeley: University of California Press.

————. 1985. *Shamans, Housewives, and Other Restless Spirits: Women in Korean Ritual Life.* Honolulu: University of Hawaii Press.

Keyes, Josa. 1985. *The Teddy Bear Story.* New York: Gallery Books.

Kim, Diana S. 1993. "Love, Armenian Style." *Los Angeles Times,* 19 August, J1, 5.

Klapp, Orrin E. 1969. *Collective Search for Identity.* New York: Holt, Rinehart and Winston.

Klein, Sybil. 1995. "The Celebration of Life in New Orleans Jazz Funerals." In *Feasts and Celebrations in North American Ethnic Communities,* edited by Ramón Gutiérrez and Geneviève Fabre. Albuquerque: University of New Mexico Press, 101–8.

Kluckhohn, Clyde, and Dorothea Leighton. 1962. *The Navaho.* New York: Anchor Books.

Kraybill, Donald B. 1989. *The Riddle of Amish Culture.* Baltimore: Johns Hopkins University Press.

Lagnado, Lucette. 1996. "Phone Eulogies, Cybermourners Make Funerals into Virtual Events." *Wall Street Journal,* 21 August, B1.

Lakota: Seeking the Great Spirit from *Native American Wisdom.* 1994. San Francisco: Chronicle Books.

Leonard, Jack. 1997. "Nun's Contributions to Chicano Heritage Recalled at Festival." *Los Angeles Times,* 2 November, B2.

Leonelli, Laura. 1993. "Adaptive Variations: Examples from the Hmong and Mien Communities of Sacramento." Unpublished paper delivered at the Southwestern Anthropology Association meeting, San Diego, Calif., April.

Levine, Bettijane. 1998. "Well Worth the Wait: Approaching the Altar Later in Life, These Happy Couples Are Rewriting the Rules." *Los Angeles Times,* 4 February, S7.

Levy, Rebecca Amato. 1987. *I Remember Rhodes.* New York: Sepher-Hermon Press.

Lewis, Thomas H. 1990. *The Medicine Men: Oglala Sioux Ceremony and Healing.* Lincoln: University of Nebraska Press in cooperation with the American Indian Studies Research Institute, Indiana University.

LiButti, Renee, and Kristine McKenzie. 1996. "Wacky Weddings." *What's On in Las Vegas,* 13–26 February, 76–77.

Liptak, Karen. 1992. *North American Indian Ceremonies.* New York: Franklin Watts.

Lorie, Peter. 1992. *Superstitions.* New York: Simon and Schuster.

Magida, Arthur J., ed. 1996. *How to Be a Perfect Stranger.* Woodstock, Vt.: Jewish Lights Publishing.

Matlins, Stuart M., and Arthur J. Magida, eds. 1997. *How to Be a Perfect Stranger.* Vol. 2. Woodstock, Vt.: Jewish Lights Publishing.

McDonnell, Patrick J. 1995. "The Day After, Parents Face a New Anxiety." *Los Angeles Times,* 8 December, A1, 28.

———. 1995. "Students Say Sad Goodbye to Two Friends." *Los Angeles Times,* 9 December, B1, 3.

McLane, Daisann. 1995. "The Cuban-American Princess." *New York Times Magazine,* 26 February, 42.

Mieder, Wolfgang. 1992. *A Dictionary of American Proverbs.* New York: Oxford University Press.

Minard, Antone. 1997. " 'Thousands of Things Worth Their Knowing': Folk Medicine in Welsh America." Unpublished paper presented to the American Folklore Society, Austin, Tex., October.

Mitchell, Rick. 1988. "Power of the *Orishas.*" *Los Angeles Times Magazine,* 7 February, 16–32.

Moore-Howard, Patricia. 1982. *The Hmong—Yesterday and Today.* Lansing, Mich.: Collection of MSU Museum.

Mulligan, Hugh A. 1997. "Something Old, Something New."

Las Vegas Review-Journal and Las Vegas Sun (Nevada), 28 September, A23–25.

Myerhoff, Barbara. 1978. *Number Our Days*. New York: E. P. Dutton.

National Association of Colleges of Mortuary Science, Inc. 1994. *Funeral Services and Ceremonies*. Dallas, Tex.: Professional Training Schools, Inc.

Navajo: Walking in Beauty from *Native American Wisdom*. 1994. San Francisco: Chronicle Books.

Ngo, Qui. 1994. "Buddhist Funeral Rites." Unpublished article, Cypress College Mortuary Science Department.

Orenstein, Debra. 1994. *Lifecycles: Jewish Women on Life Passages & Personal Milestones*. Woodstock, Vt.: Jewish Lights Publishing.

Osbey, Brenda Marie. 1996. "One More Last Chance: Ritual and the Jazz Funeral." *Georgia Review* 50 (Spring): 1, 97–107.

Paddock, Richard C. 1996. "165 Gay Couples Exchange Vows in S.F. Ceremony." *Los Angeles Times*, 26 March, A1, 18.

Padilla, Steve. 1990. "Death's New Face." *Los Angeles Times*, 5 March, B1, 8.

Perrone, Bobette; H. Henrietta Stocket; and Victoria Krueger. 1989. *Medicine Women, Curanderas, and Women Doctors*. Norman: University of Oklahoma Press.

Powers, William K. 1977. *Oglala Religion*. Lincoln: University of Nebraska Press.

Rivenburg, Roy. 1992. "An Ancient Vigil." *Los Angeles Times*, 14 September, E1, 2.

———. 1996. "Grand Finales." *Los Angeles Times*, 2 April, E1–2.

Roberts, Susan. 1994. "Blood Sisters." *New Age Journal*, May/June.

Roche, Jean. 1994. "Creative Ritual in a Hospice." *Health Progress*, December, 45–47, 55.

Rourke, Mary. 1997. "In the Spirit." *Los Angeles Times*, 21 December, E1.

Rutland, Aulica. 1997. "For a Party, It Was Pretty Lifeless."
  Missoulian (Montana), 3 November, 1.

Sahagun, Louis. 1997. "Survivors Greet Verdict with Hugs,
  Tears." *Los Angeles Times,* 3 June, A1, 23.

Sarkisian, Nola L. 1997. "Resting Easy: Culver City Casket
  Store Aims to Take the Trauma Out of Coffin Shopping." *Los
  Angeles Times,* 14 September, Westside Weekly, 1, 10.

Satzman, Darrell. 1997. "A Day for Growing." *Los Angeles
  Times,* 8 July, B2.

Sciorra, Joseph. 1991. "In Memoriam: New York City's
  Memorial Walls." In *Folklife Annual 90,* edited by James
  Hardin. Washington, D.C.: Library of Congress, 144–51.

Scott, Stephen. 1988. *The Amish Wedding.* Intercourse, Pa.:
  Good Books.

Sherman, Spencer. 1988. "The Hmong in America." *National
  Geographic,* October, 586–610.

Smith, Lynn. 1997. "Ashes to Ashes, to Ashes, to Ashes." *Los
  Angeles Times,* 10 April, E1, 5.

Smolich, Thomas H. 1990. "When a Homeboy Dies, No One
  Rests in Peace." *Los Angeles Times,* 21 July, B7.

Starck, Marcia. 1993. *Women's Medicine Ways: Cross-Cultural
  Rites of Passage.* Freedom, Calif.: Crossing Press.

Story, Paula. 1997. "Same-Sex Couples Use Festival Ceremony
  to Affirm Their Bonds." *Daily News* (Southern California),
  22 June, 12.

St. Pierre, Mark, and Tilda Long Soldier. 1995. *Walking in the
  Sacred Manner.* New York: Touchstone Books.

Sturgis, Ingrid. 1997. *The Nubian Wedding Book.* New York:
  Crown Publishers.

Sullivan, Meg. 1996. "Marriage, American Style." *University of
  Southern California Chronicle,* 22 April, 15:29, 1, 6.

Sutherland, Anne. 1975. *Gypsies: The Hidden Americans.* New
  York: Free Press.

Swartz, Susan. 1997. "A Death Without Fear." *Press Democrat*
  (Santa Rosa, Calif.), 20 July, D1, 6.

———. 1997. "Orchestrating Her Final Days on Own Terms." *Press Democrat* (Santa Rosa, Calif.), 2 March, D1, 6.

Sway, Marlene. 1988. *Familiar Strangers: Gypsy Life in America.* Urbana and Chicago: University of Illinois Press.

Thomas, James D. 1985. "Gypsies and American Medical Care." *Annals of Internal Medicine* 102: 842–45.

Trippett, Frank. 1981. "In Louisiana: Jazzman's Last Ride." *Time,* 20 April, 10–11.

"Two Iraqis Who Married Teens Get Prison Terms." 1997. *El Paso Times,* 24 September, 5A.

Walker, Sandy Moss. 1997. "Therapy Keys on Curing with Rhythm." *Daily Courier* (Yavapai County, Ariz.), 19 August, 1.

Ward, Edna M. 1992. *Celebrating Ourselves: A Crone Ritual Book.* Portland, Maine: Astarte Shell Press.

Weiner, Stacy. 1996. "Thank Heaven for Little Girls." *Jewish Monthly,* June-July, 26–31.

Willeford, Lynn Murray. 1995. "Walking the Labyrinth." *New Age Journal,* May/June, 79–83.

Winton, Louise A., ed. 1985. *Handbook of Burial Rites.* Ontario, Canada: Commemorative Services of Ontario.

Yurchenko, Marine, and Sam Abell. 1991. "Birth and Childhood." *Life,* October, 10–21.

WORLD WIDE WEB

African Immigrant Folklife Study Project, 26 April 1997
http://www.si.edu/folklife/vfest/africa/photo2.html

AIDS Quilt to Cover Mall in Washington, 19 June 1997
http://www2.nando.net/newsroom/ntn/nation/10196/nation1 2__14177.html

Belly Masks
http://www.farout.com/sprout/bellymsk

Blood Sisters, 1 May 1997

http://www.enews.com/data/magazines/alphabetic/all/new__a
ge/Archive/05194.1

Labyrinths/Veriditas
http://www.gracecom.org/veriditas/features/index.shtml

Surfers Hold "Paddle Out" Ceremony to Remember Friend, 4
December 1995
http://sddt.com/files/librarywire/DN95__12__04/DN95__12)0
4cc.html

Traditional Laotian Wedding by Siriviengphone Phengsavath
http://naio.kcc.hawaii.edu/bosp/Horizons/horizons96/23laotia
n.html

UCLA Archive of Folk Medicine
http://www.humnet.UCLA.edu/folkmed

ORGANIZATIONS

African-American Rites-of-Passage Programs:

African American Women on Tour
3914 Murphy Canyon Road, Suite 216
San Diego, CA 92123
Ph: 800-560-2298

Concerned Black Men, Inc.
Rites of Passage Manhood Training Program
1511 K Street N.W.
Washington, D.C. 20005
Ph: 202-783-5414

HAWK (High Achievement, Wisdom and Knowledge)
175 Filbert Street, Suite 202
Oakland, CA 94607
Ph: 510-836-3245

West Dallas Community Centers
Rites of Passage Project
8200 Brookriver Drive, Suite N-704
Dallas, TX 75247
Ph: 214-630-0006

COPS (Concerns of Police Survivors):
P.O. Box 3199
Camdenton, MO 65020
Ph: 800-784-2677

Feminist Spiritual Community of Portland, Maine:
1837 Forest Avenue
Portland, ME 04103
Ph: 207-797-9217

Mazon: A Jewish Response to Hunger:
National Headquarters
12401 Wilshire Boulevard, Suite 303
Los Angeles, CA 90025
Ph: 310-442-0020

Menstrual Health Foundation:
c/o Cycles of Life & Death
Tamara Slayton
P.O. Box 1613
Sebastopol, CA 95473
Ph: 707-524-4150
E-mail: IRMC1@aol.com

Missoula Demonstration Project, Inc.:
1901 South Higgins Avenue
Missoula, Montana 59801
Ph: 406-728-1613
Fax: 406-543-7769
E-mail: MDPQOL@aol.com

Natural Death Care Project (NDCP):
Jerri Lyons and Janelle Melvin, Codirectors
P.O. Box 1721
Sebastopol, CA 95473
Phone/Fax: 707-824-0268

Northwest Labyrinth Project:
Linda Sewright, Director
8403 New Brooklyn Road
Bainbridge Island, WA 98110

VIDEOTAPES

Celebration of Age: The Croning Ceremony. Context Productions. 5525 North Via Entrada, Tucson, AZ 85718.

Common Threads: Stories from the Quilt. 1989 Telling Pictures, Inc. and The NAMES Project Foundation.

OTHER SOURCES

Didgeridoo:
Rian McGonigal
2923 Kendra Drive
Prescott, AZ 86301
Ph: 520-541-7762

In Honor of Pregnant Women, Do-It-Yourself Pregnant Belly Masks. Francine Krause, P.O. Box 1024, Guerneville, CA 95446. Ph: 707-824-8357

INDEX

Abeyta, Bernardo, 171
Adoptions, 26–27
Afghani engagement and marriage
    rituals, 92, 96–98
African-American celebrations and
    rituals
    coming of age, 64–65
    funerals, 196–197
    marriage, 98–100
African American Women on Tour,
    64–65
Agra hadig celebration, 55–56
AIDS Memorial Quilt, 232–235
Alaalafaga celebration, 40–41
Alcoholics Anonymous (AA), 60–62
American Folklore Society, 88
Amish celebrations and rituals, 7–8
    funerals, 197–198
    marriage, 101–103
Anglo-American celebrations and
    rituals
    marriage, 103–104
    pregnancy, 14–15
Anne, Saint, 173–175

Apache (Mescalero) coming of age
    rituals, 74–77
Armenian celebrations and rituals
    funerals, 198–199
    future of a baby, determination of,
      55–56
    marriage, 104–106
Armstrong, Louis, 196
Artress, Lauren, 179
Asimow, Harry, 3
Astrological signs, 20, 23–24
Australian Aborigines, 185

Baci ceremony, 37, 165
Badeken (veiling) ceremony, 128
"Bad poetry" readings, 104
Ball, Lucille, 241
Bangle bracelet ceremony
    (*Valaikappu*), 10, 12
Baptism
    Ethiopian, 26
    See also Christenings
Bar mitzvah ceremony, 67–69
Bas mitzvah ceremony, 69–70

Beiju celebration, 58
Belly masks, 15–17
Bernier, Réjean, 174
Berryman, Clifford, 182
Bhansel (cleansing ceremony), 42–43
Bingen, Hildegard von, 180
Birth celebrations and rituals, 19–20
  Cambodian, 20
  Egyptian, 25
  Ethiopian, 25–26
  Hawaiian, 26–28
  Hmong, 28–29
  Japanese, 31–32
  Jewish, 32–36
  Korean, 36–37
  Lao, 37
  Mexican, 38
  Native American, 38–40
  Samoan, 40–41
  Thai, 41–42
  Tibetan, 42–43
  Vietnamese, 43–44
  See also Future of a baby,
    determination of; Naming
    celebrations and rituals
Birthday anniversary celebrations and
  rituals, 3, 5, 57
  AA "taking a cake" ceremony,
    60–62
  Indian, 30
  Japanese, 57–58
  Korean, 59–60
Birth folk wisdom, 21
Birth signs, 20, 23–24
Birthstones, 22
Boccalero, Sister Karen, 219
Bomboniere (small party favors), 124
Boys' Day, 31
Brahman celebrations and rituals. *See*
  Indian celebrations and rituals
Brit bat ceremony, 47, 48

Brit Milah (circumcision), 32–33
Broom dance, 107
Broom symbolism, 99
Brown, Willie, 147
Buddhist All Souls' Day, 200
Buddhist celebrations and rituals
  coming of age, 81–83
  funerals, 199–200
Bull, Debby, 161
Byock, Ira, 246

Caba (mantle), 113
Cajones (male healers), 175–176
Cajun marriage ceremonies, 106–108
Calles, Plutarco Elías, 175
Cambodian celebrations and rituals
  birth, 20
  funerals, 200–201
  marriage, 108–110
Campbell, Joseph, 188
"Camp Fertility" weekends, 83–85
Canning therapy, 161
Cantú, Norma E., 5, 85–87
Cascarónes (eggshells filled with
  confetti), 88
Caskets, write-on, 249–250
Caster, Jack, 233
Catholic celebrations and rituals. *See*
  Roman Catholic celebrations
  and rituals
Celestis Project, 251
Central Ohio Lung Association, 184
Chair dance, 5–6
Chambelans (male escorts), 71
Chan chan ko (red hat), 58
Chang (rice wine), 141, 142
Chapin, Sam, 104
Charivari ceremony, 107–108
Charles, Andre, 238
Chartres Cathedral, 179
Cheong-san ceremonial gown, 110

Cherokee celebrations and rituals
  birth, 38
  naming, 49
Children's Bell Tower, 235–236
Children's Day, 31
Chima dish, 142
Chimayó healing shrine, 170–173
Chinese celebrations and rituals
  funerals, 201–203
  marriage, 110–111
  naming, 45–46
Ching ming holiday, 202
Christenings
  Protestant, 52–53
  Roman Catholic, 53–54
Chuppah (bridal canopy), 128
Church of the Santo Niño de Atocha, 171
Cincuentañera ceremony, 5, 85–87
Circumcision, 32–33
Cody, Buffalo Bill, 224
Coffin, Catrina, 150
Coming-of-age celebrations and rituals, 63
  African-American, 64–65
  Buddhist, 81–83
  emerging traditions, 83–85
  Indian, 66
  Japanese, 66–67
  Jewish, 67–70
  Latina, 70–73
  Native American, 73–79
  Roman Catholic, 79–81
  Thai, 81–83
  traditional rituals and beliefs, 64–83
Commitment ceremonies, 147–150
Communion, First Holy, 79–80
Communitas (feeling of oneness), 3–4
Community Network for Appropriate Technologies (CNAT), 248

Conception dream (*tae mong*), 12
Concerns of Police Survivors (COPS), 235
Confetti (white-sugar-coated almonds), 124
Confirmation, 80–81
Conspicuous consumption, 2
Coptic celebrations and rituals. *See* Egyptian celebrations and rituals
Croning ceremony, 5, 87–90
Curing chants, 168–169
Cyberspace obituaries, 250–251

Dances *With Wolves* (film), 167
Davis, Howland, 103
Day of the Dead (*Día de los Muertos*), 218–219
Death folk wisdom, 194–195
Death rituals, 193, 196
  AIDS Memorial Quilt and NAMES Project, 232–235
  Children's Bell Tower, 235–236
  cyberspace obituaries, 250–251
  Día de los Muertos (Day of the Dead), 218–219
  do-it-yourself home funerals, 248–249
  gang members' funerals, 242–243
  high tech developments, 250
  hospice ritual, 243–246
  lapel ribbons, 232
  memorial walls, 238–239
  Missoula Demonstration Project, 246–247
  outer space funerals, 251
  Project Blue Light, 235
  reburial service, 224–225
  rededication of disturbed burial sites, 223
  sidewalk shrines, 239–241
  surfer services, 236–238

Death rituals (*cont.*)
  survivor tree, 4–5
  teddy bear comforting, 183–184
  write-on caskets, 249–250
  See also Funerals
"Decades" ritual, 88–89
Día de los Muertos (Day of the
  Dead), 218–219
Diana, Princess of Wales, 240–241
Didgeridoo (vibrational healing),
  184–188
Divorce rituals, 154
  divorce cleansing ceremony,
    156–157
  divorce party, 154–156
Do-it-yourself home funerals,
  248–249
Dreams, 12
Dresser, Mark, 67
Drypaintings, 168–169
Duncan, Susan, 151–152
Dying. *See* Death rituals; Funerals

Ear piercing, 40
Egyptian celebrations and rituals
  birth, 25
  engagement, 111
  funerals, 203–204
  marriage, 111–112
Elders, honoring of
  cincuentañera ceremony, 5, 85–87
  croning ceremony, 5, 87–90
El Niño Fidencio shrine, 175–176
Elopement, 118
El Santuario de Chimayó, 170–173
End-of-therapy rituals, 188–189
Engagement celebrations and rituals
  Afghani, 92, 96
  Egyptian, 111
  Korean, 131
Esfand (rue), 123

Ethiopian celebrations and rituals
  birth, 25–26
  funerals, 204–205
  marriage, 113–114
Evanchuk, Roberta J., 182
Evil eye, 38, 46, 91, 123, 130, 163
Expecting. *See* Pregnancy celebrations
  and rituals

Fadiman, Anne, 162
False Face Society, 166
Farrer, Claire R., 75
Feminist Spiritual Community (FSC),
  87, 88, 89
Fidencio Sintora Constantino, José,
  175
Filipino marriage ceremony, 114–115
First birthday rituals, 30, 31
First Holy Communion, 79–80
First-laugh feast, 39–40
Folklorists, 8
Folk wisdom
  birth, 21
  death, 194–195
  healing, 160
  marriage, 93–94
  pregnancy, 11
Fortune-telling, 108
Fufu dish, 51
Funerals
  African-American, 196–197
  Amish, 197–198
  Armenian, 198–199
  Buddhist, 199–200
  Cambodian, 200–201
  Chinese, 201–203
  Egyptian, 203–204
  Ethiopian, 204–205
  Hawaiian, 205–206
  Hmong, 206–209
  Indian, 209–210

Iranian, 220–221
Japanese, 210–212
Jewish, 212–215
Korean, 215–217
Lao, 217–218
Mexican, 218–219
Muslim, 220–221
Native American, 221–225
Rom (Gypsy), 225–228
Samoan, 228–229
Thai, 229–230
Tibetan, 231
See also Death rituals
Future of a baby, determination of, 55
Armenian celebrations, 55–56
Korean celebrations, 56
Vietnamese celebrations, 57

Gang members' funerals, 242–243
Garcia, Antonio "Chico," 238–239
Gay weddings, 147–150
Genfo (oatmeal-like grain), 25
Geomancers, 207
Ginsberg, Allen, 250
Girls' Day, 31
Giving birth. *See* Birth celebrations and rituals
Goddess of hysterectomy, 189–192
Godfather, The (film), 125
Godparents, 32, 52, 53–54, 105
Goldberg, Jane, 188–189
Gore, Tipper, 234
Grace Cathedral labyrinth, 179
Graffiti murals, 238–239
Grand Medicine society, 166
Grandparents, 26–27, 31
Greek Orthodox marriage ceremony, 115
Green family, 235–236
Guimond, Louis, 173

Guthrie, Arlo, 234
Gypsy funerals, 225–228

Haircut rituals
Japanese, 31
Jewish, 35–36
Hala (fruit lei), 205–206
Haley, Alex, 99
Hall, Joshua Dean, 236–237
Ham (wooden box), 131
Hamsa (hand-shaped pendant), 130
Hanai (adoption), 26–27
Happy Land Social Club, 238
Hatsubon ceremony, 211
Hatsu mairi (first temple presentation), 31–32
Hawaiian celebrations and rituals
birth, 26–28
funerals, 205–206
marriage, 116–117
pregnancy, 10
Hazen-Hammond, Susan, 78, 79
Healing celebrations and rituals, 159, 161
emerging traditions, 181–192
end-of-therapy rituals, 188–189
goddess of hysterectomy, 189–192
Hmong, 161–162
Jewish, 162–165
Lao, 165
Latina, 181–182
Native American, 159, 166–169
santiguo ceremony, 6, 181–182
teddy bear medicine, 182–184
Thai, 169
traditional rituals and beliefs, 161–169
vibrational healing, 184–188
See also Pilgrimages
Healing folk wisdom, 160

Henna designs on hands and feet,
    120–121, 130
Het boun (make offerings) custom,
    217
Hmong celebrations and rituals
    birth, 28–29
    funerals, 206–209
    healing, 161–162
    marriage, 117–120
Hopi celebrations and rituals
    funerals, 222–223
    naming, 49
Horoscopes, 20, 23–24
Hospice ritual, 243–246
Howison, Del, 151–152
Huevo (postfuneral meal), 214–215
Hulas, 116–117
Huloku (long dress with train), 116
Hu plig ceremony, 161–162
Hwan'Gap celebration, 59–60
Hysterectomy, goddess of, 189–192

Ibo celebrations and rituals. *See*
    Nigerian celebrations and rituals
Ideal Toy Corporation, 183
Imam (priest), 220
Imperial Broom Company, 99
Indian celebrations and rituals
    birthday anniversary, 30
    coming of age, 66
    funerals, 209–210
    marriage, 120–122
    naming, 46–47
    pregnancy, 10, 12
Iranian celebrations and rituals
    funerals, 220–221
    marriage, 122–124
Iraqi marriage customs, 6–7
Iroquois healing rituals, 166
Irwin, Jean Tokuda, 189–192
Italian marriage ceremony, 124–125

Japanese celebrations and rituals
    birth, 31–32
    birthday anniversary, 57–58
    coming of age, 66–67
    funerals, 210–212
    haircut, first, 31
    marriage, 126–127
Jazz funerals, 196–197
Jesa (one-year memorial), 216
Jewish celebrations and rituals
    birth, 32–36
    coming of age, 67–70
    funerals, 212–215
    haircut rituals, 35–36
    healing, 162–165
    marriage, 127–130
    naming, 47–49
    pilgrimages, 176–178
    See also Sephardic celebrations and
        rituals
Johnson, Bunk, 196
"Joining the Circle of Women"
    workshop, 64
Jones, Cleve, 233
Jumping the Broom ceremony
    in African-American weddings, 99
    in Anglo-American weddings,
        103–104
"Just Anger, A" (Piercy), 245
Juzu (string of beads), 31

Kabuto (warrior's helmet), 31
Kahili (poles topped by colored
    feathers), 205
Kahu (Hawaiian elder), 205
Kanreki (return to origins)
    celebration, 58
Kao phom hairdo, 134
Kaplan, Judith, 69
Kay, Elizabeth, 172

Ketubah (marriage contract),
   127–128, 130
Khan dong (headpiece), 143
Kilui (coverlet), 116
Kim, Young-Hoon, 146
Kinaaldá (making her cake)
   ceremony, 78–79
Kinolau (spirit forms of the gods), 27
Kittel (white smock), 127
Kluckhohn, Clyde, 168
Knight, Elizabeth, 224
Koden (monetary offering), 211–212
Korean celebrations and rituals
   birth, 36–37
   birthday anniversary, 59–60
   engagement, 131
   funerals, 215–217
   future of a baby, determination of,
      56
   marriage, 131–133
   pregnancy, 12–13
Krause, Francine, 15–17

La busta tradition, 124–125
Labyrinths, 179–181
Lakota celebrations and rituals
   coming of age, 77–78
   healing, 167
Lam vong (circle dance), 135
Lao celebrations and rituals
   birth, 37
   funerals, 217–218
   healing, 165
   marriage, 133–136
Lapel ribbons, 232
Las fadas ceremony, 48–49
Las Vegas weddings, 145–146
Later-in-life weddings, 153–154
Latina celebrations and rituals
   coming of age, 70–73
   elders, honoring of, 85–87

healing, 181–182
pregnancy, 15
Lavalava (wraparound skirt), 138
Leary, Timothy, 251
Le bal de noce (wedding dance), 106
Leighton, Dorothea, 168
Lei haku (crown of braided leaves
   and flowers), 116
Lesbian weddings, 147–150
Levy, Rebecca Amato, 163–164
Life-cycle celebrations, 1
   benefits of, 2–4, 8
   multicultural perspective on, 6–8
   new rituals to fit new
      circumstances, 4–6
Limpias (cleansings), 176
Long Wolf, Chief, 224–225
Luaus, 27
Lubavitch Headquarters, 178
Luminarias (paper bags holding
   flickering candles), 151
Lyons, Jerri, 248

Madrinas (sponsors), 71, 85–86
Maidu celebrations and rituals
   naming, 49
   pregnancy, 13
Makeba, Miriam, 98
"Marche de Mariés" (march of the
   newlyweds), 106
Marriage celebrations and rituals,
   91–92
   Afghani, 92, 96–98
   African-American, 98–100
   Amish, 101–103
   Anglo-American, 103–104
   Armenian, 104–106
   Cajun, 106–108
   Cambodian, 108–110
   Chinese, 110–111
   Egyptian, 111–112

Marriage celebrations and rituals
    (*cont.*)
  emerging traditions, 145–152
  Ethiopian, 113–114
  Filipino, 114–115
  Greek Orthodox, 115
  Hawaiian, 116–117
  Hmong, 117–120
  Indian, 120–122
  Iranian, 122–124
  Iraqi, 6–7
  Italian, 124–125
  Japanese, 126–127
  Jewish, 127–130
  Korean, 131–133
  Lao, 133–136
  Las Vegas weddings, 145–146
  Mexican, 136–137
  Nigerian, 137–138
  remarrying (later-in-life weddings),
      153–154
  Roman Catholic, 136–137
  same sex weddings, 147–150
  Samoan, 138–139
  Thai, 139–141
  Tibetan, 141–142
  traditional rituals and beliefs, 92,
      96–144
  vampire weddings, 5, 150–152
  Vietnamese, 143–144
  wedding anniversary gifts, 95
Marriage folk wisdom, 93–94
Matais (chiefs), 40
Materias (female healers), 175
Mazon: A Jewish Response to
    Hunger, 68
McGonigal, Rian, 186–188
McVeigh, Timothy, 4
Mehl-Madrona, Lewis, 159
Mehndi prenuptial ceremony,
    120–121

Memorial walls, 238–239
Menarche (onset of menses), 83–85
Menstrual Health Foundation, 83–85
Mesteth, Wilmer, 225
Mexican celebrations and rituals
  birth, 38
  funerals, 218–219
  marriage, 136–137
  pregnancy, 13
Michtom, Morris, 182–183
Midewiwin society, 166
Mikvah (ritual bath), 127
Missoula Demonstration Project,
    246–247
Miwok celebrations and rituals
  naming, 49
  pregnancy, 13
  rededication of disturbed burial
      sites, 223
Mizuhiki (colored ties), 126
Mohel (circumcision specialist), 32,
    33
Mong celebrations and rituals. *See*
    Hmong celebrations and rituals
Mop dance, 107
Morton, Jelly Roll, 196
Moser, Michele, 248–249
Mountain spirit dance, 74–77
Murdock, Tom, 180
Muslim celebrations and rituals, 8
  funerals, 220–221
Mutual-consent marriage, 118–120
Muumuu (loose, brightly colored
    dress), 138

Namakarma celebration, 46–47
Namaste greeting, 30, 122
Namazeh mayet prayer, 221
NAMES Project, 232–235
Naming celebrations and rituals,
    44–45

Chinese, 45–46
Indian, 46–47
Jewish, 47–49
Native American, 49–50
Nigerian, 50–52
Protestant christenings, 52–53
Roman Catholic christenings,
    53–54
Native American celebrations and
    rituals, 8
  birth, 38–40
  coming of age, 73–79
  funerals, 221–225
  healing, 159, 166–169
  naming, 49–50
  pregnancy, 13–14
  See also specific tribes
Natural Death Care Project (NDCP),
    248–249
Navajo celebrations and rituals
  birth, 39–40
  coming of age, 78–79
  healing, 159, 168–169
  naming, 49–50
  pregnancy, 13–14
Near, Holly, 148
New Orleans funerals, 196–197
New Orleans weddings, 100
Nicholas Green Foundation, 236
Nigerian celebrations and rituals
  marriage, 137–138
  naming, 50–52
Ninong and *ninang* (sponsors), 114
Northwest Labyrinth Project, 180
Nureen (white fabric bags), 141

Obituaries in cyberspace, 250–251
Obon festival, 211
O. Carl Simonton Cancer Center,
    186
Ofrenda (altar), 218

Oglala Sioux reburial service,
    224–225
Ojibwa healing rituals, 166
Oklahoma City bombing, 4–5
One hundredth day party, 36–37
Origami (folded paper) cranes, 58,
    126
Orisha worship, 181–182
Ory, Kid, 196
Osekihan (red rice) dish, 66–67
Outer space funerals, 251

Padrinos (sponsors), 71, 136
Paj ntaub (hand-stitched fabric), 28,
    206–207
Pak pin kao (hair decoration), 134
Partnership-in-life vows, 147–150
Patu (black wig), 141
Peot (side locks), 36
Pha kouane (flower and leaf
    arrangement), 133–134
Pidyon haben (redemption of the
    firstborn son), 34–35
Piercy, Marge, 245
Pig roasts, 139
Pilgrimages, 170
  Chimayó healing shrine, 170–173
  El Niño Fidencio shrine, 175–176
  labyrinths, 179–181
  Saint Anne Basilica, 173–175
  Schneerson's grave, 176–178
Pitts, Beth, 237
Placenta rituals, 28
Pomana (black feast), 226–228
Pomo rededication ritual, 223
Prayer Vigil Network, 239–240
Pregnancy celebrations and rituals,
    9–10
  Anglo-American, 14–15
  belly masks, 15–17
  Hawaiian, 10

Pregnancy celebrations and rituals
   (*cont.*)
   Indian, 10, 12
   Korean, 12–13
   Latina, 15
   Mexican, 13
   Native American, 13–14
   sex of the child, discovery of,
      14–15
   Thai, 14
   traditional rituals and beliefs, 10,
      12–15
Pregnancy folk wisdom, 11
Prekante ceremony, 6, 162–165
Project Blue Light, 235
Protestant christenings, 52–53
Pueblo naming rituals, 50
Pumpkin ritual, 181–182
Punahele (favorite child), 26–27

Queej (six reed pipe), 207
Queh-queh prewedding custom,
   98–99
Quinceañera (fifteen years old), 5,
   70–73

Rebozos (traditional shawls), 85
Reburial service, 224–225
Rededication of disturbed burial sites,
   223
Red egg and ginger parties, 45–46
Reincarnation, 209
Remarrying (later-in-life weddings),
   153–154
Rice-throwing, 92
Rites of passage. *See* Life-cycle
   celebrations
Robinette, Jason, 237
Roca, Fr. Casimiro, 170
Roche, Sr. Jean, 243–245
Roddenberry, Gene, 251

Roman Catholic celebrations and
   rituals
   christenings, 53–54
   coming of age, 79–81
   marriage, 136–137
   pilgrimages, 170–176
Rom funerals, 225–228
Roosevelt, Hilbourne, 103
Roosevelt, Theodore (Teddy),
   182
Roots (TV miniseries), 99
Rue, 123
Rumpelstiltskin fairy tale, 44

Saint Anne Basilica, 173–175
St. Peter's Hospice, 243
Sake (rice wine), 126, 132
Same sex weddings, 147–150
Samoan celebrations and rituals
   birth, 40–41
   funerals, 228–229
   marriage, 138–139
Sandek (godfather), 32
Sandpaintings, 168–169
Santería worship, 181–182
Santiguo ceremony, 6, 181–182
Schneerson, Rabbi Menachem
   Mendel, 176–178
Second liners, 196–197
Self-Help Graphics, 219
"Sending her home" custom, 137
Sephardic celebrations and rituals
   birth, 34–36
   coming of age, 69–70
   funerals, 214–215
   healing, 162–165
   marriage, 130
   naming, 48–49
Sewright, Linda, 180
Sex of an unborn child, discovery of,
   14–15

Shange, Ntozake, 84
Sha sha ritual, 47
Shippen family, 103–104
Shivah (mourning period), 213
Shivaree ceremony, 107–108
Shomer (guardian of the dead), 212
Sicard, Danny, 238
Sidewalk shrines, 239–241
Simchat bat ceremony, 47, 48
Slayton, Tamara, 83–84
Smolich, Fr. Thomas H., 242, 243
Sou-khoanh ceremony, 37, 165
Soul-releasing ceremony, 207–208
Spinoza Bear Company, 183–184
Spirit Catches You and You Fall Down, The (Fadiman), 162
Spittler, Connie, 89
Starside shrines, 241
Steward, Jan, 67
Stewart, Jimmy, 241
Sua (thank-you for a gift), 229
Surfing memorials, 236–238
Survivor tree, 4–5
Sweat lodge, 166–168

Tae kyo (pregnancy taboos), 12–13
Tae mong (conception dream), 12
"Taking a cake" ceremony, 60–62
"Talking stick" ritual, 244
Tallit (prayer shawl), 69
Taylor, Elizabeth, 234
Teddy bear medicine, 182–184
Teething celebrations, 55–56
Teje (mead), 113
Tela (beer), 113
Termeh (multicolored cloth), 123
Thai celebrations and rituals
  birth, 41–42
  coming of age, 81–83
  funerals, 229–230
  healing, 169

  marriage, 139–141
  pregnancy, 14
Therapeutic Sound and Music Program, 186
Tibetan celebrations and rituals
  birth, 42–43
  funerals, 231
  marriage, 141–142
Tol celebration, 56
Tomb of El Niño Fidencio, 175–176
Tomb of Rabbi Menachem Mendel Schneerson, 176–178
TWA Flight 800 explosion, 232
Txiv neeb (shaman), 161–162
"Tying the knot," 91–92
Tzitzit (jacketlike garment), 35–36

"Under the Village Tree" workshop, 64–65
Upanayanam (sacred thread ceremony), 66
Upsherin (baby boy's first haircut), 35–36

Valaikappu (bangle bracelet ceremony), 10, 12
Vampire weddings, 5, 150–152
Veriditas (Labyrinth Project at Grace Cathedral), 179
Vibrational healing, 184–188
Vietnamese celebrations and rituals
  birth, 43–44
  future of a baby, determination of, 57
  marriage, 143–144
Vision quest ceremony, 73–74

Wai greeting, 42, 135, 201, 218
Wedding anniversary gifts, 95
Weddings. *See* Marriage celebrations and rituals

West Dallas Community Center Rites
   of Passage Project, 65
White Painted Woman, 74
Whiting, Carolyn, 248
Wirthlin Group, 250
Write–on caskets, 249–250

*Y*ak kon sik (engagement), 131
Yakudoshi celebration, 57–58
Yarmulkes (skull caps), 68–69

Yochai, Rabbi Shimon Bar, 35
York Expressions casket, 249–250
Yoruba naming ceremony, 51–52
Yugal (eight-shaped, white cotton
   cord), 114

*Z*ij poj niam (bride capture) custom,
   117–118
Zinnar (red sash), 112

ABOUT THE AUTHOR

Cross-cultural customs and beliefs have fascinated folklorist Norine Dresser for over twenty-five years and have been the focus of her university teaching, research, and writing. *Multicultural Celebrations,* her most recent work, examines diverse, complex, and at times humorous facets of contemporary American culture. In *American Vampires: Fans, Victims & Practitioners,* she explores the symbolism and role of vampires. Her *Multicultural Manners* book and *Los Angeles Times* "Multicultural Manners" column demystify cross-cultural misunderstandings. The column and book earned the 1998 John Anson Ford Award for contributions toward resolving intergroup conflict, conferred by the County of Los Angeles Commission on Human Relations. *Multicultural Celebrations* documents the richness of universal ritual activity as experienced in this country. Topics of her other books and articles range from cat and horse bar mitzvahs to rumors of misplaced gerbils and invasions by *chupacabras,* literally "goat sucker," a being that is said to attack goats and other animals, reportedly sometimes even humans.

Dresser has received grants from the Smithsonian Institution, the National Endowment for the Humanities, and Los Angeles Cultural Affairs. She has appeared frequently on television as a vampire authority and participated in the groundbreaking 1995 First World Dracula Congress in Romania. She retired from the faculty at California State University, Los Angeles, in 1992 to write full-time.